Paul Cowan has been a reporter for *The Village Voice* for many years. In his acclaimed book *An Orphan in History,* he describes growing up an assimilated Jew, and retrieving, as an adult, his Jewish legacy. **Rachel Cowan,** formerly a Unitarian, is a rabbinical student at Hebrew Union College-Jewish Institute of Religion. She and Paul conduct workshops for interfaith couples and lecture widely. The Cowans, who have a daughter and a son, live in New York City.

MIXED BLESSINGS

MIXED BLESSINGS

*Marriage Between
Jews and Christians*

PAUL COWAN

with RACHEL COWAN

Doubleday

NEW YORK   1987

To Our Parents

Library of Congress Cataloging-in-Publication Data
Cowan, Paul.
    Mixed blessings.
    1. Marriage, Mixed—United States.   2. Marriage—
Religious aspects—Judaism.   3. Marriage—Religious
aspects—Christianity.   I. Cowan, Rachel.   II. Title.
HQ1031.C66   1987   306.8'43   87-480
ISBN 0-385-19502-8

"Jewish Restaurant, 43rd Street"
by Max Lerner
Copyright © 1941 Saturday Review of Literature
Reprinted by permission.
"Sit Down Young Stranger"
by Gordon Lightfoot
Copyright © 1969 Early Morning Music
Reprinted by permission.
"Marriage of Christians and Jews"
by the Reverend Ronald Osborne
Plumbline magazine, 1985
Reprinted by permission.

Acknowledgments

When we began this book, we decided to keep all the people we interviewed anonymous, with the exception of a few public figures. We do want to thank the hundreds of people who let us into their homes and their lives, and say that we hope we have done justice to their complicated stories.

We want to thank the people whose real names we used: Max, Edna, Michael and Steve Lerner; Pat and Ken Auletta and their friend Ida Tauger; Ned, Sarah, Will, and Mary Pottker Rosenbaum, and Paul, Linda and David Frank.

We asked many people for advice about this book as it was in process, and we thank them for taking the time to offer us invaluable insights: Aileen Adams, Ann Banks, Dr. Gershon Cohen, Dr. Naomi Cohen, Eve Coulson, Geoffrey Cowan, Liza Cowan, Rabbi Jerry Davidson, Tamara Engel, Howard and Rosalind Feinstein, Father Joseph Fitzpatrick, Ken Gorfinkle, Paul Gorman, Rabbi Wolfe Kelman, Rabbi Susan Laemmle, Irving Levine, Brother William Martin, Rabbi Roli Matalon, Dr. Egon Mayer, Dr. Deborah Dash Moore, Nelson Obus, Reverend Ronald Osborne, Bette Roth, Heidi Knecht Seegers, and Janet Vetter.

Rachel's sister Connie Brown Egleson, my sister Holly Shulman, and our close friend Jacqueline Gutwirth did us the special favor of reading the manuscript in two separate drafts, offering invaluable suggestions about language and structure, giving us emotional support when we most needed it. Saundra Heller, who directs workshops for interfaith couples in Denver, introduced us to many of the people we interviewed—and helped us formulate many of the ideas we used. Ingrid Russell, our friend and assistant, spent hours in the New York

Public Library doublechecking the historical quotes in chapters three and four.

Sally Arteseros, our editor, read the drafts that flowed out of us with great skill and cheerfulness. She is one of the most talented professionals we have met in publishing. More than that, she has become a dear friend.

Pam Bernstein, our agent, has constantly helped us with her good advice—and a warm, tough, reassuring manner that forced us to be as professional as possible.

Readers seldom realize that copy editors are the real workhorses of the publishing business. They read manuscripts line by line, word by word, and get almost as involved with the subjects as the writers themselves. Our copy editor, Estelle Laurence, honed our language and our information. But, more than that, she cared so much about her job and our subject that she became our conscience as we worked on the final stages of the book.

It is not easy for a husband and wife to collaborate on a book and maintain a private life and a family life, especially if one is in school and the other is holding down another job. We thank our children Lisa and Matthew for their patience with our preoccupations. And we thank each other for the gift of love under pressure.

Contents

Preface

When Jews and Christians fall in love with each other, they often feel their differences make their romance sparkle with a special brightness. But many also wonder how they can blend those differences within their households, and in their children's psyches, and still preserve the religious and ethnic qualities they hold so dear. That is the question that echoes through *Mixed Blessings*.

We began the research for the book in early spring 1981, when a Hillel director from Philadelphia heard Rachel speak about her decision to convert to Judaism, and me discuss *An Orphan in History*, the book I was writing to retrieve the Jewish legacy that had been suppressed in my family.

The Hillel director hoped that by describing the evolution of our Jewish life to Jews and Christians who were dating at Bryn Mawr, Swarthmore, the University of Pennsylvania, and Haverford, we might prompt couples to talk about themselves more freely. And, indeed, as we talked about ourselves honestly, people who had never before discussed the religious and ethnic complexities of their relationships revealed their feelings with an eager candor. We were astonished by the intensity of the emotions we encountered.

In the fall of 1981, the director of Manhattan's 92nd Street YMHA asked us to conduct workshops for interfaith couples. The American Jewish Committee arranged for us to talk to Jewish-Christian couples in six cities. Since then, synagogues, Jewish community centers, and Hillel societies have invited us to run workshops in places as far-flung as Portland, Maine; rural Vermont; Ithaca and Rochester, New York; Norfolk, Virginia; Columbus, Georgia; Baton Rouge, Louisiana;

Houston, Texas; Miami, Florida; Denver, Colorado; Los Angeles and San Francisco.

The people who come to these sessions have a broad range of feelings about their religious and ethnic backgrounds. Some of the Jews are regular synagogue-goers; others, who are not religious, express resolute ethnic pride; others are so angry at the Jewish community that they haven't set foot in a Jewish institution since their bar or bat mitzvahs. Some of the gentiles are devout Catholics or Protestants. Others talk angrily about their childhood religious training. Others consider themselves agnostics or atheists. (There is no single word that people who are not Jewish use for themselves. Therefore we have chosen to use the word "Christian" for religious people, "gentile" for nonreligious people, and to use the terms interchangeably when we're speaking generically.)

There is a theme that threads through all the workshops.

Usually even the most disaffected Jews want to raise their children as Jews. Many are aware that, according to sociologists and demographers, increasing numbers of Jews who marry in the 1980s are choosing gentiles as their spouses. Even though they themselves are intermarrying, they often are afraid that their children will be assimilated into Christian culture. They fear that if they don't insist on maintaining Judaism in their homes they will betray more than four thousand years of proud history and deprive their children of a valued legacy.

It is often impossible for their gentile partners to understand the intensity of these feelings. They wonder why so many Jews who marry Christians insist on celebrating Jewish holidays and ignoring Christmas; on sending children to Hebrew school and keeping them out of churches. Why are they insensitive to some of the deepest feelings of the gentiles they say they love? Why, the Christians wonder, are Jews so stubborn?

Why, some Jews respond, are the gentiles unable to understand the depth of their loyalty to their heritage and their people?

Those questions are very difficult for most interfaith couples to discuss. Although they can talk intimately about sex, politics, and money, about work and leisure, their romance has stirred up emotions about religion and ethnicity which they can't quite name. We have seen that couples who are in the same situation can help each other develop a vocabulary to describe their elusive feelings.

* * *

We have structured *Mixed Blessings* in three parts. The first part is a narrative—of our own marriage, of a young couple poised on the brink of an intermarriage, and of a college student who reflects on the experience of growing up in a home where her Jewish father and Protestant mother failed to provide her with a coherent sense of her religious and ethnic identity. The second section describes the role that intermarriage has played in the minds of Jews and Christians throughout American history. The third section is more practical. It is based on our workshops and interviews and is written to help Jewish-Christian couples anticipate the problems and challenges that will arise in their relationships, to furnish a vocabulary with which they can discuss them, and to help them find a pathway to a shared spiritual life. We hope *Mixed Blessings* will create a framework in which couples, their families, friends, and clergy can discuss a subject that is fraught with emotion.

We hope that it will encourage Jews and Christians who fall in love to realize that other interesting, successful people share their questions about religion and ethnicity; that discussions of those questions can be lively and fascinating, and can lead to unexpected self-discoveries; and that interfaith couples have a responsibility—to themselves and to their children—to think out solutions as carefully as possible instead of hoping that solutions will present themselves. Finally, we hope this book will encourage the Jewish and Christian communities to create forums where interfaith couples can discuss their feelings about their backgrounds as freely as possible.

We have broadened the scope of our research beyond the couples who have sought help in dealing with the tensions in their marriage by interviewing a wide range of couples who have never come to a workshop or talked openly about being in an intermarriage. Altogether we have interviewed more than three hundred couples.

We talked with old friends. We asked acquaintances in some cities we were visiting to introduce us to couples who lived in a milieu where intermarriage was taken for granted. Some of the people loved their differences. It would never have occurred to them to go to a workshop because they had no problems to discuss. Others had suppressed their feelings. They would never attend a workshop for fear of disrupting the ecology of their marriage.

Finally, we interviewed about sixty children of intermarriages who were college-age or older in order to see how their parents' decisions had affected them. Some were old friends or the children of friends. At several colleges we sought respondents by taking out advertisements in the college newspaper. We also asked undergraduates we knew to give us names of friends whose parents had intermarried.

In *Mixed Blessings,* we have used stories from our workshops and from our interviews. A few easily recognizable public figures have agreed to let us identify them. But for the most part we have disguised the names, occupations, home cities, colleges, and current residences of the people we describe.

When we conduct interviews, we think of ourselves as journalists: we listen to people describe their situations and offer suggestions only when we are asked.

As workshop leaders we have an active role. We try to talk about our own conflicts and choices in a way that allows other people to talk about theirs. Because the groups take place under Jewish auspices, many couples wonder if we will try to proselytize. Gentiles, in particular, often fear that we will try to change them instead of finding out who they are and how they feel.

We make it clear that we do not have an easy formula for the couples. Our role is not to provide solutions but to help people clarify their own ideas and values. It is obvious from our own stories, which include Rachel's decision to become a rabbi, that we have both found great meaning in Judaism. We hope that our own example will serve as a model for some other couples.

When we began this book, we had to decide what voice to use. If we always wrote as "we," each of us would lose our own individuality at moments when our personal stories differed. A third-person narrative about "Paul" and "Rachel" sounded forced.

Then when Rachel entered rabbinical school, she didn't have enough time to study and to write first drafts of chapters. So, for the most part, I have written and she has edited. That is why the book is by Paul, with Rachel.

PART I

SETTING
THE STAGE

1
Our Story

If you had been a guest at Rachel's and my wedding on an idyllic June day in 1965, you would not have imagined that the blond Unitarian woman from Wellesley, Massachusetts, a descendent of Pilgrims who came to America on the *Mayflower*, would one day be a rabbinical student or that her thin Jewish groom, whose assimilated family always celebrated Christmas and Easter and never noticed Hanukkah or Passover, would publish a book about his journey into religious Judaism. Nor would you have imagined that twenty years later we would be writing a book designed to help interfaith couples explore the kinds of religious and ethnic differences we did not discover in ourselves until long after our wedding. In 1965 we didn't consider ourselves religious people. We had no idea that we were part of a phenomenon called intermarriage.

Nevertheless, as we look at our past selves through our present eyes, we recognize that in many ways our story, for all of its quirks, resembles those of the hundreds of people we have seen in our workshops for interfaith couples and interviewed for this book—people who love each other and also love the religion and culture they grew up with.

We were married in the tantalizingly sweet months before the war in Vietnam riveted an entire generation's consciousness to images of destruction. It was a self-consciously spontaneous wedding, a "hippy wedding," some guests recall. In 1965 I certainly didn't care who

officiated. I didn't even know any rabbis to ask, so I was spared the
wound that many Jews who wed gentiles feel when a rabbi refuses to
perform the ceremony. Rachel and I wanted to design our own service and write our own vows. We felt lucky that Rachel's uncle offered
us his lovely farmhouse in rural Massachusetts for the wedding, and
introduced us to his friend, Reverend Harold Anderson, the Smith
College chaplain, who agreed to perform the wedding according to
our plan, without mentioning Jesus.

We walked down the grassy aisle to a Bob Dylan record (for me)
and Vivaldi (for Rachel). Then we paused under a sturdy butternut
tree and gazed at each other. Standing in front of our families and
close friends, we read passages from the liberal humanists whose
works formed the basis of our secular creed. I chose a passage from
James Agee's *Let Us Now Praise Famous Men;* Rachel, from Camus'
Resistance, Rebellion and Death. We each gave speeches affirming our
commitment to help make the world a more decent place. We exchanged the earnest vows we had each written.

Then, at the end of the ceremony, I broke a glass, which was the
only Jewish wedding custom I knew. Reverend Anderson said *"shalom."*

Neither of us wanted a lavish reception. Rachel had planned a
menu of chicken salad sandwiches, strawberries, and champagne—
which I later learned was standard WASP wedding fare—but I insisted that our outdoor reception be a real picnic with enough hot
dogs and hamburgers to feed our guests well. During the afternoon,
we played a seven-inning softball game.

It never occurred to us that from the point of view of many Jews we
were part of a problem that was beginning to threaten the survival of
the Jewish people. Although there is no way of ascertaining exact
intermarriage figures, it is clear that the rates are soaring. Until 1960,
only about 5 percent of the 6 million Jews in America who married
chose spouses from other religions. By the mid-1960s, more than 15
percent of the Jews who were marrying chose gentile mates. In 1986,
Brooklyn college sociologist Egon Mayer, the leading expert in the
field, estimated that the current figure hovered between 30 and 40
percent. It was as high as 70 percent in cities like Denver, Colorado,
and Phoenix Arizona, where the climate and growing universities and
industries have attracted bright, restless young people, including
many Jews. There are now about 500,000 Jews who have chosen

spouses who were not born Jewish. There are between 30,000 and 50,000 such marriages a year. Even though about one quarter of them lead to conversions to Judaism, these statistics cause many Jews to fear that American tolerance will bleach out a people who have survived more than four thousand perilous years in a particular relationship with God, and who have provided the human race with some of the most important values and ideas it possesses.

Even if I had known those statistics, I wouldn't have thought they applied to me. I still have a transcript of a 1970 interview in which I told a sociologist that "I sort of wish I had fallen in love with a Jew. I think that if all Jewish men were to marry gentile women there wouldn't be many Jews left and that would be a bad thing. But Jews seem to be marrying each other quite a bit. We shouldn't worry too much."

Soon, Rachel and I learned how strongly most Jews disagreed with that opinion.

I was at Harvard from 1958 to 1963, during the years when it was becoming normal for students to drop out of school so that they could "find themselves." There was certainly a part of myself I wanted to find. Ever since childhood I had been intensely curious about the Jewish identity that my father, the son of an Orthodox Jew named Jake Cohen, who had sold burlap bags in Chicago, had suppressed when he re-created himself as Louis G. Cowan, producer of the radio show "The Quiz Kids," the television shows "Stop the Music" and "The $64,000 Question," and who in time became president of CBS-TV. I decided to spend time in Israel to learn more about that past.

I loved working on a kibbutz near Haifa and, later, teaching the North African Jewish children whose families had just settled in the frontier city of Beersheba. I didn't learn as much about Jake Cohen's legacy as I'd hoped. The Israelis I met talked about Zionist history and building a new nation far more readily than they talked about Eastern Europe or Judaism. But I acquired something more important than a fund of specific information. I discovered that I was proud to be a Jew.

It was a private realization. I didn't see myself as part of the Jewish community. In fact, when I heard the term "Jewish community" no specific image came to mind. Was I supposed to think of all Jews? Men who wore yarmulkes? Israelis? My own Jewish friends? It wasn't a question I thought about very often. When I did, it annoyed me slightly. It seemed too parochial. In my mind, I was a citizen of the world, with no special loyalties.

But I was very pleased when a friend phoned a month before Rachel's and my wedding, inviting me to go to Tel Aviv and participate in the American Jewish Congress Dialogue between American and Israeli Jewish youth. The Dialogue would begin in early July, a week after our wedding. It seemed to be the perfect beginning of a honeymoon. Rachel, whose parents had raised her to hate fascism and anti-Semitism, and to admire the Jews who had made the desert bloom, was eager to visit the country. I longed to show it to her.

I was invited to represent politically liberal, religiously unaffiliated American-Jewish youth because I had been active in the civil rights movement in Maryland and Mississippi. I played my role to the hilt. Throughout the Dialogue, which was covered in the Israeli press, I talked freely about marrying a gentile. One day, I made the naïvely provocative remark that even though I cared very much about the continuation of the Jewish people, "for people like me, Jewish feeling is going to have to be translated; it is going to have to be taken out of the synagogue. I'm afraid it's going to have to be taken out of the State of Israel too."

One afternoon Geula Cohen, who had been a brave fighter during the War of Independence and is now a right wing member of the Knesset (the Israeli Parliament), interviewed me for a popular daily newspaper. "Why wasn't I going to move to Israel?" she asked. "Because I am committed to the civil rights movement," I said. The next week, I opened the paper, saw a picture of myself, and asked someone to translate the Hebrew language headline. "The Negroes need me more than the Jews," it read. The article also criticized my intermarriage.

As Rachel and I hitchhiked through Israel we kept meeting people who had read about us. In high school, Rachel had read *The Diary of Anne Frank*. She had identified with Anne so strongly that she would often argue with her anti-Semitic classmates. If anything, she should have been seen as a person who took on the risk of experiencing anti-Semitism by marrying me. I should have been regarded as the traitor. But she got an equal share of the criticism. Israelis and American-

Jewish tourists accused her of completing Hitler's work by marrying a
Jew.

She felt rejected by the people she had always defended. I felt an
embarrassed anger at the Israelis who had been so friendly to me, but
were so rude to my wife. We both thought we had been completely
misunderstood.

In spite of my remarks during the Dialogue, I regarded myself as a
Jew who would always fight for the Jews. For that reason I had decided to tell my draft board that I was not a pacifist. If I had been old
enough, I would have fought the Nazis in World War II and volun-
teered as a soldier in Israel's 1948 War of Independence. Rachel had
always imagined that if she had been a teenager in Europe during
World War II she would have joined a resistance group to fight
against Hitler. We thought that, as Americans who fought segrega-
tion in its heartland, Mississippi, we were combating the murderous
bigotry that had created the Holocaust. Why were we being treated
like enemies?

It was fourteen years before we went back to Israel. When we did,
my journey into Judaism had accelerated greatly, and Rachel felt such
a deep connection to the Jewish people that she had begun to think
seriously about conversion.

But at the end of the summer of 1965 we were convinced that Israel
—and many American Jews—would be hostile to us. We were happy
to return to the cosmopolitan liberal world, where we would become
Peace Corps volunteers, anti-war organizers, and journalists. We
were accepted there.

Even though Rachel was a Unitarian and I was a Jew, we were
universalists who had been raised in each other's cultural backyards.

In the sixties, we would have bridled at the suggestion—which is a
theme of this book—that differences in ethnic and religious backgrounds can become "time bombs" in relationships, especially after
children are born. We believed that distinct ethnic traits added flavor
to life, and that people who loved each other could resolve any
cultural or theological disagreement. We would have insisted that
religion created artificial divisions between people.

Neither of us was rebelling against narrow-minded families or communities. Instead, we were echoing attitudes we had absorbed in our

homes and the pleasant, accepting grade schools we had each attended.

Both of Rachel's parents were socialists. Neither of them considered themselves religious. They had won an argument with her
grandmother, a devout Episcopalian, and had refused to have Rachel
baptized. They imbued her with their skeptical view of all churches
and their feeling that religion was a crutch.

When she was a young girl her father, a brilliant mathematician,
had worked for the U.S. Navy, which meant that her family moved
often. Between moves, when her father was based at the Pentagon,
they lived in Alexandria, Virginia, and her parents sent her to the
religiously and racially integrated Burgundy Farms school, where she
celebrated the Jewish harvest festival of Sukkot and Thanksgiving,
Hanukkah and Christmas. She loved that pluralistic education.

Both of my parents were political liberals. They made it clear that
their passionate belief in social justice and philanthropy stemmed
from their Jewish backgrounds. But they never observed any Jewish
holidays at home. They never went to synagogue. They felt that
organized religions divided people. They believed that we could and
should be Jews and universalists at the same time.

My mother, Pauline Spiegel, whose German-Jewish ancestors came
to America in 1848, had particularly conflicted feelings about being
Jewish. She felt that Jews had a special, prophetic mission: it was our
duty to fight injustice. But she seemed reluctant to be identified with
other Jews. I think that was the result of her childhood, which was
similar to that of many other German Jews of her generation.

Her Chicago-born father, Modie J. Spiegel, who founded one of
the largest mail-order houses in America, was part of the generation
of German Jews that achieved considerable wealth at the turn of the
century. When he decided to move from his German-Jewish Hyde
Park neighborhood to a Chicago suburb, he happened to choose
Kenilworth. He liked the town's climate, and had no idea that it was a
more bigoted place than Winnetka or Highland Park, where Jews had
already bought homes.

According to family legend, he purchased the house from a lawyer
who hated the town and wanted to inflict Jews on it. Shortly after the
Spiegels moved there, Kenilworth's town council passed a restrictive
covenant, ruling that no more Jews could settle there. That meant
that my mother was the only Jewish girl in an entirely Christian

community. She was even more isolated than most German Jews in her generation.

But most of them felt quite isolated too. They were among the few Jews who attended New England boarding schools and Ivy League colleges in the 1920s and 30s. For example, two of my uncles went to Dartmouth in those years. My mother went to Sarah Lawrence at a time when relatively few Jews attended that college.

These German-Jewish youngsters were not raised to see the positive features of their religion or background. If anything, they learned to regard Jewishness as a social liability. That added to their sense of vulnerability when they moved away from home, into the Christian world. Sometimes their gentile classmates befriended them. Sometimes they derided them. In either case, many German Jews lived in a cultural and religious no-man's land where they felt unprotected.

I often imagine my mother's feelings as she saw the first pictures of the concentration camps—images that would stay with her forever. Since she felt so vulnerable herself, she could identify with Jews as victims in a way that she could never identify with them as ordinary people. Thus, she taught her children that we had a lifelong debt to the 6 million Jews who died in the Holocaust. We could repay some of the debt by fighting bigotry wherever we encountered it: by combating anti-Semitism and, later, by joining the Southern civil rights movement. But she seemed to dislike anything that was specifically Jewish (or "Joosh," as she'd often say in a self-mocking voice). She said that joining a synagogue—or even a Jewish country club—was too parochial for a sophisticated family like ours.

My father, who seldom talked about his Orthodox childhood, revealed a lasting pain when he described the way his parents fought over status and money as they walked home from synagogue after Yom Kippur services. "What hypocrisy!" he would say with angry disgust. "An argument on the Day of Atonement!" As a result of experiences like that, he would tell us, he believed in God, but he distrusted religion.

My parents sent me to the Dalton School in New York, a self-consciously non-denominational place. There was a Christmas pageant (I remember thinking it odd that my mother, who made an enormous production over Christmas at home, regarded the pageant as an unwelcome intrusion of religion at school). But Thanksgiving and Book Day—where classes performed plays like *Androcles and the Lion* and *Twelfth Night*—were also important ceremonies.

We used to recite a poem called "Outwitted" by Edwin Markham in our weekly assemblies at Dalton. It might have served as the motto of Rachel's childhood and of mine. "He drew a circle that shut me out/ heretic, rebel, a thing to flout/ But Love and I had the wit to win:/ We drew a circle that took him in."

Then, as teenagers, Rachel and I found ourselves in high schools where many of our classmates drew circles that shut people out.

My father hoped that Choate, a prestigious Episcopal school, would prepare me to feel at home in the corporate boardrooms where he was chronically ill-at-ease. He was bestowing on me the gift of opportunity. How could he imagine its price? During my first two years at Choate, kids would taunt me with the Yiddish accent Mr. Kitzel had used on the old Jack Benny show or call me a Fagin and Shylock—or, more simply, a kike. I didn't dare tell my father about those encounters. I thought he'd be disappointed in me for having such problems.

There was mandatory chapel at Choate. I loved that magic place, with its pews that smelled pleasantly musty on rainy days, that looked happy and sunny as Easter approached. The pageantry and the hymns used to thrill me. But often, I'd gaze at the Protestant boys, who seemed to me so thoroughly at home in their trim bodies, their well-groomed clothes. They seemed graceful and cool. I talked with my hands. I could never remember to notice whether my tie went with my suit. I was always sweating.

By junior year I was a big shot on the newspaper, the literary magazine, the debate society. My classmates began to accept me, and some of them became lifelong friends. But many perceived me as a "white Jew." They'd make disparaging remarks about the more obviously ethnic Jews in the school or the loud, ill-mannered Jews who, they said, were taking over their hometowns.

It was an odd position to be in. I certainly didn't like all of the other Jews at Choate. I didn't know the Jews who were moving into their hometowns. Nevertheless, when the Christian kids criticized Jews I felt compelled to defend them. It was the first time I felt the kind of tribal loyalty that I have come to treasure as a key of Jewish survival.

During those years I realized that it didn't really matter whether my family name was Cohen or Cowan, or whether I felt more at home with Episcopalian liturgy than I did in synagogue, or whether my classmates happened to choose me as the Jew they would accept. I liked a lot of them, but I wasn't one of them. In the recesses of my mind, in the privacy of my own skin, I was always a Jew.

When Rachel's father joined Arthur D. Little, a management consulting firm in Cambridge, Massachusetts, her parents decided to settle in Wellesley, which was reputed to have an excellent school system. As it turned out, that attempt to secure a successful future for their idealistic children was just as naïve as my father's attempt to secure one for me. In those days the environment in Wellesley was a bigoted one. Real estate agents would not show homes to Jews or blacks. Rachel frequently found herself arguing against her classmates' prejudices.

Of course, she wanted to be socially acceptable. In Wellesley, that meant she had to join a church. Her parents chose the Unitarians because the minister was a liberal intellectual, and the theology did not include the concept of Jesus as the son of God. Rachel began to teach Sunday school. The curriculum provided rational explanations for the Bible and for religion. Now she thinks that as the daughter of skeptics who moved so often during her childhood, she had a secret longing for the stability and the mystery that religious faith offers. Sometimes she felt a sense of awe during the outdoor services at the Quaker camp where she worked in the Vermont mountains, but she never found a home for it, or developed it. She always associated Christianity, or at least her classmates' upper class brand of Protestantism, with smugness and bigotry. When she went to college she never set foot inside a house of worship.

Once her Sunday school class visited a synagogue in the neighboring town of Newton. There was a bar mitzvah that day. She was captivated by the warmth of the people she met there. The lavish array of food after the service featured items that she would later learn were called bagels and lox, kugel, and strudel. Compared with this spread, which she would one day recognize as the kiddush after services, the tea and cookies after church in Wellesley seemed pallid. But that wasn't the point. To her, the food represented a generosity of spirit, an easy friendliness, that was lacking in her hometown.

Rachel and I met in Cambridge, Maryland, in the summer of 1963, during the most frightening days of the civil rights movement there.

She had just graduated from Bryn Mawr. During those months she and her sister Connie were tutoring black children who hoped to integrate the white schools. I had just graduated from Harvard and planned to become a journalist. I was writing a magazine article about the movement.

In Cambridge, we discovered that we were both enrolled in graduate school at the University of Chicago, where Rachel was going to study social work, and I was planning to read great books in the Committee on Social Thought. We decided to drive west in tandem. It never occurred to either of us that we'd fall in love. In fact, we were a little scared of each other.

When I was in my teens and twenties I usually dated daughters of intermarriages. In my fantasies, I'd get involved with blond WASPs, but when I met them at mixers or saw them in the library or in the classroom I was usually afraid of them. I assumed they would see me in the same way as my classmates at Choate had. But I had twice become intensely involved with Protestant women I met on safer ground: one on the newspaper, the other in the peace movement.

I very seldom dated Jews. It's a bias that I was unaware of then, that disturbs me deeply now. But I want to describe it since I've heard it echoed by many of the Jewish men—and women—we've interviewed for this book.

When I was in high school I read Herman Wouk's novel *Marjorie Morningstar.* Wouk's protagonist, Noel Airman, uses the name "Shirley" to describe the type of woman often referred to today as a Jewish-American princess—a JAP. These "Shirleys" seek careers on the outskirts of adventure—in theater or publishing or liberal politics —and meet the Jewish men who do those interesting jobs. When they marry them, they live in Manhattan in Greenwich Village or on the Upper West Side for a couple of years. Then, when children come along, they buy a home in Mamaroneck or Great Neck, become regular synagogue-goers, send their youngsters to Hebrew school twice a week. Whenever I dated a Jew I feared she was a Shirley in disguise who was waiting to consume my persona as an adventurous liberal journalist with her demands.

I think my attitude toward Jewish women was connected to my fear that I was unattractive as a Jewish man. I became aware of that feeling in college when I read "Time of Her Time," a novelette by Norman Mailer. In that story, Sergius O'Shaughnessy, a twenty-seven-year-old blond Irish-Catholic bullfighting teacher, brings a nineteen-year-old Jewish undergraduate to her first orgasm. Her steady boyfriend Arthur, a Jewish accountant, is "too passive" to give her that kind of sexual pleasure. Back then, I was afraid that I was possessed by a modern-day dybbuk—an adenoidal Arthur, who would shame me by emerging from whatever more attractive self I managed to create.

Besides, I was still the boy who had sat in the Choate chapel, staring at the Protestants, who seemed so graceful. Even though I couldn't be one of them, I envied them. They were America. I was an outsider. While I was still in my early twenties that was an unbearable thought. For, like most Jews who went to prep schools and Ivy League colleges at the time I did, I wanted to be an American in my professional life. I remember talking with a Jewish friend at Harvard who told me, quite coolly, that he wanted to be President of the United States and figured he could make it if he married an upper class Protestant: He did marry the woman of his dreams, and settled for becoming a multimillionaire. Most of my Jewish classmates didn't have such grandiose self-images. Some wanted to be American lawyers. Others wanted to be American doctors. Scores of us intermarried.

I wanted to be an American writer—a latter-day John Dos Passos or James Agee—and I think that, at some level of my mind, I doubted that I could roam freely through the country's heartland if I were married to a Jew. I described my ideal woman as "the glow girl of the Western pike," and when I did date gentiles I saw them as my passport to America.

When I first met Rachel, I felt my usual mixture of fear and attraction. I justified that feeling with an inverse snobbism. I told another civil rights worker in Cambridge that she looked like the kind of cool preppie who had stepped out of the pages of an F. Scott Fitzgerald novel. I didn't believe that someone who seemed as calm and self-possessed as she would be attracted to me.

Years later, she laughed when I described my first image of her. She felt disdain for the narrow bourgeois world view of the Wellesley middle class, where bank vice presidents from Pennsylvania or Ohio aspired to emulate the Boston elite. That attitude must have intertwined with her obvious intelligence to make her classmates regard her as an intellectual. The most popular boys and girls seldom invited her to their parties. She often felt like a social failure. How they intimidated her, with their endless supply of pleated Pendleton skirts and Shetland sweaters! They seemed to take their popularity for granted. They assumed it would last a lifetime. The world was supposed to be run by Republican Protestant socialites like them, not brainy Democratic outcasts like Rachel.

When she met me, she was intrigued that I was a Jew. She had Jewish friends, and was acutely aware that the Jewish people had been persecuted in history. But she did not have a fantasized image of Jews that was comparable to my image of Protestants. She did not see Jewish life as an enticing avenue of escape from the boredom of suburbia, as some gentiles do. She wasn't aware of the familiar axiom that "Jews make good husbands."

She later told me that she felt as threatened by me as I was by her. I was so intense, so filled with a journalist's self-important talk about the places I'd been and the people I'd met, that I seemed exotic and arrogant to her. Despite my image of her as a character out of Fitzgerald, she saw herself as a shy, sheltered girl from the suburbs. She feared I would perceive her as unimaginative and unworldly.

When we set out for Chicago, in two different cars, we made a plan to have a ten-minute cup of coffee at a Howard Johnson's near Pittsburgh. We stayed there for nearly an hour. We spent two hours at the next Howard Johnson's, three at the next, until finally we were more involved in talking to each other, gazing at each other, than we were in trying to reach our destination. Rachel was warmer and gentler than I'd imagined. She talked about a week she'd spent as an exchange student at a black college in North Carolina, about a paper she had written about Zionism, about her idol, Jane Addams, who had made her want to study social work near Hull House. She told me that grandmothers always liked her. I knew I could love someone who cared enough about old people to boast about that.

On that trip, she says, she began to see my brashness as enthusiasm. She was surprised that someone she perceived as worldly asked her so many questions, and listened to her answers with such interest. Because I was intense she expected me to be serious. So she was surprised that my jokes kept her laughing for minutes at a stretch. Once, she recalls, she was getting too sleepy to drive her Volkswagen, and I asked a truck driver for some No-Doz. We followed him out through the dark to his huge trailer, and I climbed up into the cabin with him to get the pills. She thought that was a bold, chivalrous gesture.

At twilight we ate at a hamburger joint in Benton Harbor, Michigan. When we were finished I told Rachel it was Yom Kippur and I was going to fast for the next twenty-four hours. It didn't occur to me to go to synagogue, or to stop traveling, as Jewish law demands. I'd never fasted before in my life, but that year I wanted to express my solidarity with the Israelis I'd met when I taught there. Rachel was fascinated that I was doing something that was Jewish. She said she would fast, too.

At about nine o'clock that night we arrived in Hyde Park, where my younger sister Holly had an apartment. Holly had an Orthodox Jewish roommate. During vacations, she'd surprised the rest of the family by talking about her growing commitment to the religion. So I was amazed when she suggested that we go to a delicatessen for a bite.

"But, Holly, how can we?" I asked. "It's Yom Kippur!"

"Paul, Yom Kippur isn't until next week," she said.

Of course, I was mortified. Rachel was interested in my intentions and did not mock my ignorance. I think this fact strengthened the love I had begun to feel for her.

It turns out that ethnically we were a fairly typical interfaith couple. In 1985, Egon Mayer concluded a study which showed that about 70 percent of intermarried Jews chose Protestants with Western European roots as their mates. Most of the remaining 30 percent chose Catholics. But our backgrounds seemed so similar that we never thought we had religious or cultural differences.

Many interfaith couples have to contend with parents who rage at the fact that they've failed to wed within the faith. We didn't have that problem. Our families seemed so delighted with our romance that we never guessed that my father and Rachel's grandmother had secret reservations.

Before we were married my father told my sister Holly that he felt a pang of remorse because I was marrying outside the religion he had stopped practicing after his bar mitzvah. The pang might have developed into a lasting ache if he hadn't been so fond of Rachel. Still, he'd sent me to Choate and rejoiced when I got into Harvard. How could he complain when I chose a wife who'd been raised in the world of his fantasies? Rachel's Episcopalian grandmother regretted the fact that her oldest granddaughter and namesake was marrying someone who would never join the church that gave her life such meaning. But her sense of decorum prohibited her from voicing any disapproval.

Besides, though our parents weren't calculating people (neither of us had been encouraged to marry for money or status), we had made a match that suited their needs as well as ours. Rachel's father was a management consultant; her mother, a children's librarian. From their point of view, my father, the TV producer, and my mother, an ardent civil rights activist, occupied a realm of wealth and power that far exceeded anything in their circles.

By contrast, Rachel's parents, whose Protestant ancestors had settled in New England in the seventeenth century, occupied a realm of psychological security that no Cowan or Spiegel had ever entered. My mother's obsession with the Holocaust was so ingrained that she urged me to learn a trade as well as a profession, in case we had to leave all our possessions behind and flee to some foreign land. My father didn't want his children to participate in the civil rights movement or oppose the war in Vietnam because he feared that Jews who offended people in power could be jailed or exiled without warning. When my brother Geoff and I spent the summer of 1964 as freedom workers in Mississippi, he begged us to write a letter to FBI director J. Edgar Hoover stating that we were going South for patriotic reasons, not subversive ones.

So Rachel had married into a rich, well-connected family with deep underlying immigrant insecurities; I had married into a less glamorous one which offered stability and deep roots in America's soil.

During our courtship and the first years of our marriage each of us discovered how much we appreciated the other's family. Rachel's was very close. But from her point of view their conversations were a little too quiet, their disputes were too indirect. She wished they celebrated birthdays and holidays with more exuberance.

By contrast, I saw Rachel's outwardly calm, rather ascetic household as a refuge from my voluble, extravagantly decorated one. Her parents were interested in us, but they didn't seem as emotionally entangled in our decisions about where we'd live or where we'd work, as my mother and father were. They didn't suffer if we went two or three weeks without telephoning them, as my father did. They didn't impose on us the relentless demands and ambitions that made me despair of ever satisfying my parents.

Rachel adored my warmhearted, protective father. She felt strengthened by the concern for us that I found somewhat smothering.

Each of us was interested in the other's religious culture, too. After we returned from Israel I got a job at *The Village Voice* and Rachel found work at a settlement house. We moved into a new apartment in the Chelsea area of New York. As a housewarming gift, Rachel bought me a copy of the Passover Haggadah illustrated by Ben Shahn. She was looking forward to using it.

In spite of the prejudice she'd met in Israel, she was still curious about Judaism. She wanted us to celebrate Jewish holidays at home. She wasn't sure what all of them signified, but she knew she liked ceremony, and wanted our future children to have more celebration in their lives than she'd had in hers. She thought it would be terrible if they grew up to be as ignorant of Jewish history and Jewish traditions as I was.

But it never occurred to her that she might become a Jew. She thought Passover and Hanukkah would decorate a life with an American core. They would be appendages to Christmas and Easter, part of a secular calendar.

When she gave me the Haggadah she assumed I'd know how to use it, and was sure I'd be pleased by it. But the book was almost as foreign to me as it was to her. Once or twice, when I was a boy, my parents made a dutiful appearance at a business acquaintance's very formal seder and they took me along. My father seemed to enjoy it. My mother was restless and eager to leave. I had no idea of what was going on. From then on I assumed all seders were long, dull events filled with words I didn't understand. I couldn't imagine myself caring enough about the unfamiliar Jewish holiday to make it enjoyable for Rachel and me.

So I took the Haggadah from her, looked at it a little doubtfully, and said, "I don't know what you do with this." I seemed indifferent to the gift she had bought me with such love. She was disappointed.

Once I urged her to go with me to the Easter service at the Cathedral of St. John the Divine in New York. I was looking forward to the Episcopal hymns that had given me such aesthetic pleasure when I heard them in the Choate chapel. But Rachel was used to the unadorned ceremony at the Wellesley Hills Unitarian Church, where the minister was dressed in a simple black robe and the sanctuary was filled with richly scented white lilies. At the cathedral, the service began when the bishop knocked on the sanctuary door with a staff. Then a procession of priests, choir members, and acolytes walked toward the altar. The bishop wore a splendid robe and a miter on his head. An acolyte preceded him swinging the censer, wafting a cloud of incense over the procession. From Rachel's New England point of view, the sights and smells seemed medieval. I was surprised when she recoiled at the pageantry I found so fascinating.

But in spite of my feelings about Passover, and Rachel's about Easter, neither of us wanted a life that was shorn of ceremony. That became clear to both of us when we had children. We decided we could celebrate Christmas and Hanukkah, Easter and Passover. We were sure that by enjoying all the holidays our traditions had to offer we would enrich our family's life.

Over the years, we had begun to see that we were not as culturally similar as we had thought on our wedding day. To our surprise, half-hidden ethnic attitudes kept emerging as issues between us.

Shortly after we settled in New York we both read Isaac Bashevis Singer's novel *The Family Moskat,* which portrays Jews who are so comfortable in Poland that they remain too long to escape the Nazis. We began to discuss the Holocaust. As a teenager, Rachel had always pictured herself as a resister. But what if we had had children? Would she have stayed to fight or would she have used her blond hair and blue eyes as camouflage to flee the Nazis and protect her young? I didn't feel I would have had that choice. I'd have been rounded up like any other Jew. I was personally imperiled by anti-Semitism. Rachel, less vulnerable, saw it as a vile form of prejudice.

In those days, the war in Vietnam posed an immediate problem. I was twenty-five, draft age, and completely opposed to the U.S. presence there. Like most young married couples, Rachel and I spent a lot of time discussing what I should do. I wasn't a pacifist. I didn't want to go to jail or leave the country. We didn't feel ready to have children. Besides, despite my feelings about the war, I believed I should serve America as a way of repaying an immigrant's debt of gratitude. Rachel thought my attitude was a little silly. She couldn't understand how a Cowan could regard himself as an immigrant. But she agreed to join the Peace Corps as a form of alternative service.

In June 1967, we were volunteers in Guayaquil, Ecuador, a muggy, dirty tropical city that we had come to love during the year we had been there. One morning the Voice of America announced that war had broken out in Israel. According to early reports, Arab bombs were falling on Jerusalem and Tel Aviv. In my imagination, they were killing the people I had come to love when I lived in Israel. In those early hours of the war, it wasn't clear that Israel would be able to overcome the combined forces of Syria, Jordan, and Egypt.

I remember walking down to the Peace Corps office, and feeling quite lonely when I realized that none of the other volunteers was as disturbed as I was. I decided to go to the Israeli Embassy, and volunteer to serve. It was another surge of the loyalty I had felt at Choate. Rachel was upset by the Arab attack on Israel, but didn't understand why I felt compelled to do anything about it. From her point of view, I was a Jew in name only, one who didn't know when Yom Kippur was or how to use a Haggadah, one who was content to have a minister marry us. And although I didn't believe in the war in Vietnam, I was ready to leave her in the tropics and fly halfway around the world to risk my life on behalf of a people who viewed our marriage as a form of apostasy. It made no sense to her. When I got to the embassy, the consul told me that I was too late. The war was already over.

It was a small difference between us, but it persisted. When we got back to the United States, and became part of the anti-war movement, I found myself increasingly uncomfortable with the left's attitude toward Israel. I was a dove, but sometimes Rachel and I would hear a criticism of Israeli military policy and find ourselves reacting very differently. She would assume that Israel was partly to blame; I'd wonder whether the criticisms contained a hint of anti-Semitism.

These political differences only cropped up occasionally. But our tensions over household details recurred so often that we sometimes wondered whether our marriage could survive them. In those days, we usually saw the traits that annoyed us in one another as willful forms of stubbornness and sloppiness that could be resolved if we would simply decide to be more considerate. Some of them were. Others were the result of sexism (I wasn't raised with the idea that husbands had to cook, clean house, or take care of children) and the sweeping changes in married life that the women's movement created. But no matter who cooked or took care of the children or tidied up the living room, chronic disagreements remained. Now we realize that many were the result of ethnic differences.

As a writer, I usually worked at home. When Rachel was a community organizer and political activist, she went to an office. I felt abandoned when she didn't call during the day. She felt smothered when I called her often.

By 1971, we had two small children, Lisa and Matt. When they had colds or mild flus our tensions got worse. I thought sick kids should be coddled. She thought I was infecting them with my hypochondria.

We could never agree on a simple grocery list. She believed in the motto "waste not, want not" and bought small portions of food. I saw generous amounts of food as expressions of love. I felt uneasy when there wasn't enough food in the refrigerator. Rachel thought I was wasteful. I thought she was stingy.

One summer afternoon Rachel and I ran into John Pearce, a psychiatrist friend, at the Martha's Vineyard Agricultural Fair. He told us that he was practicing a new form of family therapy called ethnotherapy, which helps couples understand that some of their differences have roots in their ethnic pasts. It derives from the premise that individuals are shaped significantly by their ethnic culture, not solely by particular family dynamics and internal psychological forces.

"What do you mean?" Rachel asked.

"Well, take yourselves," he said. "A Jew and a New England WASP. I'll bet that when you two have a disagreement at night, Paul wants to talk it out and Rachel wants to leave it. When you wake up in the morning, Rachel wants to spring out of bed and begin the day's activities while Paul wants to stay in bed and talk about your relationship."

The insight was accurate. When we have a fight, Rachel tries to ignore it, and I try to explore it. I hate to go to sleep until we've discussed a problem as fully as possible. Rachel gets angry at me for keeping her awake. I come from a very talkative Jewish family and Rachel comes from a reserved Protestant one, so our negotiating styles are very different. I argue melodramatically, exaggerating to make my point, trying to drag Rachel's feelings out of her. But what I see as a natural, heated conversation threatens her with obliteration. I think I'm expressing my emotions—she thinks I'm bullying her. When she withdraws or begins to cry, I feel terrible because I've been raised to think that reserved people are calmer and wiser than I am. Besides, men shouldn't hurt women. So I try to heal the wound I've inflicted, hovering over Rachel, asking her how she is. I punish her with words. She punishes me with silences.

Sometimes we can pause in the middle of a fight and laugh at these

familiar differences. But when we were first married it did not occur
to us to translate them into ethnic terms. We were, in reality, dissimilar people, spawned by dissimilar heritages. Our inability to recognize each other's feelings through the distorting lens of culture sometimes made us feel desperate, neurotic, and trapped.

But those fights were unpleasant episodes in a happy marriage. We
were so busy with politics and work, friends and family, and with the
endless details of child care, that we seldom focused on our cultural
differences and never thought about our religious attitudes. Christmas and Hanukkah, Easter and Passover were pleasant interludes in a
hectic schedule. They were not the underpinnings of identity, certainly not cornerstones of the year. If anyone had asked, we would
have said that institutionalized religion had nothing to offer us.

But I had begun to care deeply and specifically about being a Jew.
That emotion, which flickered at Choate, in Israel, and during the Six
Day War became a fixed part of my conscious life after I became
involved with Catholics who opposed the war in Vietnam.

In 1972, as a reporter for the *Voice,* I interviewed Daniel Berrigan,
the priest who had poured blood on draft cards to oppose the war in
Vietnam. He had scuttled a safe career as a college chaplain and poet
to resist the war non-violently. Now, he was a fugitive from justice,
traveling from one city to another to evade the FBI. His faith and
courage impressed me so much that I decided to keep writing about
his community, the Catholic left.

I loved being among people whose intense discussions about politics and theology were undergirded by a sweeping concern for one
another—for a friend's ailing father or newborn niece, for a former
priest or nun who couldn't quite function in the secular world. Sometimes, at night, in their apartments and brownstones, the Catholics
who were waging a peaceful revolution against war would break out a
bottle of whiskey and sing old Irish revolutionary songs like "Kevin
Barry." I felt privileged to be included in their romantic history.

I was aware that their religious culture was very different from
mine. Many of the Catholics I admired insisted that they were working with blacks at home, opposing imperialism overseas, because of
Jesus Christ. But I hadn't gone to Mississippi or joined the Peace
Corps because of Jesus Christ. One night, at a rally in a church, a
speaker chose a striking litany to punctuate his denunciation of rac-
ism and the war. "Jesus Christ is my problem," he kept saying. I had

heard that image before—in the Choate chapel, from black ministers in the civil rights movement, from religious people who opposed the war. It simply meant that Jesus was a goad in the fight for social justice.

But that night cultural awareness became culture shock. I was stunned to hear how differently the speaker's phrase rang in my ears. Jesus Christ was my problem too, but not in the way the speaker experienced it. Jesus Christ—or at least the standard Christian interpretation of him—had been a problem for me and for all Jews throughout history: during the Inquisition, in the Crusades, we had been slaughtered in his name.

I respected the men and women I met in the Catholic left. But why was I attaching myself to them, writing about them, instead of learning more about my Jewish roots?

I decided to do that by researching a piece about the poor Jews who still lived on New York's Lower East Side. In my imagination, they resembled my grandfather Jake Cohen, the Orthodox Jew whose past was such a mystery to me.

Sometimes, at night, I'd go into the tiny basement synagogues where they prayed. I got very confused as I tried to follow the service. I couldn't read Hebrew. I'd forget that the pages of the prayer book are arranged from back to front, in the opposite direction from the Episcopal prayer book I'd used at Choate. In church, people stand, sit, and kneel in unison. In those tiny Orthodox shuls, people pray at their own pace. Sometimes, I'd see some people praying raptly while others gossiped. When the congregation began the portion of the service I later learned was the *amidah* (the central prayer) they'd stand up at the same time. But each person sat down when he finished. It seemed so random. I could never figure out when to stand and when to sit, whether to look pious or engage in a conversation.

But it was an exhilarating experience for me. I felt as if those old Jews were inhabitants of my family's past.

Sometimes I'd visit their tiny apartments in low-income housing projects. On their walls, I'd see a large sign which bore the name of a local funeral home and attested to the fact that they had already paid for their coffin, their hearse, their shroud. Beneath it, there would be a smaller handwritten sign: in case of death, it would say, contact this son or daughter, that nephew or niece, in Manhattan or Long Island or Westchester County. The sign was always on the most visible part of the wall, next to the family pictures, so that whoever found the corpse would know what relative to contact.

It was a practical reminder of an unsettling reality. The youngsters never visited. "Could I write about that?" I would ask. "Not if you mention my name," the old people would invariably reply. They feared the publicity might embarrass their relatives. They might cease sending the two- or three-hundred-dollar monthly checks on which the old people depended.

When I described them in a *Village Voice* article called "Jews Without Money, Revisited" I got hundreds of appreciative letters from Jewish readers. To my astonishment, I was suddenly a very public Jew.

Rachel had never quite understood my involvement with the Catholic left. Though she liked the people I was meeting, their religion reminded her of the Christian piety that was anathema in her family. By contrast, my sudden surge of Jewish interest engaged her at once even though she had a specific reason to feel hurt and threatened.

In those days she took photographs for most of my articles. But we had agreed that she shouldn't photograph the Jews on the Lower East Side. They might have become so angry at us for intermarrying that they would never have told me their stories. But when I came home and talked about my adventures in shuls and housing projects she was fascinated.

She also saw that my experiences were awakening ethnic feelings in me. For a time, she worried that I might wander too far into the Jewish world I was discovering and adopt religious observances that would make me unrecognizable to her. Maybe my new Jewishness would exclude her. But it was a whisper of a fear. She never mentioned it to me.

It had never even occurred to me that my sudden involvement with religious Jews would provoke any change in my family's life. I didn't see any contradiction between searching for my roots on the Lower East Side and maintaining a religiously neutral household. I was trying to explore my Jewish identity, not define my faith. Those two categories still seemed distinguishable.

We assumed that we would initiate Lisa and Matt into a world that contained as much diversity as possible. Our Jewish and Christian holidays would not be religious ones—they'd just be culturally enriching celebrations. We wanted our children to feel equally at home with the black Baptists we'd known in Mississippi, the poor Jews on the Lower East Side, the Catholic radicals who were still our friends. We dreamed of raising children with rainbows in their souls.

We still love the fact that the world is a rainbow of people. But we have come to think that children need to feel immersed in one strong color so that they can take their place confidently next to the others.

For when Lisa was five and Matt three, they both asked questions that showed us that they were confused about their identities.

One night in March 1973, we were invited to a puppet show dramatizing the story of Purim. At the dramatic high point, when the evil Persian vizier Haman threatened to murder all the Jews, Matt ran across the room and threw himself into Rachel's arms, pleading for comfort. "Mom, he won't get me, will he? I'm only half Jewish."

Months later, as Rachel was tucking Lisa into bed, she looked up and said, "Mom, would it hurt your feelings if I said I was Jewish?"

Their innocent questions raised more difficult ones in our minds. What did it mean for Matt to regard himself as half and half? Or to fear that his Jewish half was threatened? What did it mean for Lisa to feel that if she identified herself as a Jew she would reject her mother?

Didn't we have to think more seriously about their religious identities? We realized that our offhand decision to profess equal respect for both religions, without teaching the substance of either, meant in practice that we were raising our children in a vacuum of information and experience. We'd been telling each other that the children could choose between Judaism and Christianity when they grew up. Gradually, we were beginning to understand that unless we reached a clearcut decision for ourselves they might never know enough to make any choice at all. Or, still worse, they might feel that choosing between religions meant choosing between parents.

Some parents don't feel these questions are particularly upsetting —they respond to remarks like Lisa's and Matt's by insisting that it's special to be both.

Frequently, though, such questions are time bombs. They eventually force people to decide whether they want to raise their children in one religion rather than in both or neither. For some couples the decision-making process is a challenge. For others it causes a painful reevaluation of their lives.

Rachel and I thought that Lisa and Matt were asking for greater clarity in their identities, and that they wanted us to make some basic decisions for them. Did we want them to be Jews or Christians?

We realized that, with our scanty seders and Hanukkahs, we weren't doing much to teach them about Judaism. While I was researching "Jews Without Money, Revisited," I'd immersed myself in the social history of Jewish immigrants. I'd read such novels as Abraham Cahan's *The Rise of David Levinsky* and Henry Roth's *Call It Sleep*, and anthropological books like *Life Is with People*. But all I knew about the religion was that I loved the sound of men praying in an Orthodox shul, the ritual of washing my hands before I ate in an Orthodox home, and listening to my host sing the Grace after meals when we were done, the sight of parents and children wishing their friends a "good Shabbos" as they strolled home from synagogue for a peaceful lunch.

How could we transmit a heritage that was outside the realm of Rachel's experience and that had been attenuated beyond recognition in my childhood? Rachel started us on the road to answering that question. In 1973, she invited our friend Jerry Raik, an actor and teacher who had enthralled our children when he told the story of the Maccabees at their day care center, to tell it again at a Hanukkah celebration in our home. From then on, every Hanukkah and Passover, she organized celebrations in our apartment for forty fascinated adults and children in which Jerry would tell the stories of the Maccabees' revolution and the miracle of the lights, or of Moses and Miriam's leading the Exodus from Egypt.

Soon we were launched on an unexpectedly exciting path. With a dozen other parents and some graduate students with strong backgrounds in Jewish education, we helped start the Havurah School, a Jewish school for about twenty neighborhood children that met once a week. The parents had agreed to assist the teachers so we began to read Jewish books and take classes in Judaism in order to figure out ways of teaching Torah to six- and seven-year-olds. We tried to make the school as joyous as possible. We helped the children interpret Bible stories in improvisational plays, or recount them over a mock television station we called WJEW. We helped plan retreats, which often coincided with the Jewish festivals of Sukkot and Shavuot. We brought the children to informal worship services in Upper West Side living rooms.

Lisa and Matt triggered something else in us. By the mid-1970s, the women's movement and the new emphasis on sexual liberation had caused an explosion in our world. Marriages that had seemed stable just a year or two earlier were in ruins. When our children's best friends' parents separated, Lisa begged us to promise that we wouldn't get divorced. We had no intention of divorcing, but words alone don't salve a young child's fears. Anyway, our children's pleas coincided with their questions about their religious identities. So we decided to light Friday night candles—Shabbat candles—as a sign to the kids that our family was very important to us. Every Friday night we would all be home together in peace.

Adopting a new custom is not so easy. Rachel bought the candlesticks, though she was terrified that the Orthodox Jew who sold them to her would tell her she didn't belong in his store. Actually, he was careful to show her pairs which had the blessings transliterated in English letters. But she felt uncomfortable uttering the Hebrew prayers. She wished she could conjure up an image of a pious ancestor covering her eyes before uttering them. I felt a little self-conscious when I put on a yarmulke, and very ashamed that I didn't know the blessings either. Luckily, we had a neighbor, Judy Rosenberg Pritchett, who could teach us the words and melody. Within a few months, we both felt at ease with the ritual. It became an anchor in our very hectic week.

Within a year, the Shabbat suppers that had once seemed to serve a secular purpose came to feel like sanctified time. Hanukkah and Passover, once pale adjuncts to Christmas and Easter, became vital moments in our family's life. Soon, they were *our* holidays. Gradually, we came to feel that Rosh Hashanah and Yom Kippur were integral to the cycle of the year.

Years later, Lisa's bat mitzvah and Matt's bar mitzvah would be two of the proudest days of our lives. These occasions seemed to emerge out of each child's very special, private self and forge a link between our individual family and the mysterious expanse of Jewish history.

But it was years before we became observant Jews: years before we both acculturated to the religion. It might have taken even longer if a family tragedy hadn't occurred in our lives.

In November 1976 my parents died in a fire. In its aftermath Jewish friends took care of our children, helped us grieve, provided us with food during the week-long shivva period, the seven days of mourning that we would never have imagined observing without their help. It was the first time I had realized how important religion—and a religious community—can be in the midst of great grief. My parents had perished. I would perish, too. Judaism, an imperishable, embracing force, took on a new value for us.

After the fire, I felt obliged to carry out a mysterious wish of my father's. He had always wanted me to write an article about Orthodox Jewish craftsmen, men who wrote Torah scrolls or produced ritual objects like the mezzuzahs Jews affix to their doors, the talesim (prayer shawls) they wear in synagogue, or the special matzoh Hassidic Jews make for Passover. I had been reluctant to do that while he was still alive. I was afraid that Orthodox Jews would denounce me because I had intermarried. But after the fire the article seemed a fitting way to honor my father.

To research the article, I knew that I needed an expert to explain the intricacies of Orthodox customs and laws. I turned for help to a Hassidic rabbi named Joseph Singer, who seemed to have stepped out of the European Orthodox world that my grandfather Jake Cohen must have yearned for. His world was such an attractive, exciting place, where religious observance and good deeds were inextricably intertwined, that I began to see Judaism and the Almighty through his eyes. His example moved me to go to synagogue as many days as possible to participate in morning prayer. That act had been totally alien to me just a few months before. But when Rabbi Singer gave me tefillin—ritual objects that pious Jews place on their arms and heads during daily morning prayer—I found that I liked winding the leather straps around my arms. It made me feel bound to Mount Sinai, and to my people. Sometimes, if I was lucky, I found a peaceful place inside myself during those minutes of prayer.

Until the fire, Rachel's Jewish involvement had been primarily rooted in our household and our neighborhood. She looked forward to High Holiday services, which, in those years, took place in the scruffy Upper West Side apartments that our religious Jewish friends saw as desirable alternatives to the formal, impersonal synagogues in which they'd been raised. It took a few years for Rachel to get used to the fact that on the High Holy Days Jews worshipped for most of a day, not an hour like the members of the Wellesley Hills Unitarian Church did at Easter. From the start, she looked forward to the singing, the discussions, the sense of community.

The spiritual foundation of the days between Rosh Hashanah and

Yom Kippur is *tshuvah* (repentance): during that time, one looks inward, seeking to make some progress on a lifelong journey toward better relations with people and with God.

At the New York Havurah, where there was no official rabbi, men and women with good Jewish educations would give sermons combining knowledge of the texts with introspection. As a matter of custom, people would ask one another's forgiveness in case they had caused each other pain during the previous year. As part of the traditional memorial service, men and women would reminisce about loved ones who had died. On Yom Kippur, especially, the songs and prayers seemed to gain a tidal force as nightfall approached.

Rachel was surprised by the intense emotions that swept over her as she sat on the floor of the crowded apartment. She loved the feeling that people's prayers were both communal and personal. They seemed like direct, intimate communications with God. She became immersed in the prayer book, which had been edited by Jules Harlow, a Conservative rabbi. All her life, she'd been troubled by an inner voice—an echo of her ancestors' Calvinism—which deemed every flaw a sin, which demanded she be perfect. By contrast, the meditations Harlow had compiled contained a patient view of human frailty and human change. They promised to help her accept her shortcomings.

These experiences allowed her to feel engaged with the Jewish community. But in those days she still called herself "a fellow traveler." She rejected the idea of conversion because she felt the act would make no sense unless it followed a religious experience which left her with the certainty of God's reality.

But my parents' death, which occurred when we were in our midthirties, forced us into our first direct confrontation with mortality. In its wake, Rachel found that she was comforted by Jewish prayer. She was hungry to learn more. She took classes in the book of Exodus, in Kabbalah, in Hebrew.

We spent the summer of 1979 in Israel. This time our rudimentary Hebrew and our thirst for knowledge prompted people to befriend us. Soon Rachel developed a sense of connection to Jews as a people.

One Saturday morning in April 1980, a small group of Havurah school parents were in the midst of discussing the story of Joseph. Once a month that year, we gathered in Jerry and Barrie Raik's apartment at 111th Street and Broadway to read from the Torah and say a few prayers. That morning, Rachel was gazing out the window at the unfinished spires of the Cathedral of St. John the Divine, to which her Episcopalian grandmother had made a contribution in honor of her graduation from college.

It suddenly struck her that this magnificent building was part of the furniture of her childhood memories, but it would never be her adult home. From now on, the Hebrew prayers and Torah readings that comprised the service in the Raiks' living room would be signposts on the religious pathway that was gradually coming into focus.

She still wasn't sure what she believed about God, but she knew that her questions about the nature of a Supreme Being were among the most important in her life. Now she was wrestling with her child-hood certainty that religion was a crutch. Would she betray her family if she became a believer? Had she fallen prey to superstition?

She had been hoping for a sign: for the kind of sudden revelation that some Christians describe as an epiphany. But the sign, she real-ized, wasn't likely to come. Instead, her belief—and her understand-ing of that belief—would deepen slowly, at a pace she couldn't con-trol.

In explaining her decision to convert, she told me that it was as if, for a long time, her weight had been on one foot—she had been an agnostic with an attraction to Judaism. Now her weight had shifted to the other foot—she was a Jew.

A Hidden Issue Emerges

It turned out that what was private to us seemed interesting to others, especially because I used my job as a reporter for *The Village Voice* as a way of exploring New York's Jewish world. In the late 1970s, I was offered a contract to write a book about my intensifying Jewish feelings. I dawdled a long time, reluctant to chart my changes, but when the book appeared in 1982, *An Orphan in History* was taken as a sign that people as thoroughly assimilated as I could find meaning in Judaism. Similarly, Rachel's conversion indicated that the ancient religion had a great deal to offer modern people who had been raised in other faiths.

In 1981, Sheila Peltz Weinberg, the Hillel director who had heard

us discuss our experiences at a Jewish retreat, asked us to speak to
students at Swarthmore, Bryn Mawr, the University of Pennsylvania
and Penn State. It began as a merry trip in the middle of a lovely week
in early spring. It had not crossed our minds that intermarriage had
affected so many people. By the time we returned home, we had
discovered an area of enormous pain and confusion.

At Penn, a Catholic woman who planned to marry a Jew and was
thinking of converting to Judaism told us that the nuns who'd had
high hopes for her as a child were now saying novenas for her soul.
She was ostracized when she attended baptisms and funerals in her
old neighborhood. Yet her fiancé was reluctant to observe Shabbat or
have a kosher home, which were the rituals she hoped to adopt. When
his parents phoned him, they always asked if "the shiksa" were there.
When they went to his parents' house, she felt insulted that they
served larger portions of food to him than to her. He was unwilling to
confront his parents on her behalf. Instead, he urged *her* to understand them, to empathize with their suffering as Jews. She felt very
lonely. Her Catholic parents and her Jewish fiancé were accomplices
to her isolation.

At Swarthmore, one young man told us his parents wouldn't let
him have the car if he dated a non-Jew, they'd lend him the secondhand car if he dated a half Jew, and the new car if he dated a Jew.
Everyone laughed at his parents' attempt to control his social life.

Then a freshman started sobbing. Stretching out her arm, she said,
"Half the blood in these veins is Jewish and I don't know anything
about it."

Several Jewish parents came to talk with us privately. One woman
told us that her daughter was marrying a Methodist. Should she
attend the wedding? She didn't want to lose the child's affection. But
she feared she'd be physically sickened by the sight of a minister
pronouncing the vows. To our astonishment, she cried as she asked *us*
where she had gone wrong. She felt like a failure because her daughter was marrying outside the faith.

Another parent had refused to speak to his son for years after he
married a Protestant. But now that there was a grandson his feelings
had changed. How could he establish contact with the child? Should
he send a card at Rosh Hashanah, and a gift at Hanukkah? Or would
those acts offend the boy's father, his Jewish son, and prevent him
from seeing his grandchild?

They all saw us as experts. But what did we know? Intermarriage had never brought this degree of pain to our families—or to us. Still, our ignorance didn't matter. People were starved to talk to anyone who would listen sympathetically.

We described their need to as many friends as would listen. Fortunately, by 1981, we had become sufficiently well known in the Jewish world that some rabbis and communal leaders took our opinions seriously. Perhaps we could help solve a problem that was important and very difficult to approach.

In 1981, Reynold Levy, the director of New York City's 92nd Street YMHA, invited us to lead five-week workshop cycles for interfaith couples, and Yehuda Rosenman, Director of Communal Affairs of the American Jewish Committee, arranged for us to conduct one-night sessions in six cities.

To our surprise, we discovered we were garnering an insight into the unspoken psychic lives of hundreds of thousands of Americans. For intermarriage is a lens through which one can see the melting pot at work as it affects one ethnic community and many individual human lives.

Many of the couples who come to our workshops or let us interview them have never before discussed their complicated feelings about intermarriage. But those who decide to be open about their emotions often talk with an intimacy that was missing when Woody Allen broke up with Diane Keaton in *Annie Hall* and when Robert Redford and Barbra Streisand quarreled in *The Way We Were*. We have heard honest disclosures of the ways Jews and Christians see themselves and each other inside the privacy of their homes. In these relationships, pressures mount as differences arise. Ancient heritages conflict behind closed doors. Even people who feel they've rejected their family's traditions in the name of modernity discover that their ethno-religious backgrounds affect the work they do, the way they think about education and food, sex, and money.

Many couples learn that they have far more powerful feelings about their heritages than they realized when they met. Often their differences are highlighted when they discuss the "December dilemma," trying to decide whether to celebrate Christmas, Hanukkah, or both, or when they seek to agree on the faith with which they'll raise their children.

Asymmetrical Responses

There are ethnic and theological reasons for that. Many Americans assume that in this country, which prides itself on pluralism, all faiths are variations on a common religious theme. Thus, the nation's values are supposed to stem from a "Judeo-Christian" tradition. The term does signify a shared belief that there is an ethical power in the universe which transcends human will; it insists that the force is represented by one God. Those are important religious similarities.

But the idea of a Judeo-Christian tradition does not suggest the differences between the two faiths. For Jews believe that God made a covenant with them as an entire, specific people at Mount Sinai, and that nothing has happened since then to create a new basis for their relationship with the Almighty. Their faith and way of life are based on their Bible, and on its later rabbinic interpretations.

Christians believe that God made a new covenant with all of humanity when he sacrificed His son, Jesus. Through belief in Jesus, every individual enters into a covenantal relationship with God. Christians call the Jewish Bible the Old Testament, and regard it as an incomplete work which prefigures the New Testament.

The Reverend Ronald Osborne, chaplain at the University of Iowa, shows the consequences of these differences in an astute essay, "Marriage of Christians and Jews," published in the Episcopal Church magazine *Plumbline* in September 1985. After years of pastoral counseling, marriage counseling, and conversations with Christian and Jewish colleagues and friends, he has come to believe that "Judaism and Christianity live and interact asymmetrically."

Osborne begins by describing the theological asymmetry. "When Christians worship with Jews there is almost nothing they cannot affirm," he writes. "They [may feel that Jesus is missing, but] they can participate fully, without reservation, in the liturgical life of the synagogue, Holy Day rituals, even family rituals.

". . . [But] when Jews worship with Christians almost nothing is accessible, almost everything is problematic. 'Old Testament' (even to call it that already denies Jewish understandings since there is to the Jewish mind but one testament always old but ever made new) readings are selected in the Christian lectionaries to interpret 'New Testament' experiences. Even the Psalms gather Christian meanings . . . Of course the distinctively 'Christian' content of Christian worship [like invocations of the Trinity] are all utterly impossible to a Jewish participant, or at least to one with theological sensitivity and integrity."

The idea of a Judeo-Christian tradition also obscures cultural and psychological differences that can prove troublesome in an intermarriage. In describing that form of asymmetry, Father Osborne reminds his readers that "Judaism is both an ethnic and religious phenomenon . . . Large numbers of Jews think of themselves as Jews and are thought of as Jews even though they have no palpable religious commitment . . . For Christians, at least in theological terms, there is no such thing as Christian ethnicity. One is not a Christian because one's mother is, as is the case in Judaism. One is a Christian because one has been baptized and seeks to live out the meaning of the baptismal covenant."

In one form or another, the cultural asymmetry that Osborne describes permeates our workshops and interviews. Time and again, we have seen that an irreducible core of Jewishness is lodged inside most Jews at the junction of ethnicity and religion. But it is often hard for them to describe it and for their gentile lovers to understand it.

For example, many couples are surprised by their intense disagreements over Christmas. A fight may flare up when the gentile wants to have a Christmas tree in the home they share. Tension may develop when they visit the Christian's family for the holidays, trim the tree, and go to a Christmas Eve church service.

The Jews in interfaith relationships often realize that, from their lover's perspective, the tree and the cross above the altar of a hometown church are part of a Yuletide experience that is filled with happy memories. Nevertheless, they often experience unexpectedly disturbing emotions when they see them. The cross and even the tree make them feel like aliens in Christian America. Sometimes, even though they know their lover isn't religious, they sit in church, glance at the cross, and find themselves thinking of Jews throughout history who were killed because they resisted Christianity. They feel an awakening of loyalty to their four-thousand-year-old history, and wonder if they are abandoning it. They realize that they may be about to marry into a religious culture which could make their children feel Christian, not Jewish. Had they fallen in love with another Jew they might never have had to reexamine their feelings about Judaism or its relationship to Christianity. But those emotions heat up in the crucible of an intermarriage, where they feel their identities are threatened. Nevertheless, they feel that they are being unfair to the gentiles they love, especially because the gentile is often willing to have a menorah in the house at Hanukkah.

Many gentiles listen to the Jews describe their reactions to Christmas, and think they are just plain stubborn. The gentiles usually see their Jewish partners as Americans whose interior feelings must surely resemble their own. They are aware of the Holocaust, but it is something they studied in school, not something their people experienced directly. They know about the Crusades, but seldom think of them as a period when Jews were slaughtered by Christians marching under the banner of the cross. They can't imagine that a modern Jew might feel part of a self-conscious minority who can never forget events that to them seem part of the distant past.

Furthermore, most gentiles can't imagine their holidays as threatening events. After all, most of them think that Jewish holidays will enrich their lives, not threaten their identities. They assume their partners to be fair-minded people who should agree to celebrate both Christmas and Hanukkah. They expect a similar open-mindedness from their Jewish partners.

Few gentiles have ever been asked to see the world through Jewish eyes before they fall in love with a Jew. They've seldom thought about the degree to which Christianity has permeated American culture. So, a Jew may explain a reluctance to celebrate Christmas by saying, "I don't want to take the chance that my children will be Christians. I'll feel like the last link in the chain of Jewish history." A Christian may answer, "why should I give in to your guilt? After all, you married me."

From their own perspectives, both partners in the relationship are right. But they seldom know how to define their differences, let alone resolve them.

In the interests of marital harmony, they remain silent about these complicated, private emotions. Feeling resigned, they remain in what we have come to call spiritual gridlock. They lack the language and the information that will help them get free.

The organized Jewish and Christian communities have responded to intermarriage in asymmetrical ways. The Jewish community is preoccupied with it. The Christian world barely notices it.

There are approximately 133 million Christians in America. Some clergy may counsel interfaith couples, but from the point of view of all the Protestant and Catholic denominations, the number of Christians marrying Jews is a statistical blip. "I don't know anyone who has married a Jew," says Daniel Cattau, former news director for the 8.2-million-member Lutheran Church of America. "I'm sure that for people who are affected, it is cause for intense personal concern. But for most of us, it's not close to home."

Ronald Osborne articulates an Episcopalian perspective. There are 3 million Episcopalians in America—and 60 million Anglicans in the world. If one of them intermarries and converts, Osborne says, "I do feel that a brother or a sister has in effect become an apostate. Someone who has shared what is, by definition, the most important set of values and beliefs there are no longer shares them." But Osborne is not worried about losing Episcopalians to Judaism because there are always new people entering the Church. "At any one time, something like one-third of all the adult Episcopalians are converts from something else. About half the clergy are converts. I'm one. I was born a Methodist. So I feel something that most Jews don't. No matter who leaves us, there will always be more Episcopalians coming along."

There are about 60 million Roman Catholics in America. Church guidelines state that Catholics who marry Protestants or Jews must give the children Catholic educations insofar as possible. But Brother William Martin, who is in charge of drawing up guidelines for Catholics who marry Jews in the New York Archdiocese, describes a personal attitude that is far more tolerant than his church's. Two of his own nephews are being raised as Jews and he accepts that cheerfully. "From a Catholic perspective, faith is a journey and if a Catholic winds up believing that he or she could serve God better as a devout Jew than as a devout Catholic, I'd have to say that's wonderful."

By contrast, Father Joseph Fitzpatrick, professor emeritus of sociology at Fordham University, describes the grief he felt when his niece married a Jew outside the church. "It was a very painful thing for her whole family. She was making a public manifestation of a withdrawal from the faith by not entering into a valid Catholic marriage. The deepest bond we have with each other is our faith—our sense of Catholic values." But, upset as Father Fitzpatrick was, he didn't see his niece's marriage as a threat to the Catholic community.

Most rabbis and Jewish leaders would see the Jew who married

Father Fitzpatrick's niece as part of a problem that threatens the entire Jewish people. For there are only 6 million Jews in America. The fact that so many of them are marrying gentiles is the focus of speeches, panel discussions, magazine articles, and sociological surveys which are part of the agenda of virtually every meeting of every Jewish organization in America. Some of these discussions focus on tactical issues. Does creating programs for intermarried people promote intermarriage? Or do outreach programs transform a problem into a possibility by creating an environment where inter-faith couples might become Jewish couples? If so, how can that be done?

The increase in intermarriage and the discussion of outreach also fuel intense debates on a crucial point of Jewish law: the question of who *is* a Jew. According to Jewish law, a Jew is someone whose mother is a Jew or someone who has been converted to Judaism according to the procedures that are established by Jewish law. Between 40 and 45 percent of all American Jews define themselves as members of the Orthodox or Conservative movements. These movements accept Jewish law as binding, and therefore maintain that there is no other acceptable view of Jewish status.

Many other Jews disagree. More than 35 percent of all Jews identify with the Reform or Reconstructionist movements, while the rest are unaffiliated. For decades, Reform and Reconstructionist leaders have been influenced by the fact that in many interfaith families, the children's religious identities do not necessarily conform to their moth-ers'. Sometimes the children of Jewish mothers and Christian fathers, although they are legally Jewish, do not consider themselves Jews at all. Sometimes the children of Jewish fathers and gentile mothers are raised as Jews and consider themselves Jewish. Furthermore, for years Reform and Reconstructionist synagogues have encouraged intermarried couples to join and have made their children eligible for bar and bat mitzvahs, whether or not they converted to Judaism. As a way of formalizing that practice and of reaching out to the increasing numbers of interfaith couples, those two movements have broken with Jewish law and ruled that a child who has been raised and educated as a Jew is a Jew, as long as at least one parent is Jewish.

Some Jewish leaders have predicted that this disagreement over status could create two separate groups of Jews "who [will be] unable or unwilling to marry each other," as the Orthodox Rabbi Irving

Greenberg has been warning the Jewish community for several years. Others argue that such fears are exaggerated since, as a practical matter, a person whose Jewish status is in question can undergo a traditional conversion and, as a communal matter, Jews have so much in common that they will figure out a way of resolving this disagreement.

The argument is pursued hotly in the organized Jewish community in the United States and in Israel. It influences some Jewish men who fall in love with gentile women to insist on conversion as a precondition to marriage. But, from the point of view of most couples who intermarry, the argument seems remote. They don't feel bound by Jewish law. If the Jewish community argues over *who is a Jew*, most couples ask a different question: *why be Jewish?*

In America today, with the dramatic rise in Jewish mobility and the decline of anti-Semitism, intermarriage rates will almost certainly continue to rise. The concern of Jewish parents and professionals will not stem the tide. Their warnings and recriminations may dissuade some Jews from intermarrying, but many others will register their disagreement with their elders as they vote with their feet—right down the aisle to the altar. From their point of view, much of the Jewish community treats intermarriage as an act of heresy at the very moment when individuals experience it as love—and as proof that Jews have been admitted into America's glowing heart.

But the fact of so much intermarriage does not necessarily mean that the next generations will abandon Judaism. The Jewish community can affect the future identities of thousands of interfaith families. That process has already begun.

During the past decade, the Reform movement has launched a well-staffed, well-financed effort to make interfaith couples feel at home in synagogues and classes, and to encourage conversion. The Orthodox and Conservative movements have few formal outreach programs, for they don't want to be in the position of taking steps that seem to sanction intermarriage. But in Orthodox and Conservative synagogues across America, rabbis and lay people are finding great excitement in teaching Jewish texts, prayers, songs, dances, and holiday observances to people who are born Jews and people who are thinking of becoming Jews.

From the point of view of the Jewish community, efforts at welcoming interfaith couples have begun to bear fruit. More than ten thousand people a year are choosing to convert to Judaism. There are now about two hundred thousand converts in America. Some sociologists predict that in forty years that number could reach as high as half a million.

But according to sociologist Egon Mayer, even though the rate of conversion to Judaism is higher than it has been in modern history, three out of every four marriages between a person who was born Jewish and a person who was not, the non-Jew does not convert to Judaism.

We're convinced that tens of thousands of these interfaith couples are longing to find ways to discuss their religious and ethnic feelings with each other. When they discover that other people share their basic confusions, they begin to see their tensions as part of the fabric of human life rather than as remnants of an outmoded age. More importantly, they learn that they aren't spiritual exiles, living on lonely islands of self-inflicted pain. They can begin to move toward finding resolutions.

Our interviews and workshops have shown us that we, like the scores of psychologists, journalists, and clerics who have begun to work with interfaith couples, have stumbled on uncharted emotional territory. We hope to assist the couples who remind us of the selves we were as they try to find their way to a rewarding shared spiritual life.

2

American Tumbleweeds

Karen and John's Tale

A mid-afternoon June prairie storm had just swept through Denver. In the midst of the downpour, a tall, graceful couple—John Halvorsen, a Lutheran from Montana, light blond, pencil-thin, with pale blue eyes, and Karen Berkowitz, a Jew from Syracuse, dark-haired, with a sleek dancer's body—hurried up the steps to the house where we were staying in the city's fashionable Capitol Hill neighborhood. Shaking water out of his hair, John looked at the large high-ceilinged living room appraisingly. He and Karen had just graduated from law school. They would be married in August, and would begin to work for Denver firms the next fall. Now, they were savoring each neighborhood they visited to see which one they preferred.

But they hadn't come to discuss real estate with us. They had heard about our work from a mutual friend and wanted to talk about religion, or at least about its place in their future. During their early courtship, each of them had felt so detached from the faiths they knew in their youth that they never discussed them. But now that they were engaged, they found themselves arguing fiercely about the religion of their future children. Karen, who is more intense than John, would keep him up until three or four in the morning as she tried to explain why she cared so deeply that their children be Jewish. John, who wanted to sleep, yielded to her insistence and stayed awake. But finally her arguments forced him to consider the validity of his religious feelings, too.

The arguments were about feelings, not facts, since they never went to church or synagogue unless they were visiting John's parents in Montana. Neither of them knew much about Judaism or Christianity. That was what made their fights so frustrating. John and Karen had just graduated from law school where they'd learned to write briefs based on information. But the subject of having children always tangled them up in religious and ethnic emotions they couldn't define.

They usually ended their arguments by resolving to drop the subject until they were ready to have children. John felt relieved when that happened. Karen felt nervous because they hadn't reached a resolution. But she was afraid to raise the subject again. It brought out her worst side, she thought. She worried that if she insisted on an immediate answer she might lose the man she loved.

John and Karen were endearingly self-mocking people whose radiant love for each other made a discussion of a ski trip—or even an hour in a grocery store—sound like an affectionate adventure. But they were caught in spiritual gridlock.

We have begun this chapter with their story because it is typical of hundreds we have encountered in our workshops and in our interviews. It suggests some of the reasons that couples with distinct religious and ethnic feelings decide to preserve the ecology of their love by keeping faith off-limits in their lives.

Karen, twenty-six, is the daughter of a doctor from Syracuse, New York. Her grandparents had belonged to an Orthodox synagogue in town, but her father insisted on joining the more prestigious, more Americanized Reform temple. He was always a little flippant about Jews and Judaism, but her mother took her heritage very seriously. She insisted that Karen go to Hebrew school through tenth grade. She sent her daughter to Jewish summer camps throughout her teens. As a child Karen took those institutions for granted, but as an adolescent she began to feel distaste for them. The people she met there seemed "over-possessive and smotheringly ambitious," she says now. By the time she was sixteen, she went to temple only on the High Holidays. She never set foot in a synagogue after she entered college.

She seldom dated Jewish boys, and that upset her mother. "She wasn't religious, but was very concerned about having Jewish grand-children and keeping our people together. We always argued when I went out with a non-Jew." Karen recalled. "I couldn't understand that kind of narrow-mindedness. But when I'm arguing with John, I have the terrible sense that I'm repeating my mother's words. I can't believe I care so much about these things."

John, twenty-seven, had grown up in Missoula, Montana, where his father, a second-generation Swedish-American, was a professor of geology at the University of Montana. Back in Minnesota, his moth-er's family, farmers from Iceland, and his father's family, craftsmen from Sweden, had belonged to a Scandinavian Lutheran church. His parents were the only members of their generation to leave home. When they migrated to Montana they joined a mainstream Lutheran church in Missoula. Then they decided that they felt more comfort-able in the relaxed environment of a small chapel on the university campus. Even that was too formal for John. "The Luther League didn't appeal to me. Most of my friends were in the Boy Scouts." He soon discovered that his most intense spiritual experiences came when he was outdoors. He went to the state university, and lived close to home. But, though his mother was a very religious woman, he accompanied her to church only on Christmas and Easter. She never got upset about that. She never tried to dictate the kind of person John should date. So there is nothing in his past to enable him to understand how his fiancée feels.

John and Karen met during their tense first year at the University of Colorado Law School in Boulder. Karen had chosen the school to get away from the family and the lover who stifled her back East. In those days, Karen, who smoked two packs of cigarettes a day, used to sit in the cafeteria so that she could smoke and study at the same time. "That's how I met John," she recalled with a happy laugh. "He had come to take a break and thought I wanted to talk. One day he was telling me about Evergreen, a neat town in Colorado where his best friend lives, and I said I'd never been there. He asked me to go up there with him. We went up as friends. When we came back we were in love. But John's a lot shyer than I am. I had to ask him for the first date."

Touching his hand fondly, she mused, "Before we went to law school, my friends and I would talk about how we were going to meet beautiful men who would all be smart and rich. My friends were disappointed. I wasn't. I found John who was tall and blond and brilliant."

"People call us an integrated couple these days," John joked, obviously admiring Karen's classically Mediterranean olive complexion.

"Yeah, I really get dark in the summer," Karen agreed, shaking the shoulder-length black hair that framed her face.

"I think we complement each other in the way we look," he said.

"We're really opposite," Karen said in her slightly breathy voice. "But we have a lot in common."

As Karen described the ways they're different, she dwelt on their years at law school—their only shared experience. In that setting, their dissimilar natures complemented each other.

"When I met John I disliked law school, but he was really unhappy there. We nursed each other through. I'm pretty high strung and compulsive. I'm always thinking about a million things I have to do tomorrow or next week. It's not that healthy. I need someone to calm me down. And John does that. He's not compulsive at all."

John felt he needed Karen's intensity. "There are some times I wouldn't do anything because I never even think about what's going on in the afternoon," he said in his wry, self-mocking voice. "Karen makes me think ahead. And also, her mind works faster than mine. When you go to law school you meet a lot of very bright people who deal with information in vastly different ways. I have to work at courses very hard. It comes much more naturally and faster to Karen."

She smiled. "The thing is that I don't remember very much. Things just go whooshing in and out of my mind. John has a much better grasp of his life and his past than I do."

When John was growing up, he spent all his summers in the Grand Tetons, where his father ran a summer geology program. From June to September, he lived at an altitude of six thousand feet. "I'm still a real mountain climber. I go mountaineering in Mexico. The mountains are my second home."

That intrigued Karen, a city girl, who spent her roughest summer on a kibbutz in Israel. She loved John's casual ease outdoors, his confidence as he drove a jeep over the narrowest mountain pass, and his ability to name whatever plant or tree they saw, or to fix things around the house. Those were not things the Jewish men she grew up with could do. "It's exciting to me that John is so competent on the mountains. I think I'll probably learn to climb now that we're not so busy in law school. He'd be a really good teacher—he's patient. My WASP friends are more stoic than I am. If I fall, I scream and cry."

"I just pick myself up and go on," John laughed.

"When I think of the life that John and I are going to have together, it's very similar to the life I would have had with another Jew," Karen said. "We're both going to be well-to-do lawyers."

But they're also going to be an interfaith couple. Sometimes they tell themselves they have so much in common that their religious problems are unimportant. They assure one another that love will conquer all. But then they ask—how?

We have developed a term for couples like John and Karen. They are American tumbleweeds, who would probably never have met in the 1940s or '50s and who seldom married in the 1960s. They are among the thousands of Jews and gentiles who rode the wave of tolerance that transformed American life in the 1970s and 1980s to a romance with a cultural stranger.

In the 1960s, there were some young Jews who fell in love with gentiles in places that would have been closed to most of their parents. For example, an increasing number were becoming part of the mainstream at colleges like Harvard, Michigan, and Berkeley. They were working side by side with Christians in professions like journalism or publishing, social work or teaching. The civil rights movement and the Peace Corps created opportunities for people of all backgrounds to live as equals in new settings for extended periods of time. The New Left and the counter-culture opened up an environment where some Jews and some Christians thought religious differences were less important than generational ones. They believed that marriages between Jews and gentiles, blacks and whites, would help create a more harmonious America.

It was the first time so many Jews and gentiles had been on equal footing. That is one reason the intermarriage rate soared from 5 percent of current marriages in 1960 to an approximate 15 percent by 1970. But the vast majority of young Americans still lived in separate worlds, divided by religious, ethnic, and sexual barriers.

Until the early sixties some private colleges still maintained quotas which limited the number of Jews they would accept. Many Jews who were admitted didn't enter the mainstream of social life. Sometimes they felt uncomfortable with gentiles. Sometimes they were excluded from the fraternities, sororities, and clubs where they would have met them. Many lived in Jewish fraternities and sororities which were permeated with the humor, the cultural references, the casual knowledge of the Jewish year that was part of all their childhoods. In that important respect, their community at college felt very much like their community at home.

Many private colleges were segregated by sex. Men and women who attended Yale and Vassar or Williams and Sarah Lawrence usually courted by telephone, dating infrequently, after long train rides. Most universities were sexually integrated, but they had strict rules governing the hours men and women could be in the same room.

In the 1960s, men, including Jewish men, were professionally and geographically more mobile than women. Women who went to college, including Jewish women, did pursue graduate educations, though they did so less frequently than men. But they usually studied the liberal arts or got degrees in such helping professions as social work, psychology, and teaching. And women usually studied near home. In those days, relatively few who came from places like Syracuse, as Karen did, traveled as far as Colorado to get a degree. Three fourths of the Jews who intermarried in those years were men.

Then, in the 1970s, most of these barriers fell. There were more ethnically integrated neighborhoods than there had been in the past, and in many high schools Jews and Christians felt more social ease with each other than they had in previous decades. Colleges had dropped their quotas restricting Jews. New state universities and community colleges opened, drawing a very diverse student body, including Jews. Most social clubs ceased to reject people on the basis of race, creed, or national origin. Although there were still Jewish fraternities and sororities at many universities, Jews could join religiously integrated ones if they chose to do so. Fewer Jews made a point of rooming with Jews. Members of all ethnic groups mingled freely.

So did men and women. In the mid-1970s many private colleges became coeducational. At colleges and universities men and women began to live in the same dorms, on the same corridors.

Affirmative action began to change the sexual composition of trade and professional schools. In the sixties and early seventies, women comprised about 5 percent of most graduate schools of law, medicine, business, and dentistry. By the mid-eighties, they accounted for 40 to 50 percent of the professional school population. And a high proportion of those women were Jews. All over America, people like Karen were breaking age-old patterns in their families. For the first time, they were almost as free to become veterinarians, accountants, ophthalmologists, computer experts, and lawyers as their brothers.

Under those circumstances, it was natural that an increasing number of Jewish and Christian teenagers and college students would date freely. And it was equally natural that some of those who met in graduate school or at work would marry. After the religious and sexual barriers fell in the mid-seventies, the intermarriage rate climbed even higher. But that statistic tells only half the story. It doesn't reveal the fact that, for the first time, Jewish women were marrying gentiles at the same rate as were Jewish men.

These changes came so rapidly that the older generation has not had time to absorb them. Coed dormitories, women dentists, religiously mixed fraternity houses: such developments are barely imaginable to people who grew up in the 1930s, '40s, and '50s.

Suddenly, American-born parents felt like immigrants in their children's new American worlds. John and Karen both felt that was true in their families.

Though Karen's father didn't oppose her wedding, her mother's relatives perceived John as a non-Jew (not as a Lutheran). They think he doesn't fit into their world.

In that respect, they are like tens of thousands of older relatives of Jews who intermarry. They are furious at their children or nieces or nephews, but they love them too. Which emotion should govern their response? Should they welcome the child and the non-Jewish spouse or maintain an attitude of disapproval? They are never sure.

Demographic explanations don't comfort them very much. When their children wed gentiles they often feel guilt as well as regret. Some blame themselves or their spouses for what they perceive as their child's transgression. They re-edit the tapes of their lives, accusing each other of religious negligence, wishing they had lit Friday night candles, or kept a kosher home, or given their children a better Hebrew school education.

And they worry about the next generation. Karen's relatives believed John when he said he was an agnostic, but they still feared that the church his parents belonged to in Montana would somehow swallow up Karen's children through an alien ceremony like baptism.

Though John's family is very friendly to Karen, they can't quite believe that the beautiful dark-haired woman their son will marry doesn't accept the divinity of Jesus. When John's mother asked herself whether her grandchildren would be raised as Christians or Jews she found herself worrying that Karen's religion would be the dominant one. Would she see her son or grandchildren in the hereafter?

But the world John and Karen inhabit is so different from their parents' that they could meet in a cafeteria, fall in love over torts, and describe the differences which would once have kept them from dating in quick, affectionate jokes about each other's looks, or more reflective descriptions of the ways their personalities complemented each other. Even when they were fighting over their future children's faith, Karen and John could perceive each other as fellow lawyers whose problem was more benign than that of some friends who were sexually unfaithful to each other, more severe than that of a couple whose tastes in politics or leisure activities were dramatically different.

But what will happen when the stakes get higher? Right now their disagreements are theoretical. But when the baby is born, what will they decide? If it's a boy, will he be baptized, have a brit (a ritual circumcision)—or neither? Will they raise the child as a Christian or a Jew?

How can they turn to their families for advice? The older generation of Christians and Jews had no experience with intermarriage. Even if they approved of the match how could they understand the terms of the disagreement? What clergy could the couple trust? Few Lutheran ministers have had experience with their problems. In Denver, there are rabbis who are skilled at counseling interfaith couples. But what if they moved to another city—as John wanted to do—and happened to encounter a rabbi who lectured them instead of counseling them.

In the end, they can't help each other much either. The American tumbleweeds know very little about each other's pasts. They might share the language of corporate law or know how to start an advertising agency together or refine laser technology as a treatment for cancer. But they are ignorant of the rudiments of each other's ethnic and religious vocabularies. They are wordless when they have to communicate in the language that expresses the substance of their very different traditions—the language that sounds such deep chords in their hearts.

John and Karen, like most tumbleweed couples, reflect the asymmetry of their religions and cultures. For example, John can go for months without thinking of himself as a Protestant. Karen can't go through a day without thinking of herself as a Jew. To her, Denver is a city where almost everyone looks like a WASP. To John, it is a place where almost everyone looks American. From John's point of view, religion does not define a person's identity: it is something a man or woman can choose to have or discard. From Karen's point of view, religion is intertwined with ethnicity: a legacy she inherited from her ancestors.

If the issue were purely theological, they could use their legal training to debate it. They could argue over whether the Torah stands alone or the Old Testament prefigures the New. But how can they get a handle on the elusive cultural difference that is at the heart of their disagreement about raising children? For that to happen, Karen would have to clarify her mixed feelings about being Jewish to John, who had known few Jews before he met her. She would have to explain why she feels a degree of ambivalence about being the daughter of an upper middle class Jewish doctor to her fiancé, who is calmly proud of his successful second-generation Scandinavian parents. And she would have to make him see why she feels a guilt about betraying her people that is completely alien to his way of thinking. John would have to listen sympathetically, remembering that—as competent and modern as she seems in his eyes—she sees herself as a member of an ancient tribe, the bearer of a very complicated legacy.

She expresses negative feelings he can't identify with when she describes her decision to drop out of Hebrew school, and leave Syracuse's tight Jewish community. "There are some angry words that people use towards Jews—words like cheap and arrogant—and I was afraid they described me. At one point during my freshman year in college, I didn't want to hang around with many Jews. I hated the fact that people thought that all Jews were rich, and that they had me stereotyped as the Jappy daughter of a Jewish doctor."

Karen became particularly uneasy when she was traveling in Europe. She thought that everyone who learned that she was a Jew assumed that she was pampered. "I rebelled. I wore earth tones and all that. I never said I wasn't Jewish, but I always thought that Jews stood out, and I felt better when people thought I was Italian."

She had even less respect for Jewish men than she had for her Jewish self. They were always off-stage when she fantasized a mate. Certainly she loved John; she was a beautiful woman who chose him from many potential suitors. Nevertheless, his appearance and background also served to buffer some complicated feelings about her own people, and even her own family. "I never really considered going out with a Jew. The last time I articulated the reason was when I was fourteen. That was when my friends and I decided that all the Jewish boys we knew were real nerds. I never met many Jewish boys after high school except when I went to Israel. But I wasn't going to live there. I went to a college that had a small Jewish population. I moved to Colorado, where there weren't many Jews. I didn't specifically think, 'I don't want a small dark Jew like my brother.' But I really did want someone light-skinned and light-haired. I know that's one of the things that attracted me to John."

As Rachel and I had done in dozens of workshops and interviews, we asked her to list the first five words that came to mind when she thought of Jewish men. At first, the words we'd heard from many other Jewish women came slowly. "Ambitious. Arrogant . . ." Then a question from her lawyer's training: "This isn't a mutually exclusive list is it? Bright." There was a long pause, something unusual for a person whose mind worked so fast, before the last two words tumbled out—"self-centered and egotistical."

John's feelings about being a third-generation Scandinavian-Lutheran were much simpler than Karen's emotions about being Jewish. When he said that his mother's family are among the wealthiest farmers in their region of Minnesota he was describing an achievement that makes him respect the people he always calls his "kith and kin." When he described his dad, a second-generation Swede who became a college professor and a dean, his proud words suggested the drive that prompted him to enroll in law school and his older brother to become a professor.

Furthermore, John, who has an even more distinctive physique than Karen, sees his appearance as an asset. He would never try to disguise his striking looks in earth-tone clothes.

"When you're six one, a hundred and twenty pounds, and have white hair, people say, 'Hey, pencil head' or 'whitey' or 'albino.' It was hard, as a kid, to be singled out like that. But by the time I got to high school and filled out a little I really liked it. It's nice to stand out. We all try to do it one way or the other—the way we dress, the way we act. A few years ago I was in Mexico, on a mountain climbing trip, and I loved to walk through the market. I used to have a white beard. People would just stare. It was really fun."

When we asked John to list the first five words that came into his mind about Jewish and Protestant women, it was clear that his cultural lenses show him a different world than Karen sees. "I think I'd have to agree with Karen that Jews are intelligent and aggressive. Maybe too aggressive. But the thing that has really impressed me is their solidarity. They have a real community feeling. One thing I've learned from Karen is that if there's a Jew in law school—even if she doesn't like the person much—she'll feel a kind of bond just because the person is Jewish."

But sometimes, when he hears Karen and her Jewish friends talk, he feels that "there is a sense of pathos associated with Jewish people. Sometimes, I get the feeling that Jewish people are trapped into being Jewish. It's not that they want to be something else. But they seem to feel," he feigned a sigh of heavy resignation, " 'Oh, I'm Jewish.' Jewishness seems to be the most important thing about Jews."

He had trouble finding five words that defined Protestants in general. "I think they're less passionate and driven than Jews. I guess I'd have to say I find them a little cold. They certainly don't have the sense of solidarity I was talking about. Then, he added, "No matter what religion we decide on, that sense of solidarity is a quality I want to pass on to my children. I want them to know the kind of family and community spirit that exists among Jews."

When John expressed approval of Jewish solidarity, Karen recalled the place she had felt it most keenly—Israel.

She had spent two summers in Israel, when she was twenty and twenty-one. She loved the land, and the sense of strength, of psychological security that the people she met transmitted to her. "I realized that Jews weren't all like the people I had grown up with in Syracuse. Being Jewish wasn't so much a religion as a heritage and a nation. I didn't want to settle there, but I knew that if I ever changed my mind I'd belong. I really felt a sense of identity there."

That experience helped transform her from the person who wanted to pass as an Italian or an ethnic neuter into one who was able to say, "I'm happy that I'm Jewish."

Then, with some sadness, she continued to muse about her sense of Jewish solidarity. "I think, 'Look at the sheer number of Jews. There aren't that many.' Deep down inside I want my kids to identify themselves as Jews."

For months she had kept that feeling to herself. Then, one night after dinner, she asked, "John, would you consider raising our kids Jewish?" After a long pause he said, "Would you consider raising the children Lutheran?" That is when their fights began.

"At first, we thought we could raise them fifty-fifty, to be Lutherans and Jews," she said. "But then we decided that wouldn't work for us. We've pretty much agreed it's going to be one thing or the other."

"Or nothing," John interjected enthusiastically.

"Well, yeah," Karen assented, sounding a little wistful. Then she added, "I don't feel that I have a keen sense of spirituality even though I went to temple for years. I want my kids to be more spiritual than I am. I don't think it *has* to be Judaism, but I am selfish in that I really *want* my kids to be Jewish.

"When I ask myself why I feel that way I often come back to the same answer. There aren't that many Jews in the world and I don't want the Jewish population to get smaller. As a gut feeling, that really upsets me. But I don't see how I can be saying that while I'm marrying a non-Jew and there's a chance that our kids won't be raised as Jews."

Then, she added, "When John and I have this argument I feel a little bit sad that I'm not marrying a Jew. This just makes things harder."

Sometimes, such statements can be daggers. But Karen and John tried to cushion them with softer, more understanding afterthoughts. Each time they approached the precipice of their different cultures, different theologies, they stepped back to safer ground.

Earlier, John had half-apologized for the fact that two sophisticated people disagreed about something as primitive as religion by saying that "Even though neither of us are very zealous about our beliefs, there's a certain cultural baggage there that we each want, selfishly, to pass on to our kids."

Now, he tried to translate Karen's words into terms he could understand. "I don't really think religion is cultural baggage," he said. "I do have a certain spirituality. I don't have to go to church. I can pray by myself. That's one of the things I like about the way I was brought up."

"It's easy for me to sit here and debate the existence of Christ, or to tell you that I have a sort of religious feeling when I contemplate a sunset, but I have a cultural basis for thinking about that kind of thing. I do think it would be hard to teach a child to be spiritual without providing some anchor to that spirituality. That probably means the child should feel rooted in an organized religion."

But what would Karen do if the religion were Christianity? Even though she said she found synagogue boring and materialistic, and Hebrew prayer meaningless, she has felt an involuntary spasm of uneasiness whenever she has gone to church, as she does when the couple visits John's family.

"The church they go to is sort of casual," she said. "They have a pulpit in front, but it feels like a small room. But the crosses bother me. I don't like to read the prayer book. John's mother looks at me once in a while to see what I'm doing and I really get embarrassed."

Then, she recalled an incident that had crystallized her emotions. "Once, at John's parents' house, we were doing a Thanksgiving service and I had to say"—she stumbled momentarily—'Jesus Christ our Lord.' Mine was the closing line of the service. I didn't want to make a big deal of it because I didn't want to hurt his mother's feelings. But I had to tell her that I didn't want to say those words because they made me uncomfortable."

What would John do if the religion were Judaism? He had been to synagogue only once. Although he didn't feel the kind of uneasiness there that Karen did in church, the Hebrew prayers made him feel like an outsider.

But Judaism as a religion makes him somewhat more uneasy than the synagogue as an institution. "I read the Old Testament in Sunday school and in religion courses at college, and I always thought something was missing. There should be more. Where's the other half? Where's the New Testament? I guess I still believe what I learned in

Sunday school as a boy. It has been a long time since I thought about it, but deep down in my bones I still believe in the divinity of Christ."

"What you think is lacking is what Karen thinks is objectionable—Jesus," Rachel said.

"Yeah, I think that's right," he answered.

As John and Karen talked, it was apparent that the fact that they were fighting made them more uneasy than the religions they were fighting about. Karen held John's thin, strong hand and said, "I don't think that either of us can reach inside ourselves and find a very deep religion. Whatever we do, we don't want to make it half-assed. But we're not going to transform ourselves into devout people."

In our experience, words like that represent a cease fire, not a peace. Karen was aware of the problem. She asked us how other couples we'd met had resolved the dilemma. What did we think they should do?

We suggested that they begin by joining a workshop for interfaith couples, sponsored by a large Denver synagogue. They should follow that with a course in Judaism. If it was taught well, it would introduce them to the ideas that Judaism could infuse in their daily lives, and enable them to discuss Jewish history and religion as a subject, not a set of inchoate emotions. By studying, and talking with other inter-faith couples in the program, Karen could find the words to tell John why she cares so much about raising Jewish children.

Likewise, we added, they should take a course in Christianity so that Karen could see the religion from John's point of view. We said we thought that John needed to decide whether Christ is important to him as a divine figure or as a symbol of a happy childhood. Was there some level of his mind where he feared for the fate of a child who didn't accept Jesus? Or did he think the spirituality he treasured had an emotional foundation outside the church where he was raised.

Looking at Karen, John said, "Those are good suggestions, but how can we make time for all that? This summer we've got our wedding to plan, then there's the bar exam to study for."

Karen, who'd always seen their disagreement as an abyss, preferred to step backward instead of approaching it directly. "We've used law school as an excuse for three years," she said, "but the truth is that we don't want to make such a big decision.

"Anyway, the excuses keep coming. We're beginning our law prac-tices. We don't have much spare time, and we like to spend the days

we have together doing things we enjoy, like skiing. Besides, we
might not even have children for five years.

"But I do know that divine intervention isn't going to come along
and tell me how to raise my child."

"We hope for divine intervention," John laughed.

"Yes," Karen said, sustaining the joke, "we pray for it—to our
different Gods. But we have to make the choice for ourselves."

Then, sounding frightened, Karen articulated the problem that
disturbed her most deeply. "We keep saying we'll try it both ways
because we're so scared of saying that we want it one or the other.
When I'm really feeling that I want my way I say, 'That's it. Jewish or
nothing. We'll break up if we don't raise the kids my way.'

"But then I realize that I love John more than any ultimatum would
be worth, and so . . . We never decide what we are going to do."

Debra's Story

If John and Karen could talk with Debra Rosenfeld, the daughter of
Suzanne Miller, a Protestant from Ganges, Michigan, and Sam Rosenfeld, a Jew from Arizona, they'd feel more urgency about resolving their religious issues. Suzanne and Sam fell in love at medical
school in the sixties, back when such courtships were not so common
as today.

Unlike Karen and John, they knew that religion was an issue in their
relationship from the time they began to court. For Sam's father was a
refugee from Hitler's Germany, and cared deeply that his son marry a
Jew. Before they got married, Suzanne agreed to convert. But her
career consumed her life. She never got around to enrolling in a
conversion class. Sam never pushed her to do so.

Debra had responded to an advertisement we had put in her college newspaper, asking children of intermarriages to talk with us. It
turned out that she was upset about her inexplicably negative response to a Roman Catholic Easter Mass she had just attended, and
her parents' impending divorce.

Debra's mother, Suzanne Rosenfeld, was a very ambitious, serious
woman who had to re-create herself entirely in order to get away from
what Debra described as her "God-fearing farm family. The stories of

her childhood make me cringe. Her parents just wanted her to go to some small community college and then become a housewife. She had to go through horrible fights when she decided to go to college and to medical school. There wasn't much her parents could do, though. She always won scholarships."

Debra perceived her slim, efficient mother as a workaholic. "When I was little, my mother was home with me a lot, but by the time I was in school, her career was taking off incredibly. She was very good at what she was doing and she got a lot of recognition all over the United States. She worked hard. She'd leave home at seven-thirty in the morning and come home at seven-thirty at night. She'd be so zonked that she just wanted to get dinner on the table and have her martini and go to sleep."

If Suzanne Rosenfeld was trying to free herself from the cocoon of her dour family, her husband Sam was very close to his charismatic father, the doctor, who had seen the dangers of Nazism as soon as Hitler took power. Sam Rosenfeld seemed to have felt a deep sense of obligation to the refugee father whose exploits dwarfed his own. "He always wanted to do well for my grandfather, and my grandfather wanted the best for him," Debra said. "He didn't want to be a doctor, but he became one for my grandfather. He was pretty unhappy in his work."

Suzanne's parents approved the marriage as much as they approved of anything in their wayward daughter's life. "They were very curious about Jews," Debra recalled. "Besides," she laughed, "they were happy she was getting married at all. She was already twenty-nine." But Sam's parents, traditional Jews, were disturbed by the match. "My parents had a Jewish wedding ceremony because my grandparents were adamant about it. My grandfather was a jovial person and he liked my mother. But my grandparents' disapproval bothered my father for a long time."

Debra was born in Cleveland where her parents were doing their residencies. She spent her first few years in St. Louis. "I remember, as a child, that my mother still talked about converting. But then her career took priority. For a while my parents tried to pretend she had converted."

When Debra and her younger brother, Mike, were in grade school, "my parents talked a lot about teaching us about religion. Then, it just kind of got lost along the way."

During this period the family always celebrated Hanukkah instead of Christmas. "We'd light the candles, then we'd get a present and sing the prayers and hear the stories.

"But then my mother's parents would send Christmas presents. Her sisters would all send presents. Friends who were not Jewish would give us Christmas presents. So we'd have this big pile of Christmas presents sitting around the house. And so we'd celebrate Christmas, too—without a tree."

Some years Suzanne's parents came from their farm in Michigan to visit. Then there was a big tree. "Mike and I would decorate it. We loved it. We loved having Christmas." When she was seven and Mike was five "we negotiated a deal with my parents. Every other year we would have a Christmas tree." But that wasn't enough for Debra. "As a kid, I was always trying to make Christmas a more festive, traditional time in our family."

She wanted the family to celebrate Hanukkah with more ceremony too, but instead they observed it in an increasingly desultory way. "We'd light the candles and say the prayers—whenever we found the time. It was so haphazard."

When Debra was ten and Mike was eight, Debra recalls, "our parents asked us if we wanted to go to Hebrew school and be bar and bat mitzvahed. They said, 'If you want to, that's up to you. You can do that.' Both of us decided not to go. A bat mitzvah seemed to mean learning Hebrew so that I could get money and have a little party. That was all we knew about Judaism. We didn't know the principles and theology of the religion. And we knew nothing at all about Christianity."

Debra doesn't think her parents realized how curious about her religious identity she was. As a child, she'd been bored when her father's parents took her to High Holy Day services, but one year in high school "I decided to find out what Judaism was like. I told my parents that I wanted to go to temple with my grandmother on Rosh Hashanah. I remember sitting there, looking around and feeling, 'All these people are Jewish. What am I?' I was very troubled by the question. It bothered me when I realized that I didn't feel that I was part of the service, I didn't understand the prayers. I looked around and saw all the people who seemed to be getting a lot of meaning out of the service. I wished I was more involved, but I felt completely disconnected from all the people there."

She wasn't able to explore that disappointing emotion in her parents' home. "I'd ask my father what it meant to be a Jew, and he would try to explain. But he didn't know very much. He would say that Judaism is a very cultural religion. He would tell us that Christians believe that Jesus Christ was the Messiah and Jews don't. All I knew, besides that, were a few Bible stories like Jonah and the Whale."

Nevertheless, Debra had a very powerful Jewish influence in her life—her grandfather and his past. She adored the ebullient, generous intellectual whose enthusiasm for life seemed to mount as he aged. "I wanted to do anything that would let me get more involved with him. Sometimes I thought of learning Hebrew or German just to please him. He gave me a tradition. When I was thirteen, he took the whole family to Europe to show us where he had grown up in Germany. He had lived in a town called Malz. The temple he had been raised in was destroyed by the Nazis, but we went to the parking lot where it once stood. We went to the graveyard where all his relatives are buried. I remember him saying 'This was my grandmother's gravestone—it was a beautiful gravestone.' But it had been destroyed by the Nazis."

The family visited Dachau that summer. "I started crying because it was so horrible," Debra recalled. "I got so hysterical that they had to carry me out of there."

The trip made a lasting impression. For years, she read all the books she could about the Holocaust. "I wanted to keep shocking myself." In tenth grade, as a history project, she interviewed her grandfather, her grandmother, her great uncle, and their refugee friends about what had happened to them in Nazi Germany. "I wrote it all down—all their different stories. I borrowed some pictures from my grandfather. He had a Nazi newspaper with a whole page about Jewish men. There was a picture of my great-grandfather. They called him a slave driver. So I put that in. I was so interested I just compiled everything. I put together an eighty-page book."

Her parents were proud, of course, but they didn't treat the project as anything special. "I didn't get any more approval for it than for a science report that my mom had helped me with."

Her memories of her grandfather were inextricably linked with Passover. "It was the only truly religious holiday my family celebrated. I got up early in the morning and started setting the table and cleaning the silver. My mother and father got up early and started cooking. My grandmother made matzoh ball soup." Toward evening, "my father got out all the yarmulkes and Haggadahs from the closet. Then we all sat down and my grandfather would tell the story. And we'd say all the prayers. I loved it."

Her grandfather died in 1981. "That year, when Passover came around, nobody felt like celebrating. It would have seemed too strange without my grandfather.

"I was sorry, but on the other hand I didn't think that Passover could ever be the same without my grandfather. He was the person who held it all together. When he died, my link to Judaism was gone."

Within the year, her parents had separated. Suzanne had been offered a lucrative research job in California. Sam had decided to teach medicine instead of practicing it. In some ways Debra was relieved that the tense marriage was over.

Now, when Passover came around, Debra would tell her friends, "My God, we used to have the greatest seders. I miss all the people around and all the cooking—but I wouldn't want to do it again." That feeling created the situation that made Easter 1984, so difficult for her.

The second day of Passover coincided with Easter Sunday, and Debra decided to try to forget her nostalgia for her grandfather and for her splintered family by going home with a Catholic friend from New Jersey. To her astonishment, she was almost unbearably upset by the Mass.

She was unaccustomed to the rituals that Roman Catholics take for granted, like dipping their fingers in holy water when they enter the church, like crossing themselves. It sounded to her as if "there were a lot of prayers about sacrifice: 'we offer this up to You,' " was a line she remembered, "and I thought, my God, this is idolatry." She interpreted one of the prayers for unbelievers to mean that " 'we hope that the heritage of Christ will save our Jewish friends.' . . . "Tears were running down my face," she said as she remembered the experience. "I didn't know why. My friend's family began to worry about me. They asked me if I wanted to leave.' I stayed, but I felt revolted by the whole thing."

After Easter, she phoned her father to see if he could help her reexamine her childhood in a way that would explain her sudden, inexplicable grief. "What did you teach when I was young that made me feel like cryng at Mass?" she asked.

Sam Rosenfeld diagnosed Debra's turbulence with clinical detachment.

"He said, 'We didn't teach you very much about religion.' When I told him how uncomfortable I was at Mass he said that was probably because I was unfamiliar with it. He advised me to go to a Jewish service one Friday night to see if I felt the same way. He was very logical about it all. He said that maybe one of the reasons I've never felt so upset by a Jewish ceremony is that I can't understand the words. He said that there's probably a lot in Hebrew prayers that would bother me too."

But her father's highly rational approach didn't help much. "I think the whole problem with religion in our family is that we tried to do both but we couldn't do either. I can't get beyond the dual heritages and religions. Mike and I would ask, 'Is there a God?' and my parents wouldn't say, 'Yes, of course there's a God.' They'd say, 'We don't know.' My mother would say she didn't believe in God. My father said that in a way he believed in God because that was what he had always been taught. So I grew up an atheist. But I wish that I had religion one way or the other."

Quite bitterly, she said, "I was given a choice. It was always 'You can choose.' But I was too young to choose. I just let it go.

"Now I wonder what I'm going to do when I get married. I think it would be hard for me to accept any religion. But I don't want my kids to grow up with no traditional family background or belief."

Debra felt a "strong desire to be part of one religious culture or another. The whole ambivalence about religion is kind of hard because I've come to feel that there must be an innate desire in people to have religion. At least there is in me. But I don't know what to believe. And nobody has helped me figure it out."

There was a time bomb lodged in her psyche—the grandfather she adored, specific Jewish experiences like the childhood seders, the trip to Malz and Dachau, which she associated with him. She knew that the time bomb had exploded on that tear-filled Easter. "When I was sitting in that Catholic Mass, the whole time I was thinking, 'My God, what would my grandfather think of me if he saw me here right now?' I think about him a lot. I feel that if I turned away from Judaism I would be doing something horrible to him."

But she added, "On the one hand I want to be loyal to his history. On the other hand, I have real problems with it because I don't know anything about it, and I can't completely accept religion as a social organization at all."

Debra still couldn't act on her feelings about the grandfather she loved, about the Holocaust, about the seders that were among her happy memories of her family without renouncing the ambivalence which was her parents' most powerful legacy to her.

Certainly some of Debra's sorrow stems from her relationship with her parents, particularly with her mother. If Suzanne had been more of a parent and less of a workaholic, she could have eased her daughter's loneliness. But Debra's problems also stem from the mixed religious signals she received as a child. In our interviews with about sixty children of intermarriages, most of those whose parents remained as indecisive about their family's religious identity as Karen and John, as Suzanne and Sam, reported similar confusion. "I feel like a bubble, neither here nor there," the child of a Jewish mother and Catholic father told us.

"I feel as if I'm always vacillating. I feel hollow at my core," said the child of a Jewish man and Protestant woman.

We know, from our work, that parents who try to preserve marital harmony by ignoring their religious differences may transmit the conflicts they are suppressing to their children. We also know that interfaith couples can confront their problems directly and arrive at considered decisions about their family's spiritual life. We present Debra's story as a way of urging them to do so—for their sake and their children's.

PART II

INTERMARRIAGE THEN: *A Historic Perspective*

3

The Price of Success

The fact that tens of thousands of interfaith couples like Karen Berkowitz and John Halvorsen are open to the possibility of making Judaism the religion of their household is a new phenomenon in the history of intermarriage. For, until 1960, even though intermarriage rates were very low, most Jews who married Christians agreed that their children could be raised in their spouse's faith. There were exceptions, of course. But, for the most part, intermarriage, which the vast majority of Jews always regarded as a violation of law and tradition, represented an exit visa out of the Jewish world. It often became one for the Jews who married Christians. It almost always did for their children.

To show how that happened, we have devoted two chapters to portraying the consequences of intermarriages that occurred in previous generations. This history also provides a view of the ways Jews have seen America and Christians have seen Jews at different phases of American history.

During the decades after the American Revolution, the several thousand Sephardic Jews who had settled in the New World were treated with great respect by the Protestant elite. Usually, the Sephardic Jews who married Christians did so in regions of the country where there were not enough Jewish men or women to provide a sufficient pool of eligible mates. As a rule, these Jews, social equals of their Christian spouses, did not convert. But the children of these intermarriages became Christians.

Then, beginning in the late 1870s, Protestant anti-Semitism became a virulent force in America. The Jews who married gentiles in those years often did so to obliterate all traces of their Jewish identities: to vanish into the safety of Christian America. Later, in the 1920s, '30s, and '40s, Eastern European Jewish composers like Irving Berlin, film makers like Samuel Goldwyn, writers like Max Lerner began to make their mark in America. Unlike most of their fellow Jews, they moved in circles where they met Christians on an equal social footing. In falling in love with Christians, they also moved into the heart of what seemed like the promised land. They didn't hide their Jewishness. It remained part of their public persona. But their spouses usually established the religious culture of the home.

During those years, there were also some working class Jews and Catholics who lived in the same neighborhood or worked in the same factory or office and who fell in love with each other and got married.

Many of the emotional subtexts in these earlier intermarriages exist in the ones we see today. But the social and historical context of contemporary marriages between Christians and Jews has changed. In the wake of the Holocaust, Jews have become acutely aware of the precariousness of Jewish survival. Many who marry gentiles still feel a fierce responsibility to keep the flame of Jewish history burning by establishing a Jewish household. That is easier to do now than it was in the past, for Jews are not as subject to bigotry as they were. They can achieve almost anything they want in America, no matter how publicly Jewish they are. Furthermore, in America today, Judaism as a religion is on an equal footing with Protestantism and Catholicism. Thus, John and Karen may have arguments over religion and ethnicity that cause them sleepless nights. But unlike the couples we describe in these chapters, their decision to live as Protestants or Jews will not determine their professional or social status.

We have chosen these stories from the American past because they furnish perspective on the present. They reflect experiences which help explain the emotions that surround intermarriage. But they do not necessarily predict the future.

Anne and Emma Lazarus: Suppressing a Precious Legacy

Emma Lazarus, a Sephardic Jew, the author of the lines that are inscribed on the Statue of Liberty, was widely known as a passionate defender of her people in the 1880s. Emma Lazarus never married, but her Jewish legacy was suppressed after her death by her beloved sister Anne, her literary executor, who did intermarry. In 1892, five years after Emma Lazarus died, Anne wed a wealthy Episcopalian painter named John Humphreys Johnston, who was part of the turn of the century Protestant elite, where anti-Semitism was the norm.

We have chosen to tell this little-known tale of two sisters because it illustrates one of the reasons Jews have traditionally seen intermarriage as a threat. Shortly after Anne married into the Protestant elite, she converted to Christianity. Years later, she dismissed her sister's Jewish wirting as "sectarian propaganda" and refused to let it be republished. She obliterated her own Jewish heritage; she helped extinguish all memories of the Jewish spark that had burned so brightly in Emma Lazarus' life. That is why her intermarriage is emblematic of a Jewish nightmare.

The lives of the Lazarus sisters—who were separated in age by a decade—also illustrate the way Christian attitudes toward Jews changed during the nineteenth century. For Emma Lazarus, born in 1849, was influenced by Protestant mentors like Ralph Waldo Emerson and the journalist-banker Edmund Clarence Stedman, who respected her Jewishness and helped her find her Jewish voice. Anne Lazarus Johnston, born in 1859, married in 1891 into a world of well-bred Protestant anti-Semites whose attitudes she adopted. Those attitudes prompted her to withhold permission for the posthumous reprinting of her sister's Jewish poetry, which she described as "sectarian propaganda."

The Lazarus ancestors were among the twenty-five hundred Jews who arrived in America before 1800. Most of this early wave of immigrants, "the grandees" as the writer Stephen Birmingham described them, were descendants of the Sephardic Jews who had been expelled from Spain and Portugal in the fifteenth and sixteenth centuries. A few were immigrants from Germany.

Emma Lazarus, the third of six sisters, was born at a time when Jews were closer, on the social scale, to the Protestants who controlled America than to the new, huge wave of Catholic immigrants, "whose alien habits," Protestant ministers warned, "are being injected into the American blood stream." She was raised in an age when Jews could be proud, religiously observant people and still feel like part-owners of America. When her sister Anne was born, Jews were still socially acceptable in America. But by the time she was a teenager, Protestant anti-Semitism had begun to make assimilated Jews think their Jewishness might be a social handicap.

The Lazarus' uncle, J. J. Lyons, was the spiritual leader of New York's Spanish and Portuguese Synagogue from 1837 to 1877. Their cousin, Benjamin Nathan, was a Sabbath observer whose home was kosher. He was also vice president of the New York Stock Exchange in 1870 and a member of the Union Club—a place that would become off-limits to Jews in thirty years. Their father, Moses Lazarus, a wealthy sugar merchant, was a secular Jew whose social circle included as many Protestant intellectuals and businessmen as it did Jews.

Like her two older sisters Sarah and Josephine, Emma never married. As "grandees," their pool of possible mates was quite small. They took it for granted that marriage to a Christian was out of the question. In the 1860s and '70s they still upheld the standard set by Rebecca Gratz at the turn of the century. Gratz, the daughter of a prosperous Philadelphia businessman who had supported George Washington, refused to marry Samuel Ewing, the minister's son she loved, because he was not Jewish. Her friend Washington Irving recounted her story to Sir Walter Scott. Scott was so affected by the tale that he not only made her the model for Rebecca in *Ivanhoe* but justified his novelist's decision to wed Ivanhoe to Rowena instead of to Rebecca on the grounds that "a character of a highly virtuous and lofty stamp is degraded rather than exalted by an attempt to reward virtue with temporal prosperity."

If the Jews who remained in New York and Philadelphia saw Rebecca Gratz as a positive model, they were dismayed by the example of many of their friends and cousins who had moved away from Northeastern urban centers and intermarried within a generation.

In 1815, Rachel Mordecai, an Orthodox Jew living in Warrenton, North Carolina, wrote Maria Edgeworth, the English novelist, that "in this happy country, where religious distinctions are scarcely known, where character and talents are sufficient to attain advancement, we find the Jews . . . form a respectable part of the community." She knew that from firsthand experience, for she had helped her father—a strict adherent of Jewish law—run a prestigious private school, whose students were mostly Christians.

But the Mordecais found it impossible to avoid intermarriage. Because there were so few Jews in the South, they couldn't provide their children with a religious education or a religious community. Because they were so far from New York or Philadelphia, they lacked ready access to religious libraries, scholars—and even, sometimes, Torah scrolls.

Most importantly, the pool of eligible Jewish spouses was even smaller in the South than it was in New York or Philadelphia. Rachel Mordecai's father Jacob had thirteen children. Of the five who remained Jewish, only two married. Six wed Protestants. Two more went a step further and converted to Christianity. Jacob Mordecai's children were typical of their caste throughout the South. In 1913, Caroline Myers Cohen began a privately circulated history of the three "grandee" families who had settled in the South in the eighteenth century with the plaintive comment that "At this date, there remain of the families of Myers, Hays and Mordecai, including the writer, only five persons professing the Jewish faith, and . . . within a few years these five will have passed away . . ."

Jews like the elder Lazarus sisters were walking a thin social line, albeit a line of their own making. From their point of view, they were the only Jews who possessed generations of background and refinement. Some of them saw marriage to a German Jew who had come to America after 1830 as downward mobility. Indeed, the "grandees" invented the derogatory term "sheeny" to ridicule the "new" German Jews, many of whose names ended with the syllables -stein or -shoen or -shine.

So, with neither Christian nor German-Jewish marital prospects, their romantic lives took place on the head of a pin. Since almost all the great aristocratic families—the Cardozos, the Gratzes, the Lazaruses, the Nathans—were interrelated, cousins were almost obliged to marry cousins. Their family trees are so involuted that one gets dizzy reading them. But many of the branches yielded no fruit—throughout the nineteenth century, each generation was full of men and women who couldn't find a suitable mate.

One can sense the depth of the grandees' feelings about intermarriage in Frances Nathan Wolff's privately published *Four Generations;*

My Life and Memories of New York for Over Eighty Years. In 1884, her brother Washington Nathan married a Protestant—after his parents were dead. She wrote, "I was thankful, if I might use that expression, that mother had been laid to rest. For I know she would have been more than heartbroken to see her son marry out of the Jewish faith. I saw very little of his wife as, at the time, I took the stand that I would not visit those who married Christians."

Emma Lazarus' diaries and journals have never been found. One has to piece together her life and Anne's from a long biographical essay by her older sister Josephine, the memoirs of her wide array of friends, and from her own writings.

Emma was a talented poet with a great gift for languages. Her father, Moses, made sure that she and her five sisters and brother had private tutors. She had learned Italian, French, German, and Spanish by the time she was in her teens. She translated Alexander Dumas, Victor Hugo, and Heinrich Heine into English. She wrote verse herself.

When she was seventeen, her father printed a volume of her work and sent copies of it to William Cullen Bryant and Ralph Waldo Emerson. He arranged for her to meet Emerson, who was sixty at the time, at the home of a mutual friend. She captivated the Sage of Concord with her intelligence and personality.

Emerson was the kind of mid-nineteenth-century American intellectual who cared about helping people from diverse backgrounds express their own voices. He was a Unitarian, an abolitionist, whose life was dedicated to liberating the spirit of the human race. The product of an innocent, idealistic age, he reveled in diversity.

He praised Emma's poetry, and made the offer that ultimately helped transform her life. "I should like to be appointed your professor, your being appointed to attend the whole term. I should be very stern and exigent."

Emma was proud that she was a Jew, but her branch of the Lazarus family thought European literature and history offered riches that were unavailable in the Jewish past.

In August 1876, Emerson invited Emma to spend a week in Concord, to "correct our village narrowness," as he wrote her. After the visit, his daughter Ellen wrote a friend that Emma was "a real unconverted Jew (who had no objection to calling herself one)." She described how much she had enjoyed hearing "how the Old Testament sounds to her"; she was delighted to learn that Emma "has been brought up to keep the Law and the Feast of Passover and the Day of Atonement. Her interior view was more interesting than I had imagined."

Emma Lazarus was as much at home in New York's cosmopolitan circles as she was in Emerson's world. She was a frequent guest in the elegant old carriage house just off Union Square in Manhattan where Richard Watson Gilder, editor of the *Century* magazine, would invite Mark Twain, William Dean Howells, and Grover Cleveland for an evening of good music and good talk. Her poetry was frequently published in *Lippincott's* magazine and her increasingly spare, biting essays were one of the staples of the *Century*.

Her friends, the elite of her age, loved spending time with her. Mrs. Constance Harrison, a Virginia-born writer and hostess, a descendant of Thomas Jefferson, wrote for the *Century*, and was part of a social circle that included Mrs. Theodore Roosevelt and Mrs. Hamilton Fish. In a memoir, *Reflections, Grave and Gay*, she described carriage rides she and Emma would take at her summer home in Lenox, Massachusetts. "Sometimes in our drives talk became so earnest that we would find ourselves halted in some grassy wayside nook, the mare's head bent down to crop rich clover, while we discussed points of mutual interest. [She] was the most feminine of women, but her eager spirit seemed to burn like an unfailing lamp . . ."

But Lazarus became increasingly dissatisfied with her own writing and sought advice from her neighbor Edmund Clarence Stedman. "She confided in me her despondency as to her poetic work," he recalled in his book *Genius and Other Essays*. She felt that she "had accomplished nothing to stir or waken or teach or suggest . . . nothing the world could not do without. Although no American poet of her years had displayed a more genuine gift than hers, I knew exactly what she meant. She had pursued art for art's sake along classic lines, and had added no distinctive element to English song."

Stedman asked her "why she had been so indifferent to the advantage which she, a Jewess of the purest stock, held above any other writer. She said that, although proud of her blood and lineage, the Hebrew ideals did not appeal to her. But I replied to her that I envied her the inspiration she might derive from them."

* * *

The course of Emma's literary career and the life of her sister Anne
were transformed by the changes taking place between Jews and
white Protestants in America.

In America, anti-Semitism was on the rise. It was directed at German Jews who had begun to migrate here in the 1830s, though not at
the more refined "grandees."

When the German Jews first came to America, it was a primarily
rural country. By the time of the Civil War, many of these Jews had
fanned out across America, working as peddlers and shopkeepers in
tiny Midwestern and Southern towns. Though they were sometimes
stereotyped as Shylocks, and occasionally made the objects of repres-
sive legislation, for the most part they were accepted as equal partners in the project of building this new land. But that attitude of
tolerance ended almost overnight as the 150,000 German Jews who
had come to America in the 1840s and 1850s achieved economic
power in post-Civil War America.

If one man symbolized the group, it was Joseph Seligman, who had
come to America in 1839 as a peddler and became one of the most
prosperous merchants and bankers in the country. During the Civil
War his textile mills had outfitted the Union Army. In 1868, President
Ulysses S. Grant wanted to make him Secretary of the Treasury.
Seligman turned down the offer. By 1874, his banking firm, J & W
Seligman & Company, collaborated with the House of Morgan and
the House of Rothschild to buy 55 million dollars in United States
bonds. In the spring of 1877, Grant's successor, Rutherford B.
Hayes, asked Seligman to help devise a strategy for refunding the
government's Civil War debt. Seligman's plan salvaged the dollar
within two years. He seemed to be at the apex of his influence. For ten
years, Seligman had been a favored guest at one of America's most
sumptuous hotels—the Grand Union in Saratoga Springs, New York,
which could house twenty-five hundred people. In the summer of
1877, he was so tired from his work in Washington that he decided to
begin his vacation there as soon as the season began.

The hotel's owner, Alexander Stewart, who also owned Manhat-
tan's largest department store, had died the previous year. Judge
Henry Hilton, a Tammany Hall politician, was now managing
Stewart's properties, including the Grand Union.

Just after lunch on June 19, Seligman and his family went to the front desk of the Grand Union, where they expected to get the key to their customary suite. When Seligman approached the desk, the manager stopped him. "Mr. Seligman," he said, "I am required to inform you that Mr. Hilton has given instructions that no Israelites shall in future be permitted to stop at this hotel."

The New York *Times* described the exchange on June 19 in the first of the articles that would rate front-page play for several days. When Seligman was denied his room, he "was so astonished that for some time he could make no reply." Then, "the banker asked the reason why Jews were thus persecuted. 'Are they dirty, do they misbehave themselves, or have they refused to pay their bills?'

" 'Oh no," replied the manager, "there is no fault to be found in that respect. The reason is simply this: business at the hotel was not good last season and we had a large number of Jews here. Mr. Hilton came to the conclusion that Christians did not like their company . . ."

When interviewed in the *Times*, Judge Hilton said he'd decided to exclude the group he called "Seligman Jews" "on business grounds solely"—to appease "the wishes and prejudices" of his Christian clientele. He stated his case particularly baldly in one interview. "Should the 'Seligman Jew' be excluded from certain first-class hotels? I say emphatically, yes. Not at all because he is a Hebrew but because he is not wanted . . . He is the "Sheeney." He has made money; he must advertise it in his person. He is of low origin, and his instincts are all of the gutter—his principals smell—they smell of decayed goods, or of decayed principles . . ."

In the weeks after the Seligman affair, Jews and Christians assumed they could reverse Judge Hilton's policy by protesting it in the newspapers and boycotting the department store Judge Hilton was managing. The Protestant minister Henry Ward Beecher, one of the most prominent clergymen in America, gave a sermon which condemned Hilton. The sermon was front-page news in the *Times*.

The boycott of the department store was so effective that Hilton had to sell it. That summer, William Cullen Bryant, then regarded as New York's sagest citizen, told Seligman that opinion was so strongly on his side that he should call off the public protest.

But Hilton, not Bryant, was in tune with his times. Within five years of the Seligman episode virtually all the first-class hotels and social clubs in America were closed to "Seligman Jews." Plainly, the post-Civil War Protestant elite was sending a message: anti-Semitism was now acceptable among the most refined people in America.

In the early 1880's Emma Lazarus' suppressed Jewish voice—the one Stedman had wanted to hear—emerged on behalf of the "Seligman" Jews and the Eastern European refugees who were fleeing from pogroms.

In 1881, Rabbi Gustav Gottheil of New York's prestigious Temple Emanu-El asked her to visit the Jewish refugees on Ward's Island. Most of her Jewish peers found them dirty and embarrassing. But Emma, angered by their tales of the brutality that had driven them from their homes, felt a kinship with them at once. She often brought them food and clothing. In her writings, she agitated on their behalf by describing their miserable living conditions in America. She had become a soul on fire.

In February, 1883, she wrote an impassioned *Century* magazine article, "The Jewish Problem." With episodes like the Seligman affair in mind, she turned her attention to the anti-Semitism that had swept across the United States in the years since Ralph Waldo Emerson had befriended her.

". . . [U]ntil the last few years, [Jews have enjoyed] a large and in some places almost entire immunity from social prejudice. And yet here, too, the everlasting prejudice is cropping out in various shapes. Within recent years Jews have been 'boycotted' at not a few places of public resort; in our schools and colleges, even in our scientific universities, Jewish scholars are frequently subjected to annoyance on account of their race. The word 'Jew' is in constant use, even among so-called refined Christians, as a term of opprobrium, and is employed as a verb to denote the meanest of tricks."

In 1879, Philip Cowen, a twenty-six-year-old New York-born German Jew, founded the *American Hebrew*. Three years later, he published Lazarus' sixteen-part essay, "Epistle to the Hebrews." Emma knew that her audience—the hundred thousand Sephardic and German Jews who were living in New York—were divided among themselves, and afraid that the strangely dressed, ill-mannered, Yiddish-speaking Russian and Polish immigrants would call unfavorable attention to them. She also knew that outbursts of bigotry like the

Seligman affair had embarrassed and frightened her readers. They were more eager than ever to blend into America. So Emma sought to restore their pride.

Her most passionate words concerned Jewish solidarity. She insisted that the "clannishness" which Judge Hilton defined as a vice was really an irreplaceable virtue. "Our adversaries are perpetually throwing dust in our eyes with accusations of materialism and tribalism and we, in our pitiable endeavor to conform to the required standard, plead guilty and fall into the trap they have set . . . *Tribal!*' This perpetual taunt rings so persistently in our ears that most Jews themselves are willing to admit its justice, in the face of the fact that our 'tribal God' has become the God of two-thirds of the inhabited globe, the God of Islam and of Christendom, and that as a people we have adapted ourselves to the varying customs and climates of every nation in the world . . .

"I do not hesitate to say that our national defect is that we are not 'tribal' enough; we have not sufficient solidarity to perceive that when the life and property of a Jew in the uttermost provinces of the Caucasus are attacked, the dignity of a Jew in free America is humiliated. . . . Until we are all free, we are none of us free. But lest we should justify the taunts of our opponents, lest we should become 'tribal' and narrow and Judaic rather than humane and cosmopolitan like the anti-Semites of Germany and the Jew-baiters of Russia, we ignore and repudiate our unhappy brethren as having no part or share in their misfortunes—until the cup of anguish is held also to our own lips."

In a personal letter to Cowen, Emma indicated her contempt for Jews who abandoned their people and their religion. "We should prove to Christian missionaries that converted Jews are probably not only the most expensive of all marketable commodities, but also the most worthless after they are purchased."

Within a few years, Emma Lazarus had earned a worldwide reputation. Just after she finished the "Epistle," she and Anne went on an extended journey through England, France, and Italy. In London, they were befriended by Robert Browning, who wrote Emma letters containing Hebrew words, and by the world-famous socialist-craftsman William Morris. The fact that Emma and Anne Lazarus met with Jewish leaders as well, and continued to agitate for Russian Jews only made them more interesting to their new group of friends.

In the fall of 1883, Emma's good friend Constance Harrison was helping to raise money for a pedestal for the Statue of Liberty. Harrison asked some writers, including Walt Whitman, John Greenleaf Whittier, and Bret Harte, to provide manuscripts that could be auctioned off to raise funds. She "begged" Emma for a poem, she recalled in her autobiography, but her friend "rebelled against writing anything to order." Instead, she "let play the summer lightning of her sarcasm on [me] . . ."

But Constance Harrison knew how to reach Emma. "Think of that goddess standing on her pedestal . . . in the bay and holding out her torch to those Russian refugees of yours. [Her] dark eyes deepened. [Her] cheeks flushed. The time for merriment was past. She said not a word more."

In a few days, the poem was ready. Constance Harrison's reference to the Russian Jews who had helped transform Emma's consciousness caused her to write the few lines for which she would be remembered:

> Give me your tired, your poor,
> Your huddled masses yearning to breathe free,
> The wretched refuse of your teeming shore.
> Send these, the homeless, tempest-tost to me,
> I lift my lamp beside the golden door!"

Shortly after Emma wrote that poem, her beloved father died.

Soon, she learned she had Hodgkin's disease. Bedridden in the Lazarus family town house, confined to the company of her sisters and a few close friends, Emma managed to rally their spirits. "Wasted to a shadow, and between acute attacks of pain, she talked about art, poetry, the scenes of travel of which her brain was so full, and the phases of her own condition, with an eloquence for which even those who knew her best were quite unprepared," Josephine wrote. Emma died on November 19, 1887. She was thirty-eight.

In 1888, her sisters convinced H. O. Houghton & Co. to publish a two-volume edition of her verse. It was organized in very much the same way as her life—the first volume contained her secular poems, and the second her Jewish verse. The introduction was a reprint of Josephine's *Century* magazine essay, a tribute to the qualities that set Emma apart from most of her contemporaries in the intelligentsia. "To be born a Jewess was a distinction for Emma Lazarus and she in turn conferred distinction on her race. To be born a woman also lends grace and a subtle magnetism to her influence. Nowhere is there contradiction or incongruity."

The family agreed that Josephine's essay should serve as Emma's eulogy. Presumably, they shared its view of Emma Lazarus' identity.

Josephine, who remained close to the editors of the *American Hebrew* and helped found the National Council of Jewish Women, remained proud of Emma's Jewish writing until her death in 1910. But Anne, who outlived the other sisters, was Emma's literary executor, and she developed very different feelings.

In 1891, Anne Lazarus married her neighbor, the wealthy painter John Humphreys Johnston who was a protégé of the noted artist John Lafarge. Several years later she converted to Anglicanism. Like her cousin Washington Nathan, who had moved to England and then to France after he married his Protestant wife, she was an outcast in her family. She lived with Johnston, adrift from her Sephardic clan.

Anne was part of a new American intelligentsia. She and Johnston, who divided their time between New York, London, and Paris, belonged to the same semi-expatriate social circle as Henry James and Henry Adams. But unlike Emerson and Stedman, who had nurtured Emma's interest in her Jewish heritage, many members of the new Protestant intellectual elite to which the Johnstons belonged were outright anti-Semites who gave a patina of respectability to the attitudes Judge Hilton represented.

In 1906, Henry James, who lived in London, visited New York, where he despaired of the future of the English language because of "the Hebrew conquest of New York." In his 1907 book, *The American Scene,* he wrote that Jews on New York's Lower East Side reminded him of "small, strange animals . . . snakes or worms . . . who, when cut in pieces, wriggle away and live as completely in the snippet as in the whole."

Henry Adams, a friend of John Humphreys Johnston in Paris, spent much of his time in Washington, where he saw Jews acquiring an increasing amount of political and economic power. As a younger man, he had been ambivalent about them. His sister, who died in 1870, had married a Jew, and he created an attractive Jewish couple in his 1880 novel *Democracy.* But at the same time he also expressed a deep prejudice. In 1879 he visited Spain and wrote, "I have now seen enough of Jews and Moors to entertain more liberal views in regard to the Inquisition, and to feel that . . . the Spaniards saw and pursued a noble aim."

By the 1890s, as he began to associate Jews with the gross qualities of the Gilded Age, his anti-Semitism grew so intense that, after the Depression of 1893 had severely affected some of his friends, he wrote that he was in a mood to help "the London mob to pull up Harcourt and Rothschild on a lamppost in Piccadilly." In the late 1890s, he sided with the French government and military when they unjustly accused the Jewish officer Alfred Dreyfus of treason. "Dreyfus himself is a howling Jew as you see from his portraits," he wrote in a letter. In 1914, he wrote his brother Brooks that the "Washington atmosphere really has become a Jew atmosphere . . . We are still in power after a fashion. Our sway over what we call society is undisputed. We keep Jews far away, and the anti-Jew feeling is quite rabid . . ."

He befriended a young Jewish actress—Elsie de Wolfe—but found her agreeable because she was "in a state of anti-Semite rebellion which is the mark of all intelligent Jews." That attitude must have affected Anne Lazarus Johnston. Anne re-created herself as a genteel Protestant. On the few occasions her Jewish cousins visited her in Europe, she was noticeably cold toward them. When her sister Josephine wrote a pamphlet defending Alfred Dreyfus, Anne wrote her a nasty letter rupturing their relationship for good.

When World War I began in Europe, many of her semi-expatriate friends faced a crisis of conscience. They hated Woodrow Wilson's policy of neutrality. They wanted America to intervene on behalf of the beleaguered British. Living in London, Henry James made his statement by renouncing his American citizenship in 1915 and becoming a British citizen. John Humphreys Johnston became a British subject a year later. Neither he nor Anne ever returned to the United States.

They had enough money to live very pleasantly. In 1906, they had moved from Paris to Venice. They settled in the elegant Palazzo Contarini, on a site where Titian had once had his studio. They became internationally famous art collectors.

After Emma Lazarus' death, she was remembered primarily for her hastily written ode to the Statue of Liberty. In 1926, an American editor, Bernard Richards, wanted to include Emma's Jewish poetry in a series that would contain the Jewish writings of French Prime Minister George Clemenceau, of the assimilated Austrian Jew Stefan Zweig, and of Georg Brandes, a Danish literary critic who had promoted Nietzsche, and written several books about his own Judaism. When Richards discovered that Emma's publishers had let her poetry go out of print, he wrote Anne Lazarus Johnston to get permission to reissue Emma's work.

Quite promptly, Anne responded with a courteous letter, which was handwritten on expensive blue stationery with a letterhead reading "Palazzo Contarini del Zaffo, Madonna del'Orto, Venezia."

She wrote Richards that she was upset that Emma's poems were out of print. But ". . . living, as I do, permanently in Italy, it was practically impossible for me at this distance to enter into [my own] publishing venture [of my sister's works] . . . I retain the copper plates and hold them intact, always having hoped that an occasion would present itself when they might be used.

"But when the opportunity comes up of republishing them, with all the necessity of advertising thereby, fresh problems arise. I now realize to the full how great a change has taken place during the interval of years that have elapsed since these volumes first made their appearance. My sister would have been the first, I feel sure, to recognize this

". . . [W]hile her political-religious poems are technically as fine as anything she ever wrote, they were nevertheless composed in a moment of emotional excitement, which would seem to make their theme of *questionable appropriateness* today. In fact, to me, it seems out of harmony with the spirit of the present times.

"There has, moreover, been a tendency, I think, on the part of some of her public, to emphasize the Hebraic strain in her work, . . . a strain of sectarian propaganda which I greatly deplore. I find this to have been merely a phase of my sister's development, called forth by righteous indignation at the tragic happenings of those days. Then, unfortunately, owing to her untimely death, this was seen to be her final word.

"But if she herself were here today, I feel sure that she might prefer to be remembered by the verses written in a more 'serene' mood. Of these, I believe that a very beautiful small selection could be made which would consist of one small volume or brochure, an attractive paper covered book of verses to be published at Christmas time . . ."

The Christian Response: The Jew Is a Social Irritant

By 1890, the anti-Semitism which had been triggered by the Selig-man episode became so pervasive that Philip Cowen devoted the Passover 1890 issue of the *American Hebrew* to a "Consensus of Opin-ion on Prejudice Against the Jews: Its Nature, Its Causes, Its Reme-dies." In February, he had sent a letter-questionnaire to one hundred clergymen, educators, and journalists. It was a plea for a diagnosis and a cure.

"In recent years," Cowen wrote, "we have seen the refusal to admit Jews to summer resorts, the exclusion of Jewish students from private schools—all at the demand of Christian patrons—the blackballing at clubs of proposed Jewish members . . . No discrimination on ac-count of character is ever made. The fact that one is of the Jewish faith seems sufficient to bar association with him. Why?" he asked. "Can you suggest what should be done to dispel the existing prejudice?"

Many of the clerics, journalists, and educators—such as Phillips Brooks, the renowned rector of Boston's Trinity Church—replied that they didn't know enough Jews to give informed answers. Some of the politically progressive writers tried to be conciliatory. A few, like Oliver Wendell Holmes, took Christians to task for their bigotry.

But many of the respondents argued that Jews were, simply, too Jewish.

The Reverend J. R. Day, a minister from New York City, wrote that "[the Jew] goes to summer resorts as a Jew; is found in parties of his own people, and therefore becomes a foreign body, an irritant in the social structure of American life.

"The remedy," he told the *American Hebrew*'s readers, "is to dis-courage everything exclusively Jewish, except your worship and sa-cred days. [Discourage] all distinctively Jewish localities in cities—all gregarious habits at American places of resort, etc.

"The German Protestant would be as quickly rejected by the best forms of American social life as is the Jew, were he to attempt to bring in his distinctively German manners and customs. There must be a merging of national peculiarities [in order] that a common plane may be reached by the diverse tribes of the earth meeting here."

These respondents proposed two different ways of treating this "irritant in the social structure. Some said Jews should be kept out of the intimate recesses of the Christian world; others urged them to marry into it. But to the proponents of the latter solution, intermarriage had one purpose: the obliteration of Jews as a distinct people.

Henry T. Finck, a biologist, criticized Jewish "clannishness" and argued that "the disadvantages of Jewish separatism are shown not only in the long, thick, crooked nose, the bloated lips, almost suggesting a negro, and the heavy lower eyelids, but in the fact (proved by statistics) that the Jews have proportionally more insane, deaf-mutes, blind and color blind than any Christians." He argued that "In my humble opinion, there ought not to be any Jews in America—that is, a hundred years hence."

Then, he proposed a solution. "Why should not the Jews intermarry with other nationalities, and seek to exist as such. . . . From an intellectual and industrial point of view, the Jews are one of the finest races in the world and their absorption by the natives in the countries where they live could not but benefit both parties concerned."

The Yonkers minister, Alvah S. Hobart, devoted his essay to the reasons that America's "natives"—the Christians—didn't even want to socialize with Jews. ". . . [M]en go to summer resorts to get rid of as many of the inharmonious things of life as is possible. . . . [T]he Christian portion of the community [has] . . . a common Sunday, they know the same preachers . . . ; they have common experiences of their home life; some of them have common desires that their daughters shall have such a circle of acquaintances as to insure a pleasing termination to the summer vacation . . . If a company of them get to talk, the presence of a Jew makes it impolite for them to bring the chiefest matters of their thought into notice. If it is Sunday, the Jew has no feeling or respect for the day. If the young people get acquainted, a watchful mother would feel it a great misfortune for her daughter to have an attachment for . . . a Jew [who] was not fitted in his deepest sympathies to harmonize with her daughter, a Christian. So it comes about that the days which were to be full of unalloyed comfort are made less so by the presence of inharmonious elements" —Jews.

E. H. Capen, president of Tufts College wrote, "While the Jews differ [from one another] on religion, they maintain their race peculiarities. They do not assimilate like other aliens; they are always Hebrews . . . This is their glory. But it renders them separate. They can never be Americans, pure and simple. In the very nature of the case, they seem to keep their nationality distinct here as they have in every other civilization of which they have formed a part. . . .

"The only thing in my judgment which can do entirely away with the social ostracism to which in many places the Jew is now subjected is a course of conduct that would take away his characteristics as a Jew. He must violate one of the most fundamental regulations of his race and take his wives from the daughters of the land. He must not seek to preserve his Hebrew stock undefiled."

A German-Jewish Response

In 1890, the *American Hebrew* was one of the Jewish publications that German Jews took the most seriously. The Christian commentators whom Cowen had enlisted for his symposium included many who represented the Protestant institutions where upwardly mobile Jews wanted to send their children. Their assertion that Jews should become more American, and perhaps marry Americans—in effect, performing emotional nose jobs—echoed opinions well-to-do Jews heard whenever they entered Protestant preserves.

Many Jews internalized these attitudes and transmitted them to their children. "We were made to feel that being born Jewish was like being born with a club foot," recalled the writer Dorothea Strauss, who was raised in a German-Jewish household in the 1920s.

In thousands of German-Jewish homes, parents tried to train their children to modulate their voices so that they wouldn't be so loud and "Jewish." They'd criticize their offspring mercilessly if they talked with their hands. They insisted on cleanliness in all things. They hired German or British nannies and, sometimes, athletic coaches, to make their children as hardy as possible. They sent them to Christian boarding schools and on tours of Europe, hoping that whatever residue of Jewishness remained would be washed away by exposure to a more refined culture.

Is it any wonder that many German Jews who grew up between 1900 and 1940 felt ashamed of their background? Most chose mates from other German-Jewish families, but some thought the only way to free themselves from the "deformity" inherent in their Jewishness was to amputate it—to sever themselves from their people. Marriage to a Christian meant they could seek refuge in their spouses' refined milieu.

Harold Hochschild, a German Jew who was born in 1892, was the head of American Metal Climax, one of the largest mining companies in the world. In his book *Half the Way Home: A Memoir of Father & Son*, Adam Hochschild described his father's strategy for gaining acceptance in America.

Harold Hochschild was raised among German Jews on the Upper West Side of New York but chose non-Jewish friends from college on. He met his Protestant wife when he was forty-eight, just before World War II. "Coming from a well-to-do Episcopalian family full of Mayflower ancestors, Mary Marquand satisfied the necessary ethnic requirements," Adam wrote. The couple had a blissfully happy marriage. But from childhood on, Adam, who spent his winters in Princeton, New Jersey, where there were few Jews, and his summers at his parents' beloved Eagle Nest, an estate in the Adirondacks where Harold Hochschild seldom invited a Jewish house guest, had to learn the little he could about his father's ancestral heritage from his Anglo-Saxon mother. Harold Hochschild rarely mentioned it.

As a boy, Adam constantly antagonized his father with a recurrent, unavoidable mistake—talking too much when other people were around. Whenever Harold Hochschild decided that Adam had been too loud, he would summon the terrified child to the imposing study where he worked at Eagle Nest, and tell him, "I thought it was quite rude when you were talking so much at the table last night. Couldn't you see it was preventing other people from having their own conversation?" Adam's mother loved the quiet good humor that her husband defined as raucousness. Nevertheless she deferred to his insistence on rebuking Adam.

When he was in college, his parents urged him to bring guests to Eagle Nest. Once he did bring four classmates home. His friends were polite, he wrote, but his father was so distant, so reserved, that Adam was consumed with the same guilt that had haunted him as a boy. Two months later, when Adam saw his father again, he understood his transgression.

". . . [T]hose four boys you brought home a few months ago. They were all Jewish. Every one of them."

Adam protested that he didn't pick his friends that way. But his father didn't believe him. "I'm just wondering if you aren't unconsciously prejudiced against *non-Jews* in some way," Harold Hochschild said.

For months, Adam defended himself in letters and conversations, "pointing to this friend and that as indications that I've been unjustly accused, and don't have any problem about non-Jews." He had not yet realized that his father "was the one with the problem."

He came to understand that after his father died, when he found a memorandum, written in 1940, in which Harold Hochschild asked himself if the United States was going in the same direction as Nazi Germany and shared his answers with a few close friends. Describing the seeds of anti-Semitism, he began by complaining that "a large proportion of Jews in America are not properly educated to American business and social standards . . . Anybody who visits restaurants, theaters, or other places of entertainment in New York, who has traveled on large pleasure cruise ships, or who has seen certain types of Jewish summer hotels or camps near similar Gentile resorts must admit that differences in behavior play a part in anti-Semitism . . . It may not be morally wrong for Jewish women to overdress or overload themselves with jewelry and makeup, but these habits are certainly repugnant to many Gentiles."

Then Adam came to the end of his father's memo—and connected it to his own childhood problem. "Young Jews should be told frankly that certain Jewish tendencies are regarded by Gentiles as anti-social," Harold Hochschild wrote; "they should be made to realize the advantages of unobtrusiveness."

"Unobtrusiveness," Adam reflected, as he read those words at his father's desk at Eagle Nest. "Young Jews. I was born two years after he wrote this. Today, as I reread the memo, sitting in his Eagle Nest chair, those words are a beam of light from the past. Of all my childhood crimes in his eyes, the one most certain to draw a summons to this very desk for a reprimand was that of talking too much when there were guests present. Was I, in Father's eyes, acting too Jewish?"

Walter Lippmann, a German Jew whose American-born father had grown wealthy in real estate, seemed to have organized much of his interior life around the image of Jews that pervaded the Protestant responses to the *American Hebrew* questionnaire. He gave public expression to the attitudes Harold Hochschild reserved for his son and his privately circulated memo.

According to Ronald Steel's biography of Lippmann, he stated his attitude toward Jews most clearly in an article he wrote for a 1922 *American Hebrew* special issue devoted to "The Better Understanding Between Jew and non-Jew in America." In the article, Lippmann blamed bigotry on newly rich, materialistic Eastern European Jews. "They are the real fountain of anti-Semitism. When they rush about in super-automobiles, bejeweled and furred and painted and over-barbered, when they build themselves French chateaux and Italian Palazzi, they stir up the latent hatred against crude wealth in the hands of shallow people; and that hatred diffuses itself . . . [they] can in a minute unmake more respect and decent human kindliness than Einstein and Brandeis and Mack and Paul Warburg can build up in a year."

Lippmann married twice—the first time to a Congregationalist who had been raised in a socialist home, the second time to an upper class Catholic woman, who had been the wife of his best friend, Hamilton Fish Armstrong. He nearly converted to Catholicism, not because he believed in its sacraments but because he was attracted by its clean sense of a moral order.

In 1933, he seized on a conciliatory speech by Adolf Hitler to urge his readers to keep the book burning incidents and other anti-Semitic persecutions that had already begun in Germany in perspective. Germans shouldn't be judged by Nazi rantings, he wrote, "any more than the Jews [should be judged] by their parvenus."

He kept his distance from those "parvenus" by joining social clubs, such as New York's River Club, that discriminated against Jews, and by refusing to accept awards from Jewish organizations. One friend of Lippmann's told Ronald Steel that he was so sensitive to his background that when they played the board game Scrabble she avoided using the word "Jew."

4
Melting Pot Marriages

By the 1920s, when German Jews like Walter Lippmann were doing everything in their power to blend into America, the Eastern European immigrants who had begun to arrive in 1879 comprised the overwhelming majority of Jews in this land.

From the moment they arrived in America, they were the targets of ugly speeches and abusive articles. Nevertheless, living in their densely populated ghettos they were more protected from personal encounters with anti-Semitism than were the German or Sephardic Jews who might experience the Christians' scorn at an elite college or in a profession like banking or the law. The newer immigrants were sheltered by their language and their neighbors in a way that the more integrated German and Sephardic Jews never had been. They never faced a shortage of potential mates. At home, at school, at summer resorts, they were surrounded by Jews of the opposite sex. The vast majority respected the laws, traditions, and family pressures that made intermarriage seem like a terrible transgression.

Most Eastern European Jews saw America as *The Promised Land,* as one of their early representatives, Mary Antin, called her extraordinarily popular 1912 autobiography. Even the anti-Semitism that seemed so emotionally threatening to the German Jews of Harold Hochschild's generation was usually verbal in character. At its worst, it was milder than the physical brutality that had terrified so many Eastern Europeans in the countries they had left behind. It did not tarnish the dream of freedom that brought them to these shores. So, ironically, even though they were scorned by many gentiles and treated as untouchables by the German and Sephardic Jews, the sun rays of acceptance they did find—and there were many—seemed like beacons that would guide them out of what Mary Antin called "the long night of history."

If they were the most despised group of Jews who came to America, they were also the most ebullient. They longed to flee the past that had imprisoned them. Sometimes that yearning was realized in creating the books, movies, songs that are still American icons. Occasionally, it was realized in intermarriage.

Mary Antin, who was born in a Russian shtetl called Plotzk in 1881 and lived there until 1894, described the immigration fever that swept over her family and friends when they still lived in Eastern Europe. It is one of the most powerful passages in her short book, *From Plotzk to Boston*, which appeared in 1899, when she was an eighteen-year-old senior at Girl's Latin School in Boston.

"America was in everybody's mouth," she recalled. "Businessmen talked of it over their accounts; the market women made up quarrels so that they might discuss it from stall to stall; people who had relatives in the famous land went around reading their letters for the enlightenment of the less fortunate folk; the one letter carrier informed the public how many letters had arrived from America and who were the recipients; children played at emigrating . . . [A]ll talked of it, but scarcely anyone knew one true fact about this magic land. For book learning was not for them, and the few persons [who had returned from America] . . . happened to be endowed with extraordinary imaginations . . . [T]heir description of life across the ocean . . . surpassed anything in the Arabian nights . . .

Antin's autobiography, *The Promised Land*, published in 1912, showed how the dream she'd had in Europe was realized when she arrived in the United States. In it, she described her new American self with the religious fervor of one who had been born again. "I was born, I have lived, and I have been made over." She had, she said, been a pious Jew as a young girl, but from the day her family arrived in Boston, America was her creed. The act of obtaining citizenship had more meaning than a brit or a baptism. The public school was her shrine.

Here is how she described her civics class. "When the class read, and it came my turn, my voice shook and the book trembled in my hand. Never had I prayed, never had I chanted songs of David, never had I called upon the Most Holy in such adoration as I repeated the simple sentences of my child's [patriotic stories]. I gazed with adoration at the portraits of George and Martha Washington, till I could see them with my eyes shut . . . As I read about the noble boy who would not tell a lie to save himself from punishment, I was for the first time truly repentant of my sins. Formerly I had fasted and prayed and made sacrifice on the Day of Atonement, but it was more than half play, in mimicry of my elders."

Her book ends with a burst of incandescent hope. "The past was only my cradle, and now it cannot hold me, because I am grown too big . . . No! it is not I that belong to that past, but the past that belongs to me. America is the youngest of nations, and inherits all that went before in history. And I am the youngest of America's children, and into my hands is given all her priceless heritage, to the last white star espied through the telescope, to the last great thought of the philosopher. Mine is the whole majestic past, and mine is the shining future."

Many native-born Americans had never been aware of the immigrants' image of their country until they read *The Promised Land.* Antin's voice captivated them. The book went through thirty-four printings and sold eighty-five thousand copies. Ellery Sedgwick, *The Nation*'s reviewer, compared it with *The Autobiography of Benjamin Franklin* and Booker T. Washington's *Up from Slavery.*

In print, Antin was discreet about the most personal details of her life. But, in reality, she not only fell in love with America, she fell in love with an American. In 1901, she married Amadeus William Grabau, a Wisconsin-born professor of biology, whose father and grandfather had been Lutheran pastors. The marriage helped her enter the promised land. In 1901, when Grabau was offered a teaching post at Columbia University, she followed him to New York and

made "gracious friends who admitted me to their tables, although I
came direct from the reeking slums."

Though Antin never wrote about her marriage to Grabau, another
woman who was born in a Russian shtetl, Anzia Yezierska, published a
short story, "The Miracle," in which she explicitly attached the emotions Antin felt for the promised land to her immigrant Jewish hero-
ine's idealized view of the Protestant teacher who befriended her in
night school. "[He] was so much above me that he wasn't a man to
me. He was a God. His face lighted up the shop [where I worked], and
his voice sang in me everywhere I went."

For their part, many Christians who worked with Jewish immigrants
harbored equally strong romantic fantasies. "I am bound by formal
education and conventional traditions," says Yezierska's lover in
"The Miracle." "You are not repressed as I am by the fear and shame
of feeling. You could teach me more than I could teach you. You could
teach me how to be natural."

Occasionally, these fantasies intersected, spawning improbable
love affairs in Jewish ghettos. As long as intermarriage existed there
—in the hazy distance—it allowed many Americans to feel a curious
kind of satisfaction. For most onlookers, these relationships meant
that democracy had succeeded—but not next door.

But in reality, many of these romances foundered on ethnic differences. According to Pamela S. Nadell, who wrote the preface to the
1985 edition of *From Plotzk to Boston,* the outbreak of the First World
War caused problems in the Antin-Grabau marriage that would eventually result in divorce. Mary Antin was loyal to America. But her
husband, the son of a German immigrant and an admirer of German
science, supported Germany. Soon, the couple began to fight terribly. In 1918, Antin, exhausted and worried about her estrangement
from her husband, "suffered an attack from what was then diagnosed
as neurasthenia and from which she never fully recovered," Nadell
wrote. In 1919, Grabau left Mary and their child. In 1920, he exiled
himself from America and became a professor in China. During the
next thirty years Antin lived with relatives in New York and New
England. She wrote very little and never saw her husband again. By
the time she was in her sixties, she had begun to think that Jewish
history might have stronger claims on her family's loyalties than she
had imagined when she wrote *The Promised Land.* According to Nadell,
Antin "wondered whether her grandchildren might someday dis-

cover that 'the faith of Israel is a heritage that no heir in the direct line had the power to alienate from his successors.' "

Anzia Yezierska—who had married and then left a Jewish schoolteacher—realized the dream she had evoked in "The Miracle" during an intense, platonic pre-World War I love affair with the Protestant educator and philosopher John Dewey. He ended the relationship, and Yezierska never got over the disappointment. Much of her later work is a wry, bitter reexamination of the hope she expressed in "The Miracle."

In *Salome of the Tenements*, a novel based on a failed intermarriage between her Jewish friend Rose Pastor and a wealthy Episcopalian named James Graham Phelps Stokes, Yezierska described some of the tensions that destroyed such relationships. In her mind, the Jew and the Protestant were "the oriental and the Anglo Saxon struggling to find a common language." "The over-emotional ghetto [was] struggling for breath in the thin air of Puritan restraint . . ."

Whatever their outcomes, marriages that involved Christians and Eastern European Jews furnished America with a powerful metaphor. Fittingly, the play *The Melting Pot*, which provided the term with which social scientists described America for decades, focused on an interfaith courtship as symbolic proof that America could heal the Old World's feuds. It was written by a Jew, Israel Zangwill, in 1908, and was dedicated to President Theodore Roosevelt. Zangwill, whose books *Children of the Ghetto* (1892) and *The King of Schnorrers* (1894) had popularized Jewish life for gentile readers, was the son of an Orthodox father and a thoroughly secular mother who had moved from Russia to London in the 1860s. At the turn of the century, he was regarded as the literary peer of George Bernard Shaw and Thomas Hardy. He divided his time between England and the United States. In 1907, he fell in love with Edith Ayerton, a gentile. Their marriage offended Jewish religious and communal leaders. And may have been the catalyst for his writing such an unabashedly assimilationist play.

In *The Melting Pot*, Zangwill's vision is embodied in the romance between David Quixano, a Jewish violinist and composer who came to New York after his family was killed in the Kishniev pogroms, and Vera Ravendal, a Russian Christian, the daughter of nobility, who was also born in Kishniev. They meet in a New York settlement house, and during their first long conversation, David announces Zangwill's creed. "America is God's crucible, where all races are forging and reforging . . . German and Frenchman, Irishman and English, Jews and Russians—into the crucible with you. God is making the American. He will be the fusion of all people, the coming superman. Ah, what a glorious finale for my symphony."

But when David meets Vera's father he recognizes the man as the general who ordered his family killed in Kishniev on the eve of Passover. He decides to end the romance. His Old World hatred is too strong to sustain his New World romance.

When David's first symphony is produced he refuses to appear before his public. For he feels that when he spurned Vera, he broke faith with the religion of the melting pot.

During the symphony, Vera begs David's forgiveness, and reclaims his love. Jubilant again, the couple decide to marry. This upbeat New World version of *Romeo and Juliet* takes place on the Fourth of July. After the finale of David's American symphony, fireworks explode in the distance and the audience greets the work with tumultuous applause.

At *The Melting Pot*'s premiere, Theodore Roosevelt, who had been in the audience, exclaimed, "That's a great play, Mr. Zangwill, a great play." For Roosevelt, a patrician New Yorker, agreed with Zangwill, the immigrant Jew, that the marriage between Christian and Jew, the child of the oppressor and the child of the oppressed, was a sign that America could work.

Zangwill's message stirred up a great deal of controversy in the Jewish community. In a 1909 sermon delivered at Temple Emanu-El, the spiritual home of New York's German Jews, Rabbi Judah L. Magnes insisted that "[T]he Melting Pot is not the highest ideal of America. America is rather the refining pot . . . In this refining process the Jew is to lose all cringing and servility. . . . But that does not mean he is to give himself over to destruction. On the contrary, here if anywhere he has the chance of clinging to all his Jewish ways and aspirations. To be regarded as a man he need not cease being a Jew. Nay, the more of a Jew he is, the more of a man he is likely to be."

In the aftermath of World War I, it didn't seem to matter whether Jews chose to call America a melting pot or a refining pot. Along with other immigrants, they were seen as impurities who crowded America's cities, who led strikes instead of working docilely, whose ghettos and tenements were spawning grounds for alcoholism, infectious diseases, and crimes. They might debate whether they should assimilate, as Zangwill believed, or acculturate, as Magnes thought. Many Protestants wondered whether they should be here at all.

In those years, a new breed of social scientist, who called themselves eugenicists, had begun to popularize the idea that marriage between American Protestants and immigrants would pollute the nation's gene pool. Intermarriage—which they regarded as miscegenation—took on considerable symbolic importance in the polemical and political effort to restrict assimilation. The eugenicist's leading theorist, an anthropologist named Madison Grant, stated their fears explicitly in his influential book *The Passing of the Great Race.* "[T]he mixture of two races . . . gives us a race . . . reverting to the lower type. The cross between the white man and the Indian is an Indian; the cross between a white man and a negro [sic] is a negro; and the cross between any of the three European races and the Jew is a Jew."

By 1924, these fears of social disruption and biological destruction swept through America. They were one reason that 6 million people had joined the Ku Klux Klan, which was then as strident in its hatred of Jews and Catholics as in its hatred of blacks. More importantly, these fears had prompted the House and Senate to agree on legislation which, in effect, ended Southern European immigration.

But most Americans still wanted their democracy to maintain respect for the ethnically diverse people who had already settled here. They might want to restrict immigration, but they didn't want to see themselves as bigots. After all, in the years following World War I, every American city was filled with WASPs, Italians, Jews, Poles, and Irish who had fought side by side in the war to make the world safe for democracy. For the most part, they wanted to believe that disparate cultures could coexist in this land—and, even, in the same household.

These feelings were reflected in the unexpected, unprecedented popularity of *Abie's Irish Rose*, a romantic comedy by Anne Nichols, a Southern-born Protestant, whose plot revolved around a marriage between an Irish Catholic and a Jew. When it opened on Broadway in May 1922, the reviews that greeted it seemed like certain signs of doom. The critic for the New York *World* predicted it would close in one night.

Sometimes, during the play's first summer, there were only five or ten people in the audience. But Nichols believed so deeply in *Abie* that she mortgaged her house in Queens and sold all her jewelry to keep the play alive. She persuaded the actors to take a temporary pay cut. She discounted the tickets, and marketed them at a Broadway drugstore. In later years, she attributed *Abie's* popularity to that decision since it brought people into the theater and created the word of mouth that soon made the play a hit.

By 1924, its success in New York—and in cities like Minneapolis and towns like Erie, Pennsylvania—was so astonishing that national magazines were assigning reporters to find out why so many Americans had found such inspiration in a work that almost all the critics had ridiculed. By then, about 3 million people had seen *Abie*. It had earned its author, Anne Nichols, about 5 million dollars. In time, its 2,327 performances made it the most popular play in Broadway history until *Tobacco Road* eclipsed it in 1937. Its success on the road has never been matched.

Its audiences were ethnically heterogeneous, according to Robert Luther Duffus, who reported on the play for the July 1924 issue of *Collier's* magazine. "It didn't seem to make any difference how many Jews or Irishmen a town had," Duffus reported.

"I think [the play] demonstrates . . . that racial and religious prejudice hasn't soured these United States," Duffus wrote. "Miss Nichols doesn't say that all prejudices are wicked, but that they are foolish. She doesn't advise you to despise people who are narrow-minded . . . but to feel sorry for them, and perhaps to see reflections of your own amusing narrow-mindedness in theirs . . . I bank more on the success of plays like this than I do on the Presidential election."

It is a patriotic play, which connects the pride Americans felt during World War I to the tolerance that had vanished in its aftermath. In the first act, Abie Levy, once a soldier, and Rose Mary Murphy, once an entertainer, mention their first meeting, which took place after Abie was wounded while fighting for America. The drama and the jokes arise as their fathers try to keep the couple apart. But by the second act it is clear that the clerics, Father John Whalen and Rabbi Jacob Samuels, who are supposed to provide a theological basis for the family feud, have actually allied themselves with the couple.

In the play's emotionally climactic scene, the rabbi and the priest reminisce about the lessons they learned when they served in the trenches during World War I. "I [comforted] a good many boys of your faith—when they couldn't find a good priest," Rabbi Samuels says. Father Whalen adds cheerfully, "Shure, they all had the same God above them. And what with all the shells bursting, and the shrapnel flying, with no one knowing just what moment death would come, Catholics, Hebrews, and Protestants alike forgot their prejudice and came to realize that all faiths and creeds have about the same destination after all." Wherever *Abie* played, that exchange drew tumultuous applause.

The play ends on Christmas Eve. Rose has given birth a month before. Abie is trimming the tree, and the couple sets out ham for Rose's friends and kosher food for Abie's. When Patrick Murphy and Solomon Levy come in unexpectedly, enraged at one another, they learn that they are grandfathers . . . of twins. The boy—whom Patrick praises as the image of Abie—will be named Solomon. The girl—who Solomon says "is just like Rosie! She's beautiful"—will be named Rose Mary.

As the Christmas bells start to ring out, a baffled Solomon Levy asks, "Vod iss it? A fire?" Patrick Murphy answers comfortingly, "Tis Christmas. Merry Christmas, Sol." Appeased, Solomon Levy offers the traditional Jewish greeting on a festival. "Goot yonteff, Patrick." It is the perfect curtain line for this wildly improbable ode to the melting pot dream.

In the America of the 1920s and '30s, of course, *Abie's Irish Rose* was still a fantasy. When Nichols wrote her play America still consisted of ethnic enclaves, where a Jew was more likely to flee from a Catholic than woo one. So the play's theme—assimilation—could provoke debates like the one between Zangwill and Magnes, but the interethnic harmony it preached was so attractive that Jewish political leaders like Rabbi Stephen Wise could praise the 1943 radio version of *Abie,* which had an audience of 20 million people, when he was interviewed by a *Time* magazine reporter. But by 1973, the rate of intermarriage was escalating, and had become a phenomenon that was seen by many as a threat to Jewish survival. The Jewish community was concerned enough to pressure CBS to drop *Bridget Loves Bernie,* a sit-com about a contemporary Abie and Rose.

Of course, when intermarriage did occur in the 1920s and '30s, most of the Jewish community consisted of people like the Solomon Levy whom we see when *Abie* begins—men and women who were more likely to mourn a son who intermarried than to wish his father-in-law "goot yonteff" on Christmas Eve. But some Jews felt the emotions Mary Antin and Israel Zangwill had described so deeply that they deliberately set out to separate themselves from their community and make a home for themselves in "the promised land." Many of those who did so entered show business and created a zesty, ebullient culture which became an icon millions of Americans shared.

One of the most famous Jews in show business, Irving Berlin, a cantor's son from Temun, Russia, came to America in 1893. The depths of his desire to assimilate allowed him to reach inside himself to find the music and words that erased the distinction between different ethnic groups, between native-born Americans and immigrants, with his ode to his adopted country, "God Bless America."

The anthem caressed the continent that he and so many of his *landsmen* saw as their Zion. It was the magic land of the spirit that Berlin evoked in his song "White Christmas"; it was the soft, beckoning vagabond land that Harold Arlen, another cantor's son, captured in the melody he wrote for "Blues in the Night." Its folk history contained the sanitized Peter Stuyvesant who sang "September Song" in *Knickerbocker Holiday*, a musical that Kurt Weill, another cantor's son, helped create; the lively, thoughtful community-spirited frontier folk whom Richard Rodgers and Oscar Hammerstein II—two German Jews from New York—glorified in *Oklahoma* and *State Fair;* the warmhearted blacks who sang "Ol' Man River" in Jerome Kern's *Showboat,* who populated Catfish Row in George Gershwin's *Porgy and Bess.*

For these Jews, America was the innocent, fresh-faced environment in which Mickey Rooney and Judy Garland cavorted in the Andy Hardy series, the brainchild of Louis B. Mayer, a Russian-born immigrant, who was so involved with those films that he'd spend hours on the set making sure that Andy didn't sass his mother, that he fell on his knees, clasped his hands, and prayed to God like the good American kids of Mayer's dreams.

Of course, these were popular songs, movies, and Broadway shows, with the sweeping themes, the panache, the hints of old-time burlesque that kept audiences entertained. Nevertheless, they reflected an underlying mood. It was as if these Jewish songwriters and film makers were describing a sparkling America they viewed through the window of a train.

When the places they portrayed so lovingly were seen through the eyes of the people who lived there, the life they glorified seemed quite grim. Imagine Irving Berlin's "White Christmas" somewhere in the rural Midwest and you have a scene from Sherwood Anderson's *Winesburg, Ohio* or Theodore Dreiser's *Sister Carrie;* put "Blues in the Night" in the South, and you're among the people Robert Penn Warren depicted in *All the King's Men,* in the world that took William Faulkner a lifetime to describe. In reality, Oklahoma must have resembled the harsh Plains States that Ole Rölvagg evoked in *Giants in the Earth* or the tense, brooding Nebraska of Willa Cather's novels; the real Porgy and Bess exist in Richard Wright's *Black Boy* and *Native Son.*

But these Jewish composers and performers had experienced America as a land of allure. They had been able to use their creative talent and awesome energy to build careers that provided them much greater wealth, more social and physical mobility, than they had imagined possible when they were young. Scores of them intermarried.

Sometimes their biographers recorded their feelings about marrying gentiles. "Groucho [Marx] never married a Jewish girl, nor did he even go out much with Jewish girls," wrote his biographer Charlotte Chandler. "He attributed this not to chance, but to choice . . . 'It always seemed to me that making love to a Jewish girl would be like making love to your sister.' "

Cinda Glenn, who had once dated Jed Harris (né Horowitz), producer of *Front Page, The Green Bay Tree,* and *Our Town,* told a friend, "Jed doesn't like Jewish girls. Ruth Gordon, Rosamond Pinchot, Louise Platt, Margaret Sullavan, me. It's a great list of shiksas. Maybe," she speculated, Jed "doesn't like being Jewish. I know he tells a lot of Jewish jokes, but jokes are either just jokes or they can hide all sorts of feelings."

Some Jews, like Irving Berlin (whose Christian wife's father had amassed a fortune of 30 million dollars), married into the elite—they made "White Christmas" marriages. Others, like George Burns, who wed a working-class Catholic he might have met near the Grand Street tenement where he was born, made melting pot marriages.

To convey the feelings underlying such marriages, and the family lives they created, we have interviewed parents and children in Max and Edna Lerner's "white Christmas" marriage and Pat and Nettie Auletta's "melting pot" marriage.

By now, the Lerners and Pat Auletta, who made these 1930s intermarriages, can take a long enough look backward to define the satisfactions and regrets they feel about their decisions to marry cultural strangers. Their children are old enough to assess the pleasures and the difficulties of being raised inside a household which blends two different religious and ethnic cultures. Though they are products of a very different age from this one, they connect the past when intermarriages were relative novelties in America and the present when intermarriage is veering toward the norm.

A "White Christmas" Marriage

In 1937, Max Lerner, the son of immigrants from Russia, a Yale graduate who wrote political articles for *The Nation* and *The New Republic* and scholarly works about Oliver Wendell Holmes and Machiavelli, met Edna Albers, the daughter of a well-to-do Episcopalian family from Connecticut. Max was twenty-nine and married. He was a professor at Sarah Lawrence College and Edna, seventeen, was one of his students.

In the 1930s, Lerner never wrote about his feelings about the Jewish people. But the Holocaust brought those emotions to the surface. His columns for *PM* in the 1940s and the New York *Post* in the '50s and '60s made him a spokesman for millions of Jews. He has spent much of his time teaching at Brandeis University and the University of California at San Diego, speaking in synagogues, attending Zionist meetings—immersed in the hurly-burly of the Jewish world. Meanwhile, Edna, a psychiatrist, a wise, self-possessed woman who treasures her independence, has maintained the refined household where their three sons, Michael, Steve, and Adam were raised.

I went to see them late one spring afternoon in 1985. Max and Edna were talking about the reasons they fell in love, in the prickly, bantering, affectionate style they display when they're together. Max was the first Jewish man Edna had ever known. "I was terrifically attracted to his intellectual exhilaration—he saw possibilities in life that I had never glimpsed," she recalled. "But the thing that made me fall in love with him was his dark 'otherness.' His history had given him qualities which made him much more interesting than anyone I had ever known."

"I was absolutely stunned by her beauty," Max said. "I had never seen such beauty in my whole life. I knew we'd have a rough time together, and we have had a somewhat rough time, but that wasn't important. Her mind was as distinctive as her looks. I knew I'd never meet anyone as special. I didn't want to let her go.

"We're very verbal, very literary, very much involved with ideas," Max added. "Jennie"—as he calls his wife—"has to listen to long discourses at dinner. I'm always excited by my work. I always bring it to the dinner table, and explain it to her. She's very good—a very tough critic."

"We never bore each other," Edna agreed. "The otherness remains. Sometimes it's infuriating. But it's always interesting."

They plainly treasure their individuality. The week after the interview, Edna would take a trip to China and Max would resume his teaching in San Diego. They are very different people who share an unquenchable zest for life.

Throughout my childhood, Max and Edna were my parents' close friends. Even as a boy I already knew that I wanted to be a writer, so I was fascinated by Max's career as a columnist. I was in awe of the author of *America as a Civilization*, a two-volume book my parents regarded as a classic. Whenever he came to dinner, I'd beg him to write a column about me. Once he did: a description of a Yankee game which he and his sons Steve and Mike, who were my contemporaries, attended with my father and brother and me. I was thrilled.

When Max sat in his spacious apartment overlooking New York's East River and described his childhood in Russia, he momentarily sounded like a character out of a Sholom Aleichem story. He is a short man—a "brachycephalic," roundhead, as he joked to his wife—and he is physically frail: he had been gravely ill with cancer in 1983. But his voice exuded infectious excitement as he talked.

"I lived in a little town called Ivinitz for my first four years, in the Minkser area of Russia. My father, Benjamin Lerner, was a gifted student, a *yeshiva bucher*, and my mother was a merchant's daughter. They met through a *shadchen*, a marriage broker. I was the fourth of four children. My father spent his time studying Jewish texts. My mother earned money for the family by running a little store.

"My father's dream was to get to Palestine, but he settled for coming to America. He came to New York City in 1903, and spent four years working in a garment loft until he earned enough money to bring the rest of us here." Max arrived in America in 1907.

From the start, the elder Lerners wanted to own their own business, as they had in Russia. They spent a decade roaming the countryside around New York in search of the American shtetl where they could succeed. "There was always some relative giving us advice. Someone had the idea that we should go to Bayonne, New Jersey, where we could rent a farm and have cows and a horse and deliver milk. We did that for a couple of years. My older brother Hyman had to work all night delivering milk. He got a rheumatic heart out of that."

The family managed to save a little money. Then, "an uncle heard of a wonderful farm in the Catskills. Sure enough, we went there, but it was a farm filled with stones." Max's brother Hyman died of rheumatic fever. "The place broke my father's back and broke our hearts."

For a few years, the Lerners turned the small farm into a boardinghouse for the tourists who came to the mountains every summer. "Then someone told my father he could establish a successful milk route in New Haven. I was nine then. He and I would drive a horse and wagon from our house in the city. We'd take forty-quart milk cans and fill them with milk we bought from farmers. We'd bring the milk home and refrigerate it. Then we would deliver it to our customers. I was my father's assistant right through high school. Then he sold his milk route and bought a little grocery store.

"He was a sweet and wonderful man, but he had no skills other than intellectual skills. He was good in shul; he was a Hebrew teacher. But he couldn't capitalize on that."

In those days, Max was standing on his parents' shoulders, scanning the country which left them feeling dazed. "The linchpin of my parents' psychology was that we were strangers in a strange land, and children were the ones who could learn the language most easily. We spoke Yiddish in the household. Every now and then, my sisters and I would break into English and teach our parents a few words. We always ate Jewish foods and sang Jewish songs.

"We became the ambassadors to the possessors. Because we were the ambassadors—and Mother and Dad couldn't handle English—we became the authority figures. It was a very close and cohesive family, but when it came to crucial decisions they were always made from the standpoint of success in America."

Though Max's parents were Orthodox Jews, "They'd say, 'Maxeleh, going to shul on holidays is all right. But otherwise, you've got better things to do.' They cared about only one thing—they loved us and it was an unqualified love. That was particularly true of me. My sisters were girls and the Messiah was supposed to be a boy. So after my brother's death, I became the Messiah. Even on Yom Kippur everyone else fasted but I didn't have to fast. I was the Messiah, but I was also the baby. One way of pampering me was to create the fiction I was fasting—and still sneak me food."

He entered Yale in 1919, just twelve years after he had arrived in America. He longed to be a Yalie. He saved his money to buy a raccoon coat and a hip flask. He didn't pledge a Jewish fraternity because he hoped to be tapped by a Christian house. But in those years, Jews—and particularly Eastern Europeans like Max Lerner— were too intense and intellectual to fit the Yale ideal.

Nevertheless, by the time he entered Yale he was completely captivated by America. In his romantic life, his dream was about "shiksas, not Jewish girls. They were the daughters of the conquerers. They represented all the values attached to the promised land. I wanted to shine in the context of this country.

"I was a very literary young man. I had read all the novels and all the romantic poetry. Except for Rebecca in *Ivanhoe*, the heroines were always what I call the possessors. In those days, all I knew was that I wanted to be dressed in slacks and a jersey and have a tennis racket and a beautiful long-legged girl next to me. We'd be going to the tennis court. She was out of Meredith's *Diana of the Crossways*. She was out of Byron and Keats and Shelley. I grew up in the haze of English romantic poetry."

Then, reflecting on himself as he was back then, he mused, "I suppose that if I could conquer the possessor, I validated myself. Otherwise, how would it be that I was married twice to non-Jewish girls?"

In 1928, he wed a Southern aristocrat, whom he had met in graduate school. According to one of her daughters, she "was never comfortable with Max's background. She thought that being Jewish was not in good taste. But she'd never met anyone like him. He was full of magnetism, excitement. He came from an unknown culture."

Lerner's mind was full of American images. "In those days," Max said, "I wooed women by talking about how I was going to go off to the Southwest and build an adobe house and have seven children. The Jewish thing didn't come until the Holocaust. And then it came very strong.

Edna is so much a product of her upper middle class Episcopalian environment that one can literally hear her background in the precise way she pronounces her vowels. She had the kind of Christian grandmother who fully expected to see *her* mother on a cloud in heaven. Edna had gone to Sunday school every week from the time she was small (in those days she thought that "God was in the organ") until she was sixteen, when she wrote a prize-winning essay on the life of Jesus. Church was part of the marrow of her family's life. She had never met a Jew until she entered Sarah Lawrence. Then, within two years, she fell deeply in love with Max, her favorite professor.

Edna said that even though Max had the "dark, extraordinary qualities" that fascinated her, "we never really talked about his being Jewish. We didn't think it was of any consequence. It never occurred to me that we wouldn't celebrate Christmas. Of course we did. But Max always got sick on Christmas. He always had a headache and went to bed. He has a terrible time buying me a Christmas present. I'm sure that's an unconscious rejection of the holiday."

As Edna remembered it, "We certainly never discussed the children's religions when they were born." Max thought they had made a choice: "We decided to impose neither Judaism nor Christianity on them, but to expose them to both." Then, with a twinkle in his eye he added, "I think Edna trusted I would take the lead in exposing them to Judaism."

Edna recalled, "I read the Bible to them and I made them memorize psalms. I wanted the children to know their prayers. I wanted them to know the Bible because I thought they should grow up with a sense of some benign force in the world. Since the force I'm familiar with is Christian, that's the package it came in. But I never took them to a Christian Sunday school because I thought that would be rude to Max. And Max never took them to a synagogue. He never went himself, so how could he take them?"

Spurred by the emergence of Nazi power in Europe, Max's suppressed Jewish feelings began to crop up in his writing. For example, on September 27, 1941, he described a scene in a Jewish delicatessen

in a poem he wrote for *The Saturday Review of Literature*. This was
before the United States entered World War II, before many Jews or
Christians could have grasped the fate that awaited European Jews.

> Here, where the swirling streams of life converge,
> and dietary laws are strictly kept,
> They sit, the subject of some future dirge,
> The dead, for whom the tears are yet unwept.

> They need no pity. Their worlds have crashed before,
> their friends thinned out, the politician's grace
> turned to dull stone. They bring old strengths to face
> the new storm-troopers striding through the door.

Throughout the war, he was one of the very few prominent American Jews to give speeches and sponsor rallies to protest the American
government's indifference to the plight of Jews of Europe. In those
days, many liberals opposed the coalition of Palestinian Jews such as
Menachem Begin and Americans like the flamboyant writer Ben
Hecht who were trying to alert people to the catastrophe that was
occurring in Europe. "I didn't give a damn about their social views,"
Max recalled with great passion. "Whenever people would say to me
'You're with a bunch of Jewish fascists,' I'd answer 'If you'll show me
some non-fascists who want to rescue the Jews in Europe I'll join
them. So far this is the only group I've found that really is dead
serious about it and I don't give a damn. I'm going to work with
them.' "

Edna shared his obsession with the events that would one day be
known as the Holocaust. She felt nothing but scorn for the people
who dismissed her husband as too militant.

Max's powerful feelings about the Jewish people did not extend to
the Jewish religion. In the 1940s and '50s, Max often extolled Israel
in his columns and lectures, but he always made it clear that he was a
secular Jew. He used to enrage his Jewish readers of the *Post* by
writing an annual description of his family's Christmas. But then he
would win them back with his unapologetic passion for Israel. In
1949, for example, he told an audience of Labor Zionists "The biggest single victory which we [Jews] have won is a psychological victory. We no longer have the sense of fear that obsessed us in 1937,
1938, 1939, and 1940. We know that we are no longer passive victims.

We have taken things into our own hands and we have done them well, and the biggest factor in our victory has been the struggle in Israel . . . [It has given me] a new sense of personal enrichment within myself, a new sense of wholeness in my personality that I didn't have before . . ."

Max was as enthusiastic about Israel and his Jewish past at home as he was on the lecture circuit. That was his strategy for transmitting his feelings to his offspring. "I never liked religious services," Max said. "I tried to communicate my sense of Jewishness by developing a kind of mythology of my immigrant days which I would recite to both sets of children—and always with a swagger."

"You tried to make them Jewish by announcing that you were Jewish and Jews were the chosen people," Edna said with a chuckle.

"I never made a secret of the fact that I had come to believe that wherever there is creativity—or any brains—it would be Jewish. Or at least part Jewish," Max agreed.

When the Lerner boys were young, there was one annual Jewish occasion in their lives—the Passover seder at Max's parents' house in New Haven. Edna used to love the event. "It was an enormous festivity. Max's mother was an observant Jew in her slaphappy way. She was not a very orderly or organized woman. The atmosphere was very different from that in my house or my mother's house, but it was such an affectionate atmosphere that we all loved it. I remember Michael saying to me, 'I have pictures in my head, and when I take them out at night and look at them the only one that doesn't fit is grandmother's house in New Haven.' That was true. Everything was helter-skelter."

It was a traditional seder, Edna recalled, "with all the rituals. Everything was done in Hebrew with no funny business about transliterations. As soon as Michael was old enough, we taught him to read the Four Questions. We did it phonetically and I helped. No one but Max had asked the questions in decades. So when Michael did it his grandparents just about fell over. I must say I couldn't help but weep with this sense of the tradition going back to the beginning. It was marvelous.

"I used to watch Max sitting there, rocking away with his father in a rather competitive fashion, mumbling a bit as if he were practicing. When his parents died, I thought Max would be eager to take over the tradition. The next year, I bought all the little hats, and I memorized what to do, and his sister came down. I thought that would be the beginning of Passover in our house. But that was it. The next year Max forgot completely. He was off lecturing somewhere."

Max agreed with Edna that those "Passovers were very moving. When my parents died, I tried once or twice to continue it but my heart wasn't in it. I have never had much use for Jewish rituals. I was out to make some dent for myself in the intellectual life in America."

"And to be an American," Edna said.

"And to be an American. . . ."

"My parents' seders were traditional and quite beautiful," he recalled with a sad nostalgia in a voice that was usually brimming with energy. "But I never caught up with Hebrew. One of the reasons I didn't go on having Passover was that I didn't know the meaning of the Hebrew words."

"You didn't make any effort to tell the boys the stories or what the holidays were."

"I didn't know. I could have found out, but it wasn't part of my ready knowledge. I wasn't emphasizing that. I always thought that if I did my best—if I tried to transmit some of my excitement about being Jewish—then I would have done whatever I could."

The bedrock of his pride lies somewhere in his own complex childhood, as Edna observed. "One of the things that has given Max security through his whole life was the sense he had of the family—the warmth and cohesiveness of this little nest of people—the potato pancakes and the matzoh ball soup."

"A warm and cohesive family and a fierce pride in the struggles of the Jews," he echoed—"those are the two things that have given me my inner fortress."

His voice became animated when he alluded to his past. "I identify with Jews on a class level. I don't identify with the affluent ones. I identify very much with the ones who have had to scramble and scratch and fight—I like that sort of rough-hewn Jew. I get along wonderfully with them."

"Where do you see them?" Edna asked.

"Wherever I lecture. Wherever I have given pro-Israel Bond speeches. Hundreds and hundreds, perhaps thousands of times, I've been with these people. I know them from the inside, and I must say I identify with them. The emotion in me is the emotion of my own beginnings and my own struggles."

His love of America and his love for the rough-hewn Jewish people swirled together when he described his taste in women. "I still like the non-Jewish style of woman better than the Jewish. My personal taste is for quietness, not garishness. But, you know, that's changed over the years." Then, in a characteristically sudden change of mood he exclaimed, "Jews are a flamboyant people. I always say, 'Thank God for our bad taste. This is our vitality.' And I care more about vitality than I do about taste."

But the Lerner household was very much tailored to Edna's tastes. The apartment was a colorful, well-organized place, with objects Max and Edna had gathered during their travels in India, South America, and Southeast Asia. But it was certainly not a flamboyant household. There was nothing "rough-hewn" about it. How did Max feel about that?

"I do my best to unrefine my household, but I fight a losing fight. If you look in my room, you'll see the authentic me. I live in a pigsty."

But was there a difference between the nourishment he got from the Jews he met when he was speaking and the Jewish nourishment he got at home?

"I don't get any Jewish nourishment from this home," he said, sounding surprised by my question.

"How could he?" Edna asked.

Then Max remembered the one serious religious disagreement he and Edna had experienced—over a bar mitzvah for their sons. "I wanted them to have one, and she was against it. And I didn't fight."

"Max thought that ceremony would innoculate them into Judaism," Edna said. "But I didn't want that. I didn't ask that the children be baptized or anything. I thought that a bar mitzvah was a tribal rite, and I didn't intend to have my children push me out."

"You took them to all kinds of churches . . ." Max said.

"Correspondingly, they could have been bar mitzvahed," Max continued. "I understand your position. The conflict wasn't that crucial. But it is part of an intermarriage. Clearly both of us have felt it and resented it for years."

Actually, Edna told me, she had seldom taken her sons to church except when they were in Europe and visited cathedrals. Besides, she didn't think the fight over the bar mitzvah had been so important. My questions, she said, had churned up feelings that Max had forgotten for years. Anyway, "Max's intense identification with Jews comes through for the children. They have that same identification. They feel they are Jewish, even though they're a lot closer to me in a religious way."

"Yes," Max said, "when the 1967 war broke out, Steve was in college and Mike was in graduate school. Independently of each other, they both decided to go over there and help out. I was very worried but very proud."

Edna was as proud of them as Max. "It was very important for them to get to the front lines," she said. "I think it helped them a lot in whatever mixed identities they have."

Occasionally, Edna worried about those mixed identities—or, at least, in her gloomy moments she brooded about the consequences of her decision to intermarry. "The longer I live, the more homesick I get for some kind of consistency and definition. I know so many people who are half-and-half. When I was a girl I lived near a lot of birthright Quakers—people whose families had been Quakers for generations—and their houses had a different atmosphere from other houses. I liked that. I like the sense that you are in an environ-ment that believes so strongly that it takes things for granted, where you *know* you are going to church on Christmas Eve or Easter instead of making a big production of it and trotting off as if you're going to a party. But in our environment people are always pulling up their roots and examining them and deciding which ones they'll let grow and which ones they'll lop off. I think that's little sad. We've become too aware—we try rationally to make choices that are not really ra-tional ones.

"Certainly my marriage is different from what it would have been if it had been a homogenous marriage. Since we're liberal people who respect each other's traditions, we create a sort of no-man's land where no one gets a Christian child's upbringing or a Jewish child's upbringing. It's part of what's making us a dun-colored culture. I like a sort of tapestry culture with vivid but friendly enclaves. But maybe the price you pay for the end of anti-Semitism is this melding that's going on all over the place."

Max doesn't worry about that homogenization—indeed, at some level, he seems to feel that Jews who intermarry are spreading the seeds of intelligence. Michael, the only one of his three sons who was married when we talked, was first wed to a woman with a Jewish father. They had one son, Josh. "I hope that he will be Jewish," Max said.

"He won't be," answered Edna, who attempts to teach her grandson psalms when he comes to visit, paying him a quarter for each one he memorizes.

"He probably won't be," Max agreed. "But I have this feeling with myself and Michael and Joshua that there really is a three-generation continuity. It isn't religious. But my basic concept is that Jews are a historical civilization—we keep the fires burning. When I look at Josh, I think of him as Jewish. He's so bright that he has to be Jewish. It's his radiance of personality. That's what's Jewish."

When I was a child, I thought of Max Lerner as being more Jewish than my parents—I guess I also assumed his sons knew more about Judaism than I did. After all, they *had* gone to those seders—something we never did. Furthermore, my mother, feeling herself too patrician and conflicted about her background to join any Jewish organization, was always amused and impressed at how much Hadassah women adored Max. I figured they adored Edna, Mike, Steve, and Adam too. I was sure the entire Lerner family had a direct experience with the ethnic Judaism that was so conspicuously absent from our lives.

I was wrong. After listening to Max and Edna describe their differences—and then hearing Mike and Steve try to make sense of them—I realized that there was a sharp contrast between being raised in an interfaith home like the Lerners' and being raised in a completely assimilated but Jewish household like ours. We had to choose between our mother's demanding German-Jewish style and our father's warm, overprotective Eastern European one; we had to reconcile their contradictory demands that we become as American as possible and remain Jewish at the same time. Those choices could perplex us. But it was not the same as the perplexity that comes when you're forced to create the identity that suits you out of your parents' very different ancestral cultures and beliefs.

Michael Lerner, the winner of a MacArthur Fellowship, is a medical researcher who lives in Bolinas, California, a tiny, unspoiled town on the Pacific coast, an hour north of San Francisco; Steve is a journalist who lives in Washington, D.C. In September 1986, he married Mary Jane Barrett. Her grandfather is Irving Berlin.

When we were teenagers, I always saw Mike as the sort of kid who had his life under control. He had breezed through Exeter, and seemed completely at home with Harvard students and faculty members. He was very good-looking. During Mike's years on the Harvard *Crimson,* he had written moderate, well-tailored articles about the war in Vietnam that made him sound more like a Kennedy-era policymaker than a student who was seeking a political identity.

Steve, who had gone to Dalton and Andover, had the same kind of self-assurance. You couldn't have a father like Max Lerner without assuming that you had easy, immediate access to any person you wanted to meet, any place you hoped to visit. But unlike Mike, who always seemed so confident of his place in America, Steve was a spiritual seeker.

Now Mike was on his own search. In his late twenties, he had felt compelled to weave the conflicting traditions his parents represented into a spiritual garment that would fit him. It wasn't easy. "I'm always aware of myself as half Jew and half Christian. It's almost as if those traditions were both inside me. One has a cross and one has a star. They're happier together than they were when I was younger, but they're still not one."

The two brothers have a great deal in common. Though Steve was now a journalist, like his father, and Mike was in health care, like his mother, they were at ease in each other's professions. They spent seven years working together in Bolinas. In 1967, without consulting one another, they each decided to fight for Israel. They were both attracted to Eastern religions. They both talked about their parents with love—and understanding.

"There is a world of half Jews," Mike said, "and we share something. We're not Jewish and we're not not Jewish. If I were to become completely Christian I'd feel as if half my reality were thrown out. The same would be true if I were completely Jewish. I'm delighted that my first wife was half Jewish—that means Josh is half Jewish. My second wife is Christian, and I'm a little sorry that if we have children they'll only be one-quarter Jewish. But if I had married a Jewish woman our children would be three-quarters Jewish. Part of me would feel I was denying the other half of my family."

Late one afternoon, I was in the Lerners' apartment, interviewing

Edna. We had just finished talking about her marriage when Mike, who was in town to deliver a series of lectures, came to meet her for dinner.

"Here comes the result," she joked, looking at her oldest son. "Hello, darling."

At once, she sought to involve him in the conversation by reminding him of the Passovers in New Haven when he had asked the Four Questions. "My eyes filled with tears," she recalled. "I felt the way I had about the church organ when I was a little girl. I felt that here we were in New Haven, and you had all these ancestors going back to Mt. Sinai, and how extraordinary that was as a tradition. I don't even know if you remember that."

"I do," Mike said in a voice that was just as crisp as his mother's. "I remember asking the Four Questions. But that was the entire Jewish religious experience of my childhood. Once a year, for a relatively short period of time, we went up to this little house in New Haven where there were these old people and this unfamiliar food . . ."

"It was awful food," Edna said.

". . . and where my father was distanced from his family by his success. The whole thing was far from luminous in its quality. My experience with Christianity was more prolonged—not just at home, with Christmas and Easter and your reading the Bible, but at Exeter, where I went to chapel every day and church on Sunday. There was an Anglicized quality to my life. I didn't feel as if I had much of a chance to learn about Judaism."

Steve remembered those seders, too. "I loved the family sitting around the table and just the whole ritual of the seder. It was such a sensual ritual, with sweet wine that I'd never had anywhere else. The food was quite foreign to me, but I liked it. I loved all the things you got to do with the plagues—those gestures with the wine. The whole point of it was to pass on this knowledge from one generation to the next—to teach the tradition of the Jews. It served its purpose. It connected me to that thread of Judaism, although in terms of education and rituals it was a very slender thread."

Neither of the brothers was even aware that their father had wanted them to have a bar mitzvah. "That would have seemed very bizarre to me," Mike said. "I experienced myself as basically brought up in a Christian world with a lot of Jewish friends and a Jewish identity. I had a way of telling myself that I was a Christian but I was a Jew. Racially I was a Jew, but spiritually I was a Christian."

For Steve, the emphasis was slightly different. "I have no hesitation in saying I'm a Jew and Jews are us. I might also say I was a half Christian. But I would never say I'm a Christian."

Steve felt the Holocaust personally. Because of his father, he became aware of the extermination of the Jews in the mid-1940s, long before most parents discussed it with their children, long before it was a required part of every Hebrew school curriculum. "My father had visited the concentration camps after the war. He brought back a strong sense of outrage. And he brought back the paraphernalia of war. We had Nazi flags. We had German helmets with bullet holes through them. We had bayonets. I was surrounded by memories of the Holocaust. I see that as the central message of my early life. I think that I lost out on a certain innocence that children naturally have. After all, I realized that my people could be rounded up and sent to gas chambers at any moment.

"Then, too, we were circumcised. I knew that the Nazis told people to drop their trousers to see if they were circumcised. They tortured and killed the ones who were. So there I was, a child looking down and seeing that I was circumcised—feeling that I was stamped for life, that I could be yanked out of my everyday world at any moment. And there was another message for me, as the child of an intermarriage. It didn't matter if I was a half Jew or a quarter Jew. *They'd* still treat me as a Jew. I learned that lesson from the start. By Nazi standards I'm a Jew even though by Jewish standards I'm not a Jew. So I might as well say that I'm a Jew."

There was never any anti-Semitism at Dalton. But Mike and Steve each encountered it in boarding school. Mike, who was exposed to it at Exeter, "sort of joined in. It was a kind of cowardice. I'm not proud of it in retrospect. I'd imitate the Jewish accents and tell the Jewish jokes. But I had a very Disraeli-like attitude towards it. I used to think, 'When *your* ancestors were barbarians in the plains of Europe, *mine* were lords in the House of David.' "

Steve, who confronted bigotry at boarding school in Switzerland, felt outraged. He was rooming with an Italian, a Canadian, and a kid from the Belgian Congo. "The Italian was a raving anti-Semite and was making cruel remarks about the only other Jew in the school. My first sentence in that room was 'I'm a Jew.' Suddenly, there was this

dead silence. It was one of those moments of intense identity realization. It wasn't that I normally went around feeling like a Jew. It was
just that when somebody didn't like Jews, I felt that I had to make it
clear . . . not that I'm half Jew or anything else. I'm a Jew.

"The same thing was true during the Six Day War in 1967. I was at
Harvard and I was listening to the radio about how all the Jews are
being pushed into the sea. I thought, 'I'm not going to listen to the
radio while this thing happens. I want to be there and fight.' It was in
June—I had some exams—but I decided to go anyway. My parents
advised that I get credentials, so I called up *Ramparts* magazine to get
a press card. Just before leaving I heard that Michael was going, too.
We finally got there on a stripped-down military plane out of Rome. It
was one of the last planes that got in.

"Of course, the Israelis didn't need me. I wrote something that
Ramparts didn't like because they decided it was pro-Israel. That was
the way I felt at the time—very connected to the country—and to the
Jewish tradition."

Michael felt much the same. "My Judaism was expressed when
Steve and I flew to Israel in 1967, into a very dangerous situation,
because we wanted to help. I was acting out of my racial identity, not
my spiritual identity. *That* was the way I could affirm my Jewishness:
by risking my life as a Jew when there was a palpable threat to the
Jewish people. At that moment I didn't have any question about my
identity. I was unambiguously proud to be a Jew."

But Mike was troubled by the social distance he felt from many of
the Jews he has met. He thought it stemmed from a silent message
both his parents conveyed. For in spite of Max's identification with
"rough-hewn Jews," in spite of his belief that Jews were brighter than
other people, his oldest son saw clearly that "my father chose a wife
who came from a higher social class than he did. The whole Jewish
experience seemed to be one that he had moved away from." Further,
"I felt that my mother wanted me to inherit my father's exuberance
and vitality towards life and lack of fear—and combine that with a
gentlemanly perception of the world."

Mike often felt uncomfortable when his father brought home students from Brandeis. From his Exeter-bred perspective, "They didn't
look right or sound right . . . Being half Jewish, I didn't want to be
like them. I wanted a Judaism that was absolutely above reproach.
Now I think that attitude is part of the baggage I'm carrying from my

childhood. It's the aspect of being Jewish that I was carefully taught not to be."

After Mike graduated from Harvard, he got a Ph.D. in political science at Yale and became an assistant professor there. Meanwhile, Steve got a job as a staff writer for *The Village Voice,* where his articles were almost always played on the front page. So both young men, in their different ways, seemed destined to fulfill their parents' dreams for them.

Then their careers took utterly unexpected detours. In the late 1960s, they both began to travel professional and spiritual paths that worried their parents and startled their friends. Mike thinks his decisions were partly related to the questions he felt as the child of an intermarriage. Steve feels that his were the result of circumstance.

Sitting in the living room of his weathered wooden cabin in Bolinas, Mike recalled the reasons he had left Yale, New Haven, and the life he was expected to lead. "By the time I had finished graduate school and was teaching at Yale, the sixties were rolling around. I was teaching courses on the counter-culture—and a revolution was taking place on the campus. I became the junior faculty member who was most interested in these issues."

He was working with the sociologist Kenneth Kenniston on a book about young radicals when he began to notice a personal trait that troubled him. "I could argue all sides of any issue, but I could never find a single truth. I felt hollow at the center. I think that was partly because I didn't have a single tradition that I could define as my core." That void became a physical pain, which he felt he must cure. "I'd discovered a spiritual yearning inside myself that surprised me. It really wasn't part of my agenda."

He was recalling that pain in the most tranquil of settings—a simple living room furnished with secondhand country furniture, looking out over lush green hillsides. As we sipped herb tea and talked above the gentle lull of chimes that hung on the porch, a deer was grazing only twenty feet away.

"I thought I'd take a year off from Yale and see what the counter-culture was like in California. Then I realized that there was an enormous amount for me to learn there. The place was just filled with people involved with Buddhist studies and all kinds of spiritual traditions, and those were the people who could teach me. So I decided to stay. It was like walking off a cliff. I was giving up a great job that I had trained for forever. My parents thought that I was crazy. In career terms, it just didn't make sense. But it felt like the path of my heart."

In his first year in California, he had met a hyperkinetic child who was cured by a change of diet, and the encounter influenced him profoundly. "I decided that rather than study political science I was going to study the way nutrition affects mental disorders in children." From that beginning he went on to found Commonweal, a nationally recognized center for the study of healing techniques. His pioneering work in health—on alternative cancer therapies, on helping troubled children, in holistic and behavioral medicine—won him a MacArthur Fellowship in 1983.

Steve's break with his career path was more accidental. In 1969, his *Voice* pieces prompted a book publisher to give him a large advance to travel through Asia and write about his experiences. Much of his journalism was—and is—determined by his childhood obsession with the Holocaust. "I'm always looking out for the underdog, always trying to figure out ways to help." He had no idea that the book offer —a marvelous professional opportunity—would enable him to discover a spiritual framework for that lifelong quest.

While researching his book, "I spent a couple of years just wandering around. I did a lot of reading in Yoga and Buddhism. I found it very attractive as a philosophy, not as a religion. I began to see how to deal compassionately with other people without being martyrized. I was always struck by the fact that the central image in Christianity was the crucifix. I never liked that. I thought Buddhism would teach me the techniques of meditation and Yoga—the techniques that make you self-aware so that you don't hurt other people, so that you actually do things that help other people." But, Steve added, "I never joined a religious group or found a guru. I think Mike is much more attracted to a strictly religious path than I am."

At Yale, Mike had discovered that he was a spiritually oriented person. But how could he choose between Judaism and Christianity? "I couldn't be a Christian and deny my Judaism, and I couldn't be a Jew and deny my Christianity. I just couldn't do it."

When he was in California, he read Aldous Huxley's book *The Perennial Philosophy,* and developed "a deep religious belief that there is one spiritual truth and many paths to that truth. He found "one of the purest expressions of the Perennial Philosophy in yoga. It was grounded in physical, mental and ethical precepts that I found empirically help me live a better life. It fascinates me to think that if I had been born into a single religious tradition I would not have had to embark upon a search for a way to reconcile the Protestant and Jewish traditions of my parents.

"In Yoga, I saw a spiritual alternative that included both of the above. The religion showed me a way that I can be at peace with both of these aspects of myself. I can explore them both and they don't conflict."

Once, Mike was torn between his parents' cultures. Now, he seemed to have balanced them, though he felt that Judaism as a religion "is an aspect of my life I haven't fully explored yet. It feels as if there's a switch inside me that hasn't been reconnected. But I think it will be."

He's concluded that his complicated psychological experience has left him with an unusual ability to serve as a mediator between people, faiths, and ideologies that are ordinarily in conflict. That is what he does at Commonweal, where he's constantly seeking to synthesize conventional and alternative methods of health care.

He described the impulse when I told him how difficult it had been for me to understand his moderate views on Vietnam when we were on the *Crimson.* I thought the war was immoral. He had argued that it was unfortunate.

He reminded me that his father had held hawkish views about the war. "I felt that he was aware of an important aspect of the truth that other people were ignoring. I still feel that. But that goes back to the continuous sense I have that if somebody expresses one aspect of the truth, that's fine with me, but I happen to see all the other possible ways you can view the situation.

"That's one of the realities of being the product of an intermarriage. It's a constant vision of different truths from different perspectives. I'm constantly involved in a quest to make peace between very different experiences of life. That's just what I was given to deal with."

A Melting Pot Marriage

Nettie Tenenbaum and Pat Auletta—who were married in 1936—spent their entire lives in the kind of rooted, traditionalist setting that Max Lerner had left behind—off Surf Avenue, Coney Island. For much of her life, Nettie's family owned a candy store; Pat's father owned a barbershop. For much of their marriage, Nettie and Pat worked together day and night to build up the sporting goods store, ice skating rink, and beach umbrella concession that would support them and their children, Richard, Ken, and Bonnie.

When Pat and Nettie met, their families both lived on West Seventeenth Street, the dividing line between Coney Island's Jewish and Italian communities. It was an unusually tolerant block. If Nettie had lived on Twenty-third Street, near her Jewish friend Ida Tauger, where agnostic families pulled down the blinds if they ate on Yom Kippur, she would never have been able to date an Italian like Pat with the impunity she enjoyed on her own block. If Pat had lived on Stillwell Avenue or West Twelfth Street, the Italian section, where most adults and children still accepted the Church's contention that the Jews killed Jesus, he'd have risked constant beatings if he'd courted a young lady named Tenenbaum. But on West Seventeenth Street most Jews and Italians had been shaped by Coney Island's special environment to live side by side, in affectionate harmony. Living on that melting pot block, all three Tenenbaum girls married Italians; two of three Auletta men married Jews. In effect, they were part of the same extended Southern European ethnicity.

They even shared a common enemy—the upper class Protestants who had once tried to make Coney Island a Gilded Age resort for the very rich, who now described amusement parks like Steeplechase, where Pat Auletta worked, as terrifying testimony to America's decadence. These were the people who were using the specter of dangerous Italians and Jews to agitate for immigration restriction. ". . . [T]he hair on most heads along Coney Island is black," complained a progressive young *New Republic* writer named Bruce Bliven in 1921. The "native American stock," which had historically formed the foundation of American manners," was forced to yield "before displays of love-making on the beach," he added.

Pat Auletta recalls such prejudice. Until 1921, when the Boardwalk was built, there were only private beaches. "The WASPs controlled the best of them. We couldn't get in."

Nettie Tenenbaum Auletta is dead now, but when her sister Rose Tenenbaum Dellaquilla and her best friend Ida describe her, she emerges as the sweet, high-spirited daughter of Jewish parents who were so cut off from their pasts that her only culture was the one she found on Coney Island.

In 1905 Nettie's mother, Sarah Horowitz, an eighteen-year-old girl from a shtetl in Russia, was exiled from her country because she was a socialist who had distributed leaflets against the Czar. In Berlin, her temporary haven, she fell in love with Solomon Tenenbaum, one of fourteen children, whose wealthy, aristocratic parents owned tobacco farms and factories in Dresden and Poland. It was a bittersweet romance, since the Tenenbaums disapproved of the penniless Eastern European radical, and Sarah's visa only allowed her to stay in Germany for six months. "My father gave up everything to come to America with the woman he loved," Rose said.

Sarah and Sol arrived in New York in 1906. Neither of them had any family members here. Sol's family, furious, seldom wrote him, and Sarah was too poor to dream of seeing her parents again. They were both Jews, of course, but beyond that fact the aristocrat from Germany and the socialist from Russia had little but their love in common. They weren't religious enough to join a synagogue—or, as Rose remembers, political enough to get involved with a party.

Sol was a traveling salesman before he opened the candy store. Sarah bore five children. First they moved to Ocean Parkway from East New York. Then, in 1914, Rose said, Sarah became nervous and depressed. "Someone told her to move to Coney Island since bathing in the water would be good for her nerves. I guess they were right. I don't remember her being unhappy after that. And, in those days, Coney Island was a lovely place to live."

If Sol and Sarah felt displaced, they disguised their moods when they talked to their offspring. Sometimes, Rose remembers, a nostalgic expression would cross Sol's face when he heard classical German music or a Jewish song like "Eili, Eili"; sometimes Sarah would get angry when she discussed the pogroms; sometimes they'd laugh together when they reminisced about the happy-go-lucky, morally loose women they had known in Berlin. But, for the most part, their years in Europe seemed misty and vague to their children.

Rose remembers a childhood filled with sudden outbursts of laughter. Sarah loved the custom of April Fools' jokes—she'd make up a new one for each child every year. Nettie was a sweet, rather serious girl, but Rose and her brother Eddie loved to make up silly little skits. The entire Tenenbaum family was enchanted by Charlie Chaplin, Harold Lloyd, Buster Keaton, Our Gang.

"I thought of my parents as very romantic. My father always missed his life in Germany, He had been rich and happy there and he had to struggle when he got here. But he loved my mother very much—they were very sentimental about each other. Nettie and I always knew that we would marry for love."

Pat Auletta, the love of Nettie's life, had been entranced by her long before she noticed him. He misses her terribly. At lunch one January day, he sat in Gargulio's restaurant, his favorite haunt, easing his sorrow by reminiscing about the past. The next day, his son Ken, a columnist for the New York *Daily News*, would begin a three-week tour to promote his best-selling book *Greed and Glory on Wall Street: The Fall of the House of Lehman.* But for now, Ken forgot the dynamics of book-peddling, while he and I listened to Pat describe his Italian childhood and Ken's mother, the Jewish wife he had adored.

As a child, Pat was terrified of his father, Ed, an Italian immigrant from the town of Auletta, near Sorrento, and a barber. He was cruel to his gentle, devoutly Catholic wife Anna. But Pat and his father did have one thing in common. "He loved Coney Island. He loved the excitement and the tourists. That's the one part of him I take after."

As Pat recalls it, Ed Auletta's barbershop was an enclave of prejudice on a block where harmony reigned. "He was a vicious man. He never made anti-Semitic remarks to me—but that was because he never talked to me directly, only when he made a command. I used to listen to him and his friends when I worked at the barbershop. In those days, before the safety razor came in, it was a real neighborhood hangout. Everybody used to come there, and I'd have to give them numbers to wait their turn before they were shaved. Many times they skipped their turn just so they could continue whatever they were talking about. They were all Catholics. Jews didn't exist as people for them. My father would use an expression, *amazza cristo*, which in English means those who killed Jesus Christ. That was a favorite of his, and of the crowd that came into the shop. I saw so much hatred all around me, I just couldn't tolerate it. I had to get out."

As a teenager, Pat worked as a waiter at Steeplechase Park, earning about forty dollars a week in tips. There he began to see Coney Island as a place full of "fascinating schemers—guys who came here in the summer to make a quick kill, and then left in the off-season." Sometimes he worked as a shoeshine boy outside his father's barbershop. He still remembers the day he took his shoeshine box on board a boat where men were gambling on deck. "Scarface Al Capone was shooting craps. He asked me to get him a pack of Camels at the other end of the boat. He gave me a dollar tip."

When he wasn't working he hung out at the Cardinals or the Tigers, social clubs in the basement of an apartment house where teenagers, mostly Italian guys and Jewish girls, danced to the Benny Goodman and Ted Weems songs they played on their record players. In those huge rooms with their shiny, highly waxed floors, guys played cards in smoke-filled back rooms or danced with their girlfriends or bantered until their words sparked a fight. Stanley Tauger, Ida's husband, who was one of the few Jewish men in the Cardinals, remembers "Pat used his hands pretty rapidly. No one messed around with him until Nettie reformed him. Then he quit fighting completely."

Pat had had a crush on Nettie since he first saw her at a high school basketball game, where she broke a fingernail trying to catch a ball. "But I couldn't approach her as long as she was going out with somebody. That wasn't my code. I used to sit in my father's barber chair in the dark, and just wait until she walked by on her way home. I could hear the tap of her high-heeled shoes half a block away. I could picture her blond hair, and her walk, which was so erect."

One night, Pat was standing outside the shop when Nettie walked by. She had been arguing with her boyfriend, and she wanted to talk. They both felt the electricity between them. Then a few months later, when Nettie's sister Sally got married—to an Italian—Pat helped her brother Louis prepare for the wedding reception. "We made some homemade booze out of rum and ice water, and we had a lot left over. I slept over at the Tenenbaums' that night. It was summer, and Louis and I stayed out on the porch, counting the stars. I was showing off. I'm one of those drunks who laughs and clowns around. Nettie came

over to me, and thanked me, and kissed me. That was the beginning . . ."

Pat still remembers the green and white outfit she was wearing on
their first date. He had been working eighteen hours a day, seven days
a week, and now he had about a hundred and twenty-five dollars'
worth of tips in his pocket: enough money to impress her. He hailed a
taxi—a great extravagance in 1936—and asked the driver to take him
and Nettie to Junior's—"the most popular restaurant in Brooklyn.
She was bashful. I forced her to get a sandwich. She left half of it on
her plate, she was so nervous."

Soon, the two were "keeping company," dancing together at the
Cardinals, holding hands on the boardwalk while they watched Benny
Goodman perform in person at Half-Moon Park. On special nights,
they'd take the subway into Manhattan—which seemed like another
city—and spend a dollar to listen to music at the Paramount and eat a
hot dog at Nedick's. Sometimes, they'd take a boat ride up the Hud-
son to West Point, where the men would play softball and the women
would laugh for hours over a game of mah-jongg.

One day, afer Pat Auletta had gone into Manhattan to apply for a
job at the Board of Education, he gazed into the window of a jewelry
shop at a wedding ring he liked. It cost a hundred and twenty-five
dollars. He felt lucky that day—he had gotten a job—so he decided to
bet a dime on the numbers. When he read the *Mirror* the next morning he discovered that he had won fifty dollars. He decided to look for
a similar ring.

"I got up one bright, early morning and decided I'd be the first at a
pawnshop on the Bowery." He asked Nettie to come with him. He
thought he might have a surprise for her. "In those days, many
pawnbrokers believed that if they didn't make a sale to the first
customer their day was ruined. Sure enough, I went into a pawnshop
and asked the broker to take out his best ring. It was worth two
hundred and forty dollars. I said, 'That's the one I want.' But I only
had my fifty dollars.

"The pawnbroker said, 'You're the first customer.'

"I said, 'How well I know I'm the first customer, brother. I'm going
to bleed you to death.'

"He said, 'Two hundred and twenty-five dollars' and I told him he
was out of his mind. Then he told me to make an offer, and I said,

'Twenty-five dollars.' Back and forth it went. Finally, I got the ring for sixty dollars. I proposed to Nettie that day."

He was a little nervous about breaking the news to his mother. For Anna Auletta went to Mass every day and filled her house with statues of saints. But instead of rebuking Pat, "She wished me luck and said, 'I love Nettie, and I hope what you have is better than what I had.' "

"I think all the misery I saw between my mother and father made me realize that you didn't have to marry one of your own in order to be loving to one another."

"It didn't matter to Nettie that I was a Catholic. Her parents didn't seem to care either except that, with typical Jewish thinking, they wanted their daughter to marry a doctor or a lawyer. We Italians wanted to make money, but we never thought of sending someone to school to get a degree." Still, Sarah and Sol always tried to make Pat feel part of their family.

Nettie never experienced the community pressure that affects most Jews who intermarry. But Pat did experience pressure from Catholics. Though he wasn't religious, he was always connected with the Church somehow—usually in sports—and there he encountered the attitudes he had avoided in the clubs on West Seventeenth Street. "People there were as bigoted as the people in the barbershop. Someone found out that I was going to marry a Jew and they sort of isolated me from the crowd. Then they apologized and tried to be my friend again." But traces of prejudice persisted for years. "Whenever I was in the church or in a restaurant, and would hear someone use a word like 'kike,' I'd think of my wife. Sometimes I hit the person."

Neither Nettie nor Pat considered getting married in a church or a synagogue, since neither of them wanted the other to convert. "If either of us had been religious, we couldn't have been married," Pat Auletta said reflectively. But he was estranged from his father's cruel Catholicism and from the bigotry he had heard from the pulpit; Nettie had never even been to a synagogue. West Seventeenth Street, Coney Island, was their world.

They got married in City Hall, and Sarah and Sol, pleased that their oldest daughter was so happy with *her* Italian husband, gave the wedding party.

They never considered raising their children either as Catholics or as Jews. "They could do as they pleased when they got older," Pat said. "You know, I think one of the great things that helped my children to understand the marriage is that at the time of school holidays the Catholics had their day and the Jews had their day. Of course, it was nice for my kids. They took both days off. But I think it also gave them a respect for both religions."

Ken Auletta agreed with his father—for him the act of staying out of school on Yom Kippur "meant that you had to declare that you were Jewish on that day," he said as we were finishing lunch at Gargulio's. That took some courage in his boyhood world, which was primarily composed of tough Italian kids.

When he was in his parents' house, he felt as much like a Tenenbaum as an Auletta. "We lived with the Tenenbaums for the first thirteen years of my life. It was a stoop house. We lived in the back. My grandparents lived in the front. We all ate together. I know all about gefilte fish."

During the pleasant Coney Island dusks, his parents and the Tenenbaums would sit in the living room or on the front porch listening to the radio and chatting. Most nights at about 8 P.M., Pat Auletta walked to the corner to buy the night owl edition of the *Daily News.* While the grown-ups talked in soft, comforting voices, Ken and his brother Dick and their friends would play stoop ball or Johnny-on-the-Peg on the fire hydrant in front of Ken's aunt's stoop, a few doors away. P.S. 80, their school, was around the corner, and Our Lady of Solace, which they sometimes thought of as their church, was just up the block about a hundred feet from the house. The Tenenbaums' candy store—where you could get Mellow Rolls for a nickel, a big chunk of Nestle's candy for two cents—was across the street. When Ken was a boy, Anna Auletta lived across the street, behind the barbershop her husband had once owned.

Friday nights had a special quality. Ken and his brother would go out with Pat, who didn't care about the Catholic prohibition against meat, but liked to hang around with the men who observed their fish day at Gargulio's or at Totonnes' pizza parlor. "Dick and I would sit in the front while my dad sat in the back with all these old Italian guys eating octopus or squid, which had been specially cooked for them. My mom would stay at home and play canasta or mah-jongg with her friends."

On Sundays, his family joined the rest of the Auletta clan at Aunt Lizzie's or Uncle Mike's or Anna Auletta's house. Sometimes the Tenenbaums would join them. "Part of the family would have gone to church. We'd arrive around one o'clock, after services, and be there the whole day. They didn't have a TV set, so we didn't watch the football game, as we would have ten years later. We just sat around and ate a huge Italian meal and talked. By five o'clock, we'd get hungry again and have a snack. Then we'd go home." It was almost as if Ken could reach out and touch all the important places in his life.

But from the mid-1940s on there was a frightening undercurrent in the family's life. Ken, who as an Auletta was an Italian to most of his friends in grade school, lived with the tragedy that Sol and Sarah Tenenbaum could never forget—and could never discuss.

Now they were even more silent about their past than they had been when Rose and Nettie and their siblings were growing up. Once in a while, Ken remembers, Sol would show him some German marks, but the money was really a memory of a memory. Sol never discussed the past the marks must have reminded him of.

By the time Ken was in elementary school, everyone in the Tenenbaum-Auletta household knew the worst. Sol's parents had died before Hitler came to power, but eleven of his siblings had perished in the Holocaust. One cousin had escaped to London, two brothers were somewhere in South America, but Sol didn't know how to get in touch with them. One of Sarah's brothers had come to New York, but he couldn't tell Sarah what had happened to her parents or her sisters who were still in Russia. If Sol's and Sarah's words had failed to furnish Ken an image of the lives his European Jewish relatives had led, their sad silence conveyed an image of their death. "In my house, the Holocaust existed totally. I knew that if they were coming for the Jews, they were coming for me."

How could he communicate that feeling to the Italian kids in his neighborhood? He didn't want to antagonize them since their care-free style represented an attractive alternative to the hard-working life his parents demanded.

One rare afternoon, he recalls, his mother took him and Dick for a picnic on the beach. But usually, while his friends were playing touch football on the sand, or cruising the beach for girls, or body surfing, he had to work in his father's sporting goods store or at their umbrella concession on the beach. "I resented my parents for that," Ken says. "I rebelled by hanging out with the tough kids."

By then, West Seventeenth Street had grown a little less tolerant, a little harsher, than it was when Pat Auletta and Ida Tauger were young. "Except for the Jewish enclave on my block—the Tenenbaums and their friends—it was mostly an Italian neighborhood," Ken says. "Most of the kids were tough guys. My name was Auletta. I was a good athlete so the Italian kids saw me as one of them. I would hear mumblings of 'they killed Christ' around Our Lady of Solace Church. I would hear Jews called fags because they didn't fight back. They'd be told to walk across the street. They couldn't compete with Italians in athletics, in fighting, in hanging out. They may have been better at books, but who cared about books?

"The street guys aspired to be mobsters. The mob was a big influence there. Their goal was to stand in front of the candy store on the corner and watch the wise guys in the Cadillacs—and eventually to drive the Cadillac."

Ken had no aspirations to be a mobster, but if he'd even begun to inch in that direction, Pat would have stopped him. "He had a strap—for sharpening razors. He got it from his dad. It was a useful thing to have. He'd tell me, 'If I see you on the same side of the street with those kids, I'm going to hit you with the strap.' I was terrified.

"But I was a strong kid—I hung out—I was accepted by the guys who would sneer at the Jews. The conflict I felt was that at night I would go home to my grandfather and grandmother whom I loved. They *were* Jews—and they were two of the gentlest people I knew. But the kids on the street extolled toughness."

When Ken was in high school, he was a good pitcher. He thought he had a realistic chance of becoming a professional ball player. If that didn't happen, he wanted to be an FBI man until he realized he'd have to learn something about law or accounting to join the Bureau. He still thought studying anything was a sign of weakness. That created tension between him and his brother. For Dick Auletta—today a successful public relations man—liked books. "He got into Brooklyn College—he was the first member of the Tenenbaum or Auletta family to do that. He was different from the kids I knew on the street. Most of them had brothers who were tough. If they got into fights, their brothers would stand up for them. But my brother was home reading. I was humiliated. In some way I might have identified that humiliation with Jewishness."

Eventually, Ken impressed the Oswego State College baseball coach with his skill: the coach convinced him to enroll at that school. He was away from Coney Island, away from his parents' demands and the pressures he felt on the street, in an environment where people saw value in books. He discovered that he loved to read and learn. "When I began to care more about my mind than my body, I felt more in touch with the Jewish part of myself." He began to feel an identification with the Jewish kids on campus. But it was an identification that took the form of friendship, not cultural or religious activity. In those days he was convinced that all religion was superstition.

Not that he thought about the subject very much. When he graduated from Oswego, a teacher's college, he enrolled at Syracuse University, where he edited an underground paper, led civil rights marches, and got involved in Robert Kennedy's campaign for the United States Senate.

While he was in graduate school he met Howard Samuels, who later became Secretary of Commerce under Lyndon Johnson, and became close to the businessman-politician. He managed Samuels' unsuccessful 1970 and 1974 Democratic primary campaigns for governor. In 1971, John Lindsay named Samuels the first chairman of the Offtrack Betting Corporation, and Auletta became his executive director.

When he was at OTB, he met Amanda Urban, a marketing specialist who had gone to exclusive private schools, and graduated from Wheaton College, which, in those years, mostly attracted Protestants. Binky—as Amanda is called—was known for her intelligence and vivacity. Those were the qualities that captivated Ken when they met.

In 1972 it was still secretly thrilling for a Tenenbaum or an Auletta to go out with an "American."

He recalled the first night he went to her parents' house and his awareness of feeling alien. "The place represented 'Waspdom' to me," he said. But he quickly felt comfortable with her family.

Each family gave a party before the wedding. The Urbans' was at their country club. Ken's immediate family were the only guests from Coney Island. They weren't used to celebrations where food meant canapés, and drinks meant martinis. The extended Auletta family threw its party at Gargulio's, where the bar was full of all the beer and wine and hard liquor one could drink, where there was a huge buffet of sliced mozzarella and peppers, scungilli, and pasta with a special artichoke sauce Ken loved. The band played all night. The two families were cordial, but it was clear that they came from different universes.

Ken and Binky had a special plan for their honeymoon. Ken wanted to visit his grandfather's hometown, Auletta, Italy. Since he had been a child, he had imagined the day when he'd be welcomed as a prodigal son by his grandfather's people. Sure enough, the town existed, and as the couple drove there Binky took a photograph of the small sign that bore her husband's family name. But no one cared that he was there. He and Amanda stayed in a small hotel, the Americas. "All my life I had dreamed of the great meal we'd be fed in Auletta. It was awful. They cooked us what tasted like spaghetti out of a can. We went to the church where I had imagined generations of Aulettas getting married. Someone had stolen the crucifix." The mayor was out of town so they couldn't examine the family records, but Ken realized that there were no families called Auletta in town. His grandfather had simply adopted the name of his birthplace when he came to America. "Why should they be excited that you're here?" Binky asked between peals of laughter. "It was as if your grandfather had taken the name Philadelphia."

If Europe had remained the same place Ken's grandparents had left, he and Binky might have gone to Dresden to meet his Tenenbaum relatives or to Russia to meet the Horowitzes. But the kinsmen who might have given texture and meaning to his fond feelings for his grandparents were among history's ghosts.

Now, Ken visits Pat Auletta every week or two, and moves as easily among the people who work at Gargulio's and the Brooklyn politicians who hang out there as he does among bankers and media celebrities.

But he doesn't know how to transmit his sense of rootedness to his daughter Kate. That's a natural outcome of the decision that kept his parents' melting pot marriage together. He was raised in a place, not a faith, and he can't pass that knowledge on. He can tell Kate stories about Coney Island, but she'll never know the particular smells of the Tenenbaums' house or of Nannie Auletta's apartment on a Sunday afternoon or the swagger of the Italian kids who hung out on West Seventeenth Street. And he has no solid vessel—no set of traditions —to be sure his daughter has an anchor inside herself. "I wish I could go back thirty-five years and talk to my grandparents. I have so many unanswered questions. I want to understand the religious past I grew out of."

Then, self-critically, he adds, "Right now we're not raising our child as anything, much to Binky's consternation."

When he was in his late teens, he was influenced by *Crime and Punishment*—particularly by Raskolnikov's feeling that there are limits on rationality. "Theoretically, I believe in the importance of faith, of living in a society that accepts a common sense of spiritual values. I'm troubled about abortion. I'm open to school prayer. I respect religious values. But I'm not sure I actually *feel* the same way as people who have those values."

He has inherited his parents' discomfort with "houses of worship. I never spent much time in synagogue, but I knew a lot of kids who went to Catholic school. I would see them get hit by rulers. I recoiled, it seemed so barbaric. I still see religion as superstition. I'm still carrying around anti-religious baggage from my childhood. But for Kate's sake I've got to get rid of it. I've got to work out the importance of faith, the non-quantifiable parts of human relationships."

It is unlikely that he'll free himself from the feeling he shares with his father that the Catholic church is a bigoted place. It's unlikely that he'll reach past his pleasant memories of the Tenenbaums, and his rage at the anti-Semitic forces that destroyed their families, to search for a Jewish life. He and Binky will probably raise Kate in something more akin to the Protestantism that Binky knew when she was young than the amalgam of Judaism and Catholicism that Ken took for granted in Coney Island.

As a journalist, Ken feels a proud sympathy for both of the groups that sometimes seemed in conflict when he was a boy. Like Mike and Steve Lerner, Ken is—and will always be—strengthened by his ability to understand and explain his parents' cultures. But neither he nor his family is likely to embrace either one.

PART III

INTERMARRIAGE NOW: *Working it out*

5

Time Bombs

The ecology of intermarriages in the 1980s is very different from the ones we have described in the two previous chapters. In our workshops and interviews, Jews almost always display a pride in their religion and ethnicity that was so conspicuously absent when Anne Lazarus Johnston talked about Emma's Jewish writing, or when Harold Hochschild and Walter Lippmann wrote about themselves and their people. The Jews and the Christians we meet are far more conscious of the desire to infuse their families' lives with their religious and cultural heritages than the Lerners or the Aulettas were when they married. They are far more likely than their counterparts in earlier generations to argue about which faith will be ascendant in their households.

Jews, including those who intermarry, worry that their 4,000-year-old history will be extinguished: the Holocaust serves as a constant reminder that survival is perilous. Their desire to transmit identity from one generation to the next has been intensified by the renewed interest in religion and ethnicity that has become such an important part of American life in the past two decades. Furthermore, nowadays Jews like Karen Berkowitz meet gentiles like John Halvorsen as American tumbleweeds, not as latter-day versions of the Harold Hochschild who wanted to escape into Christian America. They are on an equal social and economic footing with their mates as they try to decide whether to raise their children as Jews or Christians.

Just as many Jews who marry gentiles are often surprised to discover that they feel an inexplicably powerful commitment to Jewish survival, so many Christians who wed Jews come to the sudden, unexpected realization that they care more than they had thought about Jesus, about the church, about the meaning of Christmas and Easter.

Often, these religious and cultural feelings are suppressed when a Jewish-Christian couple falls in love. They come to the surface as marriage approaches or when children are born. We call these feelings time bombs in an interfaith relationship. In this portion of *Mixed Blessings* we suggest ways of anticipating these emotions and understanding them. And we suggest ways of transforming potential conflicts into a shared spiritual life.

When Jews and Christians first fall in love, they usually regard themselves as individualists who will be able to transcend the specific cultural demands of the pasts that shaped their beliefs and laid claims on their loyalties. But that is a more difficult task than they imagine, for at some profound level of self and psyche, most will always be attached to the religious and ethnic tribes in which they were raised. They'll remain Americanized Eastern European Jews or German Methodists or Italian Catholics or Chinese Buddhists. They love the cultural assumptions that permeated their households when they were young: the background music of ordinary life, which a child takes for granted, which an adolescent or young adult tries to forget. If couples don't acknowledge such assumptions in the same way that people acknowledge music—as an interior melody that can't be articulated in words—they can damage the ecology of an intermarriage.

If a struggle over religion does begin, it often takes couples by surprise, thrusting them into confusing, seemingly endless discussions. For suddenly they discover that they are not interchangeable parts of an American whole, but two people whose different pasts have endowed them with a distinct set of feelings. How should they discuss their differences? How can each understand the ethnic and religious context in which the other's emotions exist?

Their first disagreements are likely to be over the external features of religious identity—over the holidays they will celebrate, or the way they will raise their children. Then, as they get older, they may find that the joys of having children, the complexities of finding work that satisfies them, the sorrow of losing loved ones, may cause them to feel a more powerful personal need for religion than they could have imagined when they were married. Sometimes, they become involved with a synagogue or church they thought they'd left behind when they left home. When that happens, an important part of their life is suddenly unfamiliar to their spouse. They have violated the tacit agreement about religion they had made when they got married.

But, as important as religious differences are, they are just one part of the complex array of emotional forces that come into play in an intermarriage. For the partners in a relationship may find that although they don't have specific religious disagreements, they are still troubled because their ethnic assumptions come into conflict. We see this time and again in our workshops. When we describe our own WASP-Jewish conflicts over food, health, emotional privacy, or our style of arguing, the couples laugh with the relief of recognition. Then they begin to talk about cultural differences of their own.

Our understanding of the way conflicts over religion and ethnicity can overlap has been deepened by the ideas contained in ethnotherapy, a family therapy technique that was developed in the early 1970s by Dr. Price Cobb, a black psychiatrist, and adapted for use with Jews by his assistant, Dr. Judith Weinstein Klein. The insights of ethnotherapy were broadened and promoted by Irving Levine and Joseph Giordano of the American Jewish Committee.

Ethnotherapy helps people understand that many of the emotional experiences they assume are universal are actually shaped by a particular cultural background. It also helps them see that their self-images are deeply influenced by the way society perceives the ethnic group to which they belong. It reminds people that religious and ethnic differences are inevitable, not shameful. Thus, ethnotherapists argue that when people from different cultural backgrounds fall in love, rejoice together and grieve together, raise children together, they aren't doing so as undifferentiated white bread Americans, but as men and women whose response to issues as major as life and death, as minor as food or the best way to spend leisure time, have been influenced by their cultural heritages.

In a book called *Ethnicity and Family Therapy*, Monica McGoldrick, Director of Family Training at Rutgers Medical School, described her experiences counseling interfaith couples and highlighted the role cultural differences play. "Couples who choose to [intermarry] are usually seeking a rebalance of the characteristics of their own ethnic background. They are moving away from some values as well as toward others . . . During courtship, a person may be attracted precisely to the fiancé's differentness, but when entrenched in a marital relationship the same qualities often become the rub . . ."

When couples are under stress, she wrote, "[they] react to each other as though the other's behavior were a personal attack rather than just a difference rooted in ethnicity. Typically, we tolerate differences when we are not under stress. In fact, we find them appealing. However when stress is added to a system, our tolerance for differences diminishes. We become frustrated if we are not understood in ways that fit with our wishes and expectations. WASPs tend to withdraw when upset, to move toward stoical isolation, in order to mobilize their powers of reason (their major resource in coping with stress). Jews, on the other hand, seek to analyze their experience together; Italians may seek solace . . . in emotional and dramatic expression of their feelings and a high degree of human contact. Obviously, these groups may perceive each other's reactions as offensive or insensitive although within each group's ethnic context their reactions make excellent sense. In our experience much of therapy involves helping family members recognize each other's behavior as a reaction from a different frame of reference."

When Jewish-Christian couples suppress or ignore religious or ethnic feelings they set the time bombs that can explode in any intermarriage. We are not sociologists. Our sample of workshops and interviews is not large enough to allow us to estimate the percentage of interfaith couples who experience unexpected tensions in their relationships. There are no definitive studies of current divorce rates in marriages between Jews and Christians, although a few 1960s and 1970s studies—in California, Utah, and Indiana—showed that the Jews, Mormons, Protestants, and Catholics who were surveyed did divorce spouses from other religions at a somewhat higher rate than those from their own. A 1984 study by the National Opinion Research Center showed a positive correlation between marital satisfaction and marriage to a spouse from a similar religious background.

We are not arguing that marriages between Christians and Jews can't work, nor would we want to. Many of our friends are happily intermarried. But we are insisting that, for many people, religion and ethnicity are sufficiently important that they must be taken seriously.

The time bombs that explode are usually ignited by the stress that develops at the moments when interfaith couples are faced with important choices, or difficult losses. They often go off 1) during the December holidays—or more precisely, from the moment the first Christmas decorations group in late October and trigger what has come to be called the December dilemma; 2) when marriage approaches; 3) when a child is born; 4) when a child asks about its identity; 5) when a loved one dies.

With such potential for misunderstanding, it is no wonder that time bombs go off in intermarriages. (In fact, it is a wonder they don't go off more often.) The best way to avoid these explosions is to be aware of their potential—and of the moments they have occurred in the lives of other Jewish-Christian couples who assumed that their love would conquer all.

Courtship

Some Jews and Christians become aware of their ethnic and religious incompatibility while they are courting. They may discover that a lover is an unconscious bigot. They may become aware that the man or woman they'd regarded as an attractive fellow professional has deep religious or ethnic loyalties which they cannot share. Or they may realize that they will feel like a traitor if they leave their family religion or their spouse doesn't join it.

Many couples don't experience these feelings at all. If there are disagreements, they emerge much later in a relationship. Others detect them, then dismiss them.

Many try to resolve them through negotiations. They try to hammer out their own and their future children's beliefs as if they were bargaining over an eight-hour day. But you can't negotiate faith: a committed Jew and a religious Catholic can't simply split the difference between them and decide to be Unitarians. The discussion might end in tears or in a tacit agreement not to raise the subject again. It is seldom resolved.

Sometimes couples use religious conflicts as a smokescreen which allows them to avoid other issues. Perhaps they fear intimacy. Perhaps they're intrigued by each other but don't love each other enough to wed.

Sometimes couples who are courting say that the only intermarriage issue that troubles them is their parents' disapproval of the relationship. They are hurt and angry when their parents refuse to meet the person they are dating or threaten to boycott the wedding.

They usually react to their parents' rage by ignoring their own disagreements. For the opposition seems like bigotry. They now perceive themselves as soldiers in the army of love and regard their wedding as a rebellion against narrow-mindedness, and bad manners. Instead of surrendering, they resolve to fight harder.

But occasionally hostile parents do manage to ignite the time bomb. We have decided to describe two relationships where that happened because both provide an x-ray view of tensions that would have made both couples miserable if they had married.

In one instance, an Episcopalian from the South had a strong desire to remain a Christian and held subtly disdainful feelings about Jews. But in her desire to be urbane, she had discarded her religious practice. Her fiancé, who had tried to leave his ethnic past behind him when he went to Dartmouth and Harvard Business School, ignored her attitudes when they manifested themselves in comments about his mother's taste in food and house decoration. But when his mother refused to invite the young woman to her home for a Passover seder they both had to confront their deepest feelings—the bomb had been ignited.

The time bomb that exploded in the other relationship typifies a problem we see frequently in our workshops. In every group there is at least one child of a Holocaust survivor. Often these people have had trouble gauging the claim the past has on them. As courtship proceeds toward marriage conflicts with parents frequently develop. As they are forced to choose between parents and lovers, they often discover that Jewish loyalties intensify. Often the gentiles who love them will pay a high price for the fact that these children of survivors are so out of touch with their feelings.

Molly and Tom: Guess Who Isn't Coming to the Seder?

Molly Perkins, thirty-four, was born in Atlanta, Georgia. Her Epis-copalian parents had lost much of the family fortune during the Depression. Molly was always aware that they weren't as wealthy as most of their friends, but they belonged to the same church, same social clubs, and attended the same balls as the rest of the city's elite.

As a girl, she'd enjoyed the life of Protestant high society. She had liked going to church on Sunday. "I wasn't at all religious, but I always had this image that I'd walk down the aisle with my father and that after the wedding I'd have a reception at his social club. I must have imagined that wedding eighty-seven times with eighty-seven different grooms."

But she thought she said good-bye to all that when she enrolled at Smith and became a feminist and a political radical who felt scorn for religion. At twenty-five she moved to Boston and embarked on what she expected to be a lifetime career in the theater. She lived with Tom Schwartz, a graduate of Dartmouth and Harvard Business School, who'd been raised in a Conservative Jewish home in the Boston suburbs. Molly and Tom were both agnostics whose tastes in jokes, people, books, and plays made them feel like soul mates. Tom, who represented hi-tech businesses, thought Molly's career as an actress was "racy." Molly was amazed that Tom could make the business world seem interesting to her.

After they had lived together for two years, they began to talk about getting married. Often they would argue about the two hurdles they would have to cross on the way to the altar—Tom's family and the way they would raise their children.

Tom was very close to his mother, but his mother had no use for his Protestant girlfriend. As Molly recalled it, "At first, he didn't want to introduce me to her, and I asked him, 'Why not?' People's mothers had *always* liked me. I was great to bring home. I would always write thank-you notes. Finally, Tom told me that his mother was upset that I wasn't Jewish. None of the Jewish families I'd known in Atlanta had felt that way.

"At first, I thought that when Tom's mother met me she would forget that I wasn't Jewish and just like *me*. But that didn't happen— she didn't like me and she was rude about it. It was the first time I experienced the tribal thing."

Both women were aware of the complex blend of social class and inherited culture that divided them. "Tom's family had more money than my family did—but they were very newly rich. My family is old poor. My mother is the kind of person who might be serving hot dogs, but the silver would be out. It wasn't that she was trying to look like she was rich—it was just that a certain level of etiquette, a certain standard of living, were *de rigeur*.

"I was raised to think you didn't talk about money, but Tom's family talked about money a lot. I feel embarrassed to say it, but I thought their taste was really tacky. I remember going out there once for Thanksgiving dinner. They had a beautiful table that Tom's mother always bragged about. But it was covered with a plastic table-cloth. There was plastic on the lamps. When I remarked on that to Tom, he laughed. But he loved his mother a lot. In retrospect, I think he was hurt."

Tom and Molly loved their life in their Back Bay apartment and they wanted to get married. But they couldn't decide what sort of family they would raise.

The conflict was as stark as possible: "Tom didn't want our children to be Christians and I didn't want them to be Jews. At first I thought they should be raised without religion, but I couldn't shake my own warm feelings about my upbringing in Atlanta." Once Tom suggested they be raised as Unitarians, but Molly just "snorted and said that's no compromise at all. It fuzzes both religions out. It's not Christian, really, and it's certainly not Jewish."

At the least, Molly wanted a Christmas tree. But Tom wouldn't allow a tree in his home. Molly thought that was part of the psychological complexity that made him so interesting and so attractive. "Dartmouth had really gotten to him. He'd loved the fraternities, and the tweed jacket, pipe smoking routine. He was really struggling with that. But his ethnic identity was strong. He was always talking about the Holocaust and Eastern European-Jewish history."

When Molly suggested they call the tree a Hanukkah bush, he got furious and said, "That's for assimilated Jews." Soon, the specter of the tree began to haunt their relationship. It was as if they were experiencing the December dilemma all year round.

"I thought I'd change his mind one year when I took him to Atlanta for Christmas. My parents welcomed him. We had a big Christmas tree. We had all the parties. There was a big Christmas Eve dinner of roast beef and Yorkshire pudding. There were Christmas presents under the tree for him. We had an open house on Christmas Day with eggnog. It was all very Waspy. I thought he'd enjoy it. But he was uncomfortable the whole week we were there.''

The time bomb, which Molly called "the straw that broke the camel's back," exploded during Passover 1980, when Mrs. Schwartz refused to invite Molly to the family seder. It was her tactic for sabotaging the wedding and it worked.

Molly was enraged. "I said, 'What do you mean your mother asked that I not come?'

" 'Well, she doesn't want you.'

"I said, 'Are you going?'

" 'Yes,' he said, 'I can't miss Passover.' "

With chagrin, she said, "I remember yelling at Tom about Jews being stubborn. I guess I had just had his mother up to my ears. I couldn't stand this stubbornness, and this refusal to accept me and let me in. So I said, 'You Jews are assimilated as much as you want to be. You're keeping yourselves separate.' As soon as those words came out I thought, 'Oh, God, what have I said?' But I was really angry.

"I felt, 'Damn it, *these people:* they're stubborn, they won't fit in, they won't compromise.' Once I'd thought those qualities were admirable —they had allowed Jews to survive without a country for two thousand years—but suddenly I felt, '*They* really think they're better than anybody else. They ask for what they get. They *will* be different. They *will* set themselves apart. They *will* be pushy and rude. Well, what do they expect?'

"I think, at some level, I felt that my family—we WASPs, we Episcopalians—had bent over backwards to accept Tom. If we had wanted to, we could have been snobby and anti-Semitic. But we were irreproachable. I kept thinking that Tom and his family should be grateful that we talked to them. But they'd turned the tables. I thought, 'How dare they not be grateful that my family and I had accepted them?' "

Then, she added, "I hate remembering that. It's so snotty, so cruel. But I do harbor those feelings somewhere inside me. And Tom saw them. He told me I was wildly anti-Semitic. In his mind, it placed me in the camp of those who had always persecuted Jews. I guess that was the real end of the affair."

A week after they broke up, "Easter rolled around," Molly recalled.

"We were still living in the same apartment, since neither of us had a new place to live. It was uncomfortable: what do you say to someone whose bed you're sharing after you've broken up with him? Besides, after that experience with Tom and his mother I was getting Waspier by the minute.

"So, I decided to get up and go to church. I went to an Episcopal church for a two-hour service that knocked my socks off. I remember the bishop knocking at the sanctuary door and those huge doors being thrown open—then he said, 'Christ is Risen.' I thought, 'Ooh, maybe He is.'

"That was April. I didn't go back to church because I was involved in a show. But when it was over in May—and I'd finally moved out of the apartment—I expected to fall apart. So I went to visit my grandmother and went to church with her. I thought I was being a good girl. Then I went home to Atlanta and went to my old church with my parents. I didn't think of myself as religious, but I loved the experience. So when I got back to Boston I started going to church. I've never stopped."

The next year Molly became a divinity student and was ordained as a minister upon graduation. She now has a pulpit in the Midwest. Tom married a Jewish woman, and they're active in their synagogue in New Jersey. Mrs. Schwartz, who still lives outside Boston, feels an abiding sense of relief that she has never had to talk about "my daughter-in-law, the Reverend."

Sheila and Phil: She Was the Love of My Life

Sheila Eisen, the only child of Holocaust survivors, came to one of our early workshops with her fiancé Phil Angelli, a Catholic from New Jersey.

As they told the story, her parents were their problem. Although the couple was engaged, Sheila's parents refused to meet Phil and said they would disown Sheila if the wedding took place. Phil, whose parents had left the Catholic church because it was too narrow-minded for them, was enraged. He wanted to help free Sheila from what he regarded as her parents' bigotry. They didn't resolve their dilemma during the workshop cycle. But a time bomb went off later on.

Sheila was raised on Long Island in a home that "felt European Jewish first, American second. My parents' entire social circle consists of other survivors. They spend a lot of the money they earn putting up monuments to the dead, or sending checks to the gentiles who helped them in the war."

Outwardly, she had a typical American-Jewish childhood. She went to Hebrew school for seven years, but her social life revolved around the friendships she made in public school. Being a cheerleader made her very popular. But inwardly she was haunted: "My mother always told me to marry a Jew because a non-Jew would turn on me."

After Sheila had studied mass communications at NYU, she went to work in an advertising agency. When she settled in Manhattan, she was so busy that she ordered almost all her dinners at the local deli where Phil Angelli, an aspiring actor, was working to make ends meet until he got a decent role in a play. "He is a big, tubby guy—I wasn't particularly attracted to him. But suddenly I realized I loved spending time with him."

Phil had always felt a special affinity toward Jews. When he was fourteen, he got involved with a theater group at a local temple. "I spent a lot of time at that temple. I liked it. I've always considered myself more of a universalist than anything else. But I could never understand why so many of my Jewish friends said they would only marry Jews. Why would someone close off all their options at seventeen?"

When he got to know Sheila, he realized that "she was the great love of my life. I'd never been able to open myself up in the way I did to her."

Soon she felt the same way. "After we had been pals for about six months, going to movies and theater together, I felt a slap on my face saying, 'wake up, shmuck, you love this guy.' But at the same time, the other side of my mind was saying: 'This is not a good thing that he's not Jewish. Do you want to go home and tell your parents about it?' "

Sheila tried to warn Phil about the dangers that lay ahead. "I told him it was going to be a long uphill battle—a combination of *West Side Story*, *Romeo and Juliet*, and the soaps we were always watching together. They'll never let us come to their house together. They'll refuse to meet you or talk to you on the phone. They'll do everything they can to break us up."

But Phil couldn't understand how they could do that. "Why did she care so much about her parents' opinion? I know they suffered, and I feel very badly for them. I knew they believed that if their daughter married a gentile, the gift of life they had received when they survived the camps would be in vain. I thought about converting for a long time. But they wouldn't even meet me for dinner. They didn't care who *I* was. As far as they were concerned, I was just another *goy* who was completing Hitler's work. Why would I give up my identity if I was going to be treated like that? How could they be such bigots after they had suffered that kind of persecution?

"But Sheila's parents had this hold on her. Sometimes, we'd wake up in the morning after a wonderful night at the theater or just be joking around with each other and her parents would call up. She would argue with them angrily, but when she hung up she'd begin to cry. I'd say, 'Your love for me is your decision, not theirs. I don't see them in this bed here with us this morning.' She would agree with me for a while. But then the guilt would come back."

Actually, Sheila felt liberated by Phil's arguments. "You know that part of Helen Epstein's book *Children of the Holocaust* where she says, 'they were not parents like any other parents, and we are not children like any other children'? That stuck like granite in my mind. I always felt set apart. I always wanted to tell my children about what my parents had suffered. But Phil taught me suffering is not confined to Jews."

Phil was a loving man who could make Sheila laugh, who delighted in buying her flowers and a good meal when she was feeling depressed, and in holding her close. "Our relationship was like the best of those Hollywood love movies in the forties," Phil said. Within a year, they were man and wife in everything but name. They shared the rent on their apartment as well as a joint bank account. Phil became an assistant TV producer. He took Sheila on a wonderful vacation on the *QE2*. In August 1982, they became engaged.

"I didn't tell my parents until after Yom Kippur," Sheila said. "I didn't want to spoil the Holidays for them. They had come over to my apartment—Phil was away somewhere—and brought me enough food for a small disaster. The room was filled with the flowers Phil had left so that I'd think of him when he was gone. When I told them we were engaged my father shot me a look of hatred and anger that I'd never seen on his face before. The look was directed at *me*—the daughter he loved. After about twenty minutes, he grabbed my mother and said, 'Come on, Rose, let's go.' It was devastating for both of us."

For the next three months, Sheila's mother called her every day, telling her that she was killing her father and her. Whenever Phil overheard the conversations, he told his fiancée that Jews had been killed by bigots. Why were her parents being bigots? Caught in the crossfire, Sheila began to see a psychiatrist. "Finally, I realized that I was trying to protect both Phil and my parents. I didn't know how *I* felt any longer. I realized that the person I was really hurting was myself."

The time bomb exploded after a cousin of Sheila's—another child of survivors—had invited them to her wedding. "We were both very excited," Sheila said. "Phil and I had been living together for two and one half years and he had never met my parents. They were going to be there."

But then, a week later, Sheila's cousin called back; she didn't want *her* parents to know that she had invited Phil. Sheila would have to take responsibility for the presence of her gentile fiancé at the event. She panicked at the idea.

"I didn't want her to have all that anxiety on her wedding day. I figured you only get one wedding day to remember. So I went down to the theater where Phil was taking acting lessons and I told him not to come. There would only be fifty people, and they'd all be staring at him: my parents would be uncomfortable and he would be uncomfortable. Of course, he thought I had betrayed him in favor of my parents. Maybe I had."

"I was shocked," Phil recalled. "I asked her, 'Are we engaged?' She said, 'Yes.' I said, 'If we are married we go places as one. We are a unit.' Until then, I had been angry at her parents, but not at her. I thought *we* had something special, that we were battling for an ideal of love. Suddenly, I realized that I could never trust her when it came to a choice between me and her parents. That tore us apart."

The couple argued non-stop for three days. As Phil recalled it, Sheila kept crying hysterically and apologizing. "But I had lost trust. That was the end."

Six months later, Sheila had fallen in love again—with a Jewish businessman who had been a classmate in high school. "It's like magic," she said. "I've been walking around, pinching myself ever since."

Phil was still bitter, though he tried to keep his anger directed at Sheila and not her people. "If you get stiffed by an Irish cab driver, you'll probably hate all the Irish for a while. Then you'll remember that he was an individual." Then, wistfully, he recalled the love of his life with a phrase which suited his universalist faith. "She understood my craft—I believed in her. We were like two flowers with the same root. And then an arbitrary gardener decided to uproot the garden and plant the flowers on opposite sides."

The Wedding Takes Place

When a Jew and gentile marry, the wedding arrangements can be the source of terrible tension. Who should preside? A rabbi? A minister? Both? A judge or justice of the peace? Sometimes the answer to these questions can shatter childhood dreams. In one workshop, the daughter of a Hebrew school principal, who'd always imagined that she would be married by dancing Hassidic rabbis, decided that it would be unprincipled to have any religious presence at all when she married her Protestant fiancé. There was no honest way she could agree that an intermarriage could be performed "according to the law of Moses"—a crucial part of the Jewish marriage contract. Another Jew permanently antagonized his devoutly Protestant mother-in-law who'd arranged for her minister to perform the wedding. He insisted that he was a Jew and Jews should be married by rabbis.

A Catholic man, who was married by a justice of the peace because his Jewish in-laws refused to come if the wedding included a priest, told his wife that he "needed to feel that someone was blessing us." Though she felt uneasy in churches, she thought her parents had been unfair to the man she loved. She agreed to let a priest marry them secretly the day after their public wedding.

Some parents will never attend an intermarriage, no matter who officiates. They feel they cannot condone their child's act of betrayal. That kind of rejection can cause couples agony. In one of our workshops, a Jew and a Catholic went all the way from New York to Hawaii to get married because they hoped the long voyage to a beautiful place would let them experience their love for each other instead of the pain of parental disapproval.

By the time a couple actually set the date for a wedding, parental objections rarely prevail. Courtship is over by then. The couple is too committed to each other—and their decision to get married—to feel anything but anger at the interfering parents.

If one or both members want a religious wedding, that anger can extend to the clergy. Sometimes that's true of Catholics who are marrying Jewish divorcés since priests are forbidden to perform a wedding if one of the partners has been divorced. More frequently it is true of Jews, who feel hurt when a rabbi refuses to perform an intermarriage. The majority of rabbis don't perform intermarriages even though they are painfully aware the decision hurts and angers the couples involved. For according to Jewish law a Jewish wedding unites two Jews. It reaffirms the covenant which God established with the Jewish people at Mount Sinai. A wedding which includes someone who is not a Jew, who is not part of the covenant, may be holy but its holiness is not specifically Jewish. These rabbis feel that Jewish law and tradition make it impossible for them to sanctify such unions.

Often, in interviews and workshops, we argue that clerics would be violating their conscience and perhaps risking their jobs if they agreed to perform weddings that their religion forbids. But, from the point of view of the couple who have been spurned, our defense of the clergy sounds theoretical and somewhat heartless. At that point in their relationship, they have decided they will have nothing to do with the religious communities that seemed so hostile when they wanted sanctification for their union.

Nevertheless, we urge couples to think carefully about that feeling, which is very much akin to the anger at the Jewish community we experienced after our honeymoon in Israel. Are they using their conviction that they have been betrayed by narrow-minded rabbis or priests as a way of transforming anxieties about their own religious and ethnic tensions into anger at a common enemy? Are they writing off an entire religious community because of one unhappy experience?

After the wedding there is usually a period when religious issues subside. For most childless couples relish their independence. They can be vagabonds in time. They have no responsibilities to parents or children.

Many say they seldom thought about their religious differences, or that they ignored their parents' disapproval until a baby was born. But children mark the beginning of a new reality. Most vagabonds are forced to turn into burghers overnight. They feed their children at fixed hours, try to choose homes that are near good day care centers or schools, rely on parents they once rejected to babysit for their youngsters long enough to let them enjoy a few romantic hours of freedom.

By then, many Jews and Christians who marry are forced to face the internal truth they avoided during their courtship, their wedding, and the years when they were childless. They realize that, in their new role as adults, as nurturers, they understand their own parents better and want their approval. They realize that their children will need links to the past to create identities in the present. They care about those identities.

The birth can raise an immediate religious question. Should there be a baptism or a christening, or a brit [a ritual circumcision] if the child is a boy, or a baby naming in synagogue if she is a girl? Discussions of these rituals can transform the silent language through which each partner conveys ethnic and religious attitudes into a shouting match.

Most Jews see the prospect of a baptism or christening as a sign that their child will be separated from them and join a different people. The act that can be so inspiring to their Protestant or Catholic spouse often fills them with guilt.

For the gentile, a brit is a frightening, confusing way of welcoming a male child into the world. For, unlike a hospital circumcision, it is celebrated in a festive atmosphere, in public. Jews watch as the *mohel* [the specialist in ritual circumcision] cuts off the boy's foreskin. They say *mazel tov*—congratulations—while he is still crying. From their point of view, the brit represents God's covenant with Abraham: the baby has just joined the Jewish people. The gentile often wonders how he or she could have consented to letting the baby be subjected to such a foreign ritual.

The couple may face another difficult issue when a child is born. If the mother is not Jewish, there may be a lot of pressure on the couple to agree to convert the baby to Judaism according to the rituals established by Jewish law. (Jewish law requires circumcision of a boy, and immersion in the mikvah, or ritual bath, for a boy or a girl.) If the baby is not legally converted, the Orthodox and Conservative movements of Judaism will not recognize him or her as a Jew.

Some parents feel that conversion is a logical part of the decision to raise the child as a Jew. Others resent the law or think it is irrelevant. Some mothers worry that the formal act of conversion will make them feel set apart from the rest of the family.

By the time the birthing ceremony takes place the marriage has gained its own momentum. The couple has too much stake in each other and their new family to let this argument disrupt a marriage. But in reality, the problems that arise when a child is born and when a baby begins to speak are more wrenching than those that arise during courtship.

Thus, Molly Perkins and Tom Schwartz can forget each other; Phil Angelli can retain a bittersweet memory of his relationship with Sheila Eisen. But the couples we are about to describe, Lars Swenson and Judy Horowitz, and Ted and Margie Kaplan, didn't recognize the power of their religious and ethnic loyalties until they had children. When their time bombs went off, they were forced to make decisions for a third person, not just for themselves.

The time bombs did not destroy either marriage. But they forced the couples to make compromises that left each partner feeling somewhat lonely and dissatisfied.

Lars and Judy: Can a Devout Christian Raise an Observant Jew?

Lars Swenson and Judy Horowitz were prototypical American tumbleweeds. She was an urban Jew who seldom went to synagogue; he was a religious Lutheran from a farm in Nebraska. They met as a doctor and lawyer in Los Angeles. They were opposites whose cultural differences attracted them to each other.

Lars, thirty-two, grew up in a small Midwestern town where his grandparents and his parents were pillars of the church. It was a very conservative environment. At home, men would stand in the living room talking about farm prices while their wives did the dishes in the kitchen. No liquor was permitted in the house. It was a milieu where premarital sex was regarded as sin. Lars loved the security it afforded, but he was a restless person who wanted to travel widely and meet a broad range of people. In college, he decided to become a doctor.

When he was in medical school in Los Angeles, some friends invited him out for a Chinese dinner. He sat next to Judy Horowitz, thirty-one, a tax lawyer who had always lived in the city, near her parents. "I was smitten," he said.

"You said you were impressed that I gave you my phone number that night," Judy recalled. "That was a perfectly natural thing for me to do."

Lars, who was used to demure women, saw the act as an appealingly aggressive one. "Besides, I felt a physical attraction . . ."

"He said that my jeans were too tight," Judy laughed.

"I liked her *zaftig* quality," he said, using naturally the Yiddish word for appealingly plump. "I come from a family of lean people."

When Judy met Lars, she had just divorced a Jewish man, "who relied on his parents for money and drifted from one job to another while I was in law school. It was hard for me to respect that." So, when she met Lars, "I was intrigued by this guy from a farm in Nebraska who had such big dreams. He was sure he would become a great doctor. It was exciting to meet someone who seemed so idealistic and courageous."

It had never occurred to Judy that, from Lars's perspective, the mere fact of her Judaism made her alluring. But when he described his early attraction to her he said, "I thought I was doing something exciting—in a bad sense—when I began to go out with a Jewish attorney from a big city. It was everything I wasn't supposed to do.

"My mother always said that she didn't care who I married as long as it was a nice Christian girl. So, when I told her about Judy, I said two out of three isn't bad. She's nice and she's a girl."

But she certainly wasn't a devout Christian like Lars and his family. She was a Jewish agnostic.

That difference became a conflict when they moved to New York, began to live together, and got engaged. They came to one of our workshops to try to work it out.

One episode symbolized their problem. Lars, a man of faith, was interested in Judy's Judaism. He liked going to High Holiday services and Passover seders. That year he asked her to accompany him to a

Good Friday service at a church he had just joined. She agreed to do so, but when she got to church she developed a fierce headache. She said that there was something in the nature of a Christian service that disagreed with her. Feeling sorrowful, Lars left with her.

Wouldn't the conflict deepen when a baby was born? She didn't want to be a religious Jew or let the children be Christian. He couldn't let his children be atheists. Nevertheless, they were sure that their love was so powerful that any problem would work itself out.

That summer, they got married in the United Nations chapel—a neutral place—by a Unitarian minister—a neutral person. Judy was satisfied. "It was a non-denominational service—Shakespeare and the Old Testament. It was very nice." Lars felt he had made a compromise. "We just didn't think we could do justice to both Judaism and Christianity in the wedding service, so why even try? Our decision to have a Unitarian minister seemed like the lowest common denominator." But he was pleased with its outcome. He thought the ceremony had a "beautiful spiritual feeling."

Judy became pregnant the next fall. For a time they thought the problem of the child's upbringing would resolve itself, just as their wedding had. Now that they were married they had learned to relax with each other. That year they were able to resolve the "December dilemma" much more easily than they had settled their dispute over Easter. Maybe they wouldn't have to feel one another's pulse whenever a religious holiday rolled around after all.

Judy's mother and brother had come to New York to visit them. "We had a Hanukkah party, and then we talked about getting a Christmas tree," Lars said. "But I didn't want to offend my mother-in-law. So we bought a fern. But then Judy's mother said, 'How can we not have a Christmas—Lars must really want one.' So *she* decorated the fern.

"It was a special day," Lars said. "We had put together a sort of last minute Swedish Christmas dinner. We had dried fruit in a bag, which was always our appetizer at home, and ate roast pork, then whitefish and lutefish. Then we had cauliflower and cheese sauce, which had been a tradition in my family. We exchanged a few Christmas presents.

"Judy and her family wanted me to have the same kind of Christmas I had at home. That meant reading from the New Testament. They urged me to do that. On Christmas Eve, my father reads the Christmas story from Luke, so that's what I did."

"We were surprised at how short the Christmas story was," Judy said. "We were used to the Haggadah."

They could find a way of enjoying the holidays together. They could even joke about their differences. But what would happen in the future, when a new person was in the house? They hadn't resolved the question when their daughter Eve was born.

"For a while, we thought about raising her with neither religion," Lars said. "But I didn't like that. I was raised as a religious Christian, and I think if I converted I'd be a religious Jew. I'd always be a religious something. It's more important for me to have my children raised religion/Jewish than religion/nothing or religion/both.

"I met a woman in New York whose father was Catholic and whose mother was Jewish. She told me that they were very happy, and that they had raised her with neither. She was very flippant about faith. She said, 'When I want to be Jewish I can be Jewish. When I want to be Catholic I can be Catholic.' That bothered me. To me, you're one or the other—you can't be both. You can't believe in Christ *and* be Jewish. It's a contradiction in terms."

But how could he avoid duplicating that contradiction in his own home? He was searching for the formula that would resolve that question.

He'd learned through experiences like the one on Good Friday that, "It would be difficult for Judy if our children were raised Christian. She would feel alienated. I'm more comfortable with Judaism. So we've decided to send Eve to Hebrew school, and make it clear that the Jewish holidays are the family holidays.

"But I can't give up my Christian beliefs. So we've decided to tell her that Christmas and Easter are *Daddy's* holidays."

Judy's feelings were much simpler. "I was willing to teach Eve both religions, and tell her she didn't have to believe in anything except the Golden Rule. But we had to make a compromise. If Lars insists that Eve have formal religious training, then let it be in a religion that I'm comfortable with in my conscience."

Can Lars live with that decision? Or will he always feel that he's walking on a narrow precipice between his intense religious feelings and Judy's strong ethnic ones?

As he talked, it became clear that he was already having more difficulty than he wanted to admit. Just after he finished describing the agreement he and Judy had reached about Eve, he said sadly that he rarely went to the church he joined when he arrived in New York. "I feel cut off, especially now that we've made the decision to raise Eve as a Jew. I miss it.

"I don't want to announce her birth to my church back home either. I don't want them to criticize me because my daughter is a Jew.

"Once I told my parents that my children might be raised as Jews. But I don't want to tell them that we've actually made the decision. It's not the kind of thing I want to mention in a phone call or even a letter. I think they would be very upset because she won't be baptized. In their minds, baptism is the way of affirming a baby's place in the family of God."

They decided to name Eve in a synagogue, and arranged to bring her there one Friday night. On Thursday, Lars telephoned the rabbi to postpone the event. He didn't want it to take place behind his parents' backs. But he didn't know how to tell his parents that it would take place at all.

Would he be betraying them? Would he be cheating his daughter and an important part of himself? He couldn't answer those questions.

Eve is two now. She has neither been named in a synagogue nor baptized in a church.

Ted Kaplan: "My Son Had to Understand the Jewish Me"

For Lars and Judy, the newborn child they loved was an embodiment of existing religious differences they could not resolve. For Ted Kaplan, the son of Orthodox Jews from a working class neighborhood in Brooklyn, the birth of a child marked the beginning of a religious reawakening. But he was just as troubled as Lars.

We met him after we spoke in a Cleveland synagogue, and talked for hours about the tension between his desire to explore his Jewish self and share it with his son, and his wife Margie's feeling that Judaism posed a potential threat to their marriage.

Margie had met him at the point when he was at the greatest psychological distance from his Jewish identity. When they got en-

gaged he was trying to re-create himself as a Midwesterner with a
Jewish background. He talked sarcastically about his upbringing as a
traditionally observant Jew. How could she—a Protestant from the
rural Midwest—have imagined the transition he would undergo when
he had a son?

Ted went to a yeshiva until he was eleven and switched to public
school. His home was kosher. His father was an important figure in
his community's religious life. "I was brought up playing in shul.
That was great fun."

But in late adolescence, Ted grew restless as he realized there was
an America beyond his Jewish world. He blamed his parents for
confining him to their Jewish ghetto. In the summer between his
senior year in high school and his freshman year in college, he and his
parents drove to Amish country. "One morning at breakfast I ordered a piece of ham. I wanted to see what it tasted like. Rage came
over my father's face. He could see the message I was giving him."
Here, Ted's voice was sad and lethargic.

When he entered Brooklyn College, he wrote a paper for a psychology class about the early roots of religion. "I read Freud's *Moses and
Monotheism,* and argued that the only basis for belief was psychological. My parents were furious. Then I fell in love with American literature. I was probably taking a cue from my parents. They loved this
country—they were the kind of Jewish immigrants who used to dress
in their best clothes on Election Day because they wanted to show
respect for a land that had given them such freedom. But when I tried
to talk to them about Emerson's transcendentalism or Whitman's
religion of democracy, they got frustrated and angry. I still don't
know whether they thought I should be devoting myself to Torah and
Talmud, or to learning a profession and making money, or whether
they were jealous that I really had a chance to be part of the country
they dreamed of.

"But I know that I was always angry at them, too. Now I think that
by rejecting the religious part of myself I was rejecting them. It hurt
all three of us."

Ted decided to study American literature in Indiana, Theodore
Dreiser's home. At first, he tried to conceal his identity as a Jew and as
a New Yorker. "When I was in Indiana, people could quickly hear my
accent. I was trying to get away from the image New Yorkers have of
being aggressive. So I worked on my voice. I tried not to pronounce

certain things too harshly, and I tried to talk in a low register so my accent wouldn't stand out."

But, by his third year in graduate school, he had become uncomfortable in his disguise. "During one spring break, I had gone to a psychological encounter group when I suddenly realized it was Passover. I began to wonder why I'd rejected my parents so forcefully when I loved them so much. I remember calling them up that night— they were in the midst of their seder—to tell them that I loved them. I felt terrible that I wasn't at a seder."

His fleeting experience at Passover buttressed his pride in his ethnic identity, though he never imagined it was a harbinger of renewed religious feelings. "I began to realize that what people called Jewish aggressiveness was the drive that had helped so many Jews succeed. I asked myself why I wanted to erase that from my personality. So I went out and bought a New York Yankee hat. I figured if I have the accent already I can't hide it. I might as well accept who I am."

That was a personal discovery. It was a way of accepting the identity he had been born with. But it didn't push him toward any involvement with the Jewish community.

At graduate school, Ted had become aware that he was avoiding Jewish women. "I had so many stereotypes of controlling, obnoxious Jews that I couldn't imagine myself marrying one."

In 1972, he met Margie, a tall, slim Protestant woman whose father was a professor of Romance Languages. "She seemed undemanding. She's not academic, but her father is. She could accept the fact that I was a graduate student, struggling for a Ph.D., and not in business making millions. She accepted me. She made me feel good about myself."

When he told his parents that he planned to marry Margie, they were furious. That intensified Ted's sense of guilt and sorrow, love and rage.

"I went through horrendous times with them—they fought with me, they argued with me. They wrote me long tomes of letters asking what was I going to do with my children. I said Margie and I would raise them with love and give them equal religions. But I didn't understand the issues. Even though I was raised Orthodox, I didn't understand the symbolism of a Jewish wedding.

"It's so strange to look back at that ceremony," he continued. "We were married by a judge, and I remember cringing when he said he was marrying us under God. This was at the rehearsal. I stood there, wondering whether I should let him say that at the actual ceremony. I did, but I felt embarrassed and threatened."

After Ted and Margie had been married for six years, their first son, Jake, was born. To Ted's astonishment, the religious feelings he thought he had left behind him surged through him now that he was a father.

"I realized that Jake could not really understand me if he didn't understand and know the Jewish part of me. I couldn't teach him until I found out for myself who *I* was as a Jew. I told Margie what I wanted. Suddenly it was clear to me that my son had to be Jewish. I could not tolerate it if he weren't. But this realization came six years after we were married. It wasn't fair to her."

Ted's self-discovery frightened Margie. She felt isolated whenever she entered the synagogue where Ted had begun to worship. Terms Jews take for granted made her feel excluded.

"The rabbi is a terrific person," Ted said. "He gives provocative sermons and he's a great storyteller. But he always talks about Jews and non-Jews, as if the world is divided into those categories. Even though Margie isn't religious, she thinks he should use the word Christian since it's a term of respect. She thinks he's really conveying a message that pits the Jews against the rest of the world."

Margie felt uncomfortable when the rabbi talked about Jewish ethics, even though, from Ted's point of view, he was using a language the congregation understood to urge them to be more moral people. "She doesn't think that ethics are either Jewish or Christian," he said. "From her point of view they're universal. So when the rabbi exhorted the congregation to act according to the Jewish ethical tradition, her response was that Christians had virtues, too. She'd say, 'We were taught to be just as good and ethical as the Jews.'

"When she goes to synagogue she gets worried that our son will pick up the idea that Jews are good and Christians aren't."

Now Jake Kaplan is five years old. Ted has begun to take him to temple most Friday nights and plans to enroll him in Hebrew school. Margie won't let her son be educated in Ted's temple.

"Luckily," he said, "she had been at a bar mitzvah at a synagogue twenty-five minutes from where we live where the rabbi was a woman. That appealed to Margie, who is a feminist. She saw that there were a

lot of interfaith couples, and felt confident that no one would catego-
rize people as Jews and non-Jews.

"She doesn't want to go to any synagogue herself. But she agreed
to let Jake go if I did the driving. That seemed like a fair compromise.

"But now that I've embarked in this Jewish direction I can't stop.
It's frustrating to go back and see that I've forgotten everything I
knew as a kid. I'm learning how to pray in Hebrew again and how to
read Torah again. Two weeks ago I began to say morning prayers and
lay tefillin. I hadn't done that since I was sixteen."

But, he said sadly, "Margie talks about how much I've changed. She
says, 'Your attitude now is not the attitude of the man I married.'
She's right, but there's nothing I can do."

Once Jake was born and the time bomb exploded, the common
ground upon which they once stood opened into a gulf. For Margie
had no way of hearing the language that always resounded in Ted's
mind—the ongoing dialogue with the parents and the tradition from
which he once seemed to feel so estranged.

"My pain now is that I can't move into Judaism as fast as I want
because I'm married to somebody who has a whole different perspective on life than I do. If I move too fast I have to reject her or leave her
behind. I'll have to spend time in places where she feels like an
outsider, an inferior. I understand why she feels that way. At one level
I agree with her. But that doesn't affect my own desire to become
more Jewish. What do I have to do to be sure that my son accepts
himself as a Jew and doesn't reject his mother as a Christian? How can
I keep peace with my wife and still be true to my Jewish self?"

A Child Speaks

Many intermarried parents experience the birth of a child as the
moment when they have to make a religious choice. But others want
to wait a few years longer. Many still don't feel that they have to make
a choice at all.

After all, an infant or toddler isn't going to be affected by a decision
to celebrate Christmas or Hanukkah, or to join a church or a synagogue. It will always matter if a boy is circumcised, but he won't
remember whether the procedure was done by an intern or a *mohel*.

Baptism is theologically important for Christian families, but the infant won't recall the event. Those arguments are over children, but they essentially concern parents.

The situation changes dramatically when the child begins to speak. For its early questions provide the first clear view of the new family culture. Until they arise, all the nervous discussions about childrens' identities are speculation. You can't predict what a child's disposition will be like, or whether it will be spiritual or practical, or what kind of relationship it will form with each parent. But by the time a youngster is three or four he or she has acquired enough of a personality to show you that a song you've always sung, a burst of mirth or anger, a story you've told, or a prejudice you've displayed can be the seed that spawned a growing consciousness. That consciousness can be a mirror for the religious and ethnic identities parents have created—or failed to create.

By the time children are old enough to ask about their identities, most patterns of a marriage are already established. Couples have negotiated their wedding ceremonies, the details of housekeeping, child care, wage earning, bill paying. They know what they'll do when one wants to make love and the other feels too tired. They have learned whether they can live with an annoying habit, like chronic lateness or bad table manners, or whether those habits may be the first step on the route to the divorce court.

But when the new person in their home asks questions which indicate uncertainty about his or her religious or ethnic identity, the interfaith couple may feel its marital ecology is imperiled. If the child asks a question indirectly, the couple may fail to acknowledge its importance or dismiss it as a cute remark. If the question suggests urgency, as our son Matt's question about Haman did, it may provoke such doubt and disagreement that the parents ignore it altogether.

But they shouldn't. All youngsters need to feel secure. Often, when they ask questions about faith, they are seeking emotional reinforcement. But when children of intermarriages combine remarks about faith with questions about identity they are trying to discover where they belong, as well. They are trying to ascertain *their* religion, *their* ethnicity, *their* place in a world that seems quite puzzling. They need to hear answers that show them their parents are comfortable with whatever spiritual choices they have made.

If the couple has postponed resolving religious and ethnic differences until the child speaks, the challenge to do so now may seem overwhelming. For if they take the questions they hear seriously, they will have to face the issues they have ignored. That can demand considerable self-discipline and considerable courage. They may have to read the books about religion and culture they've been avoiding; unearth the loyalties and biases they've been burying; make the leap of faith (or the admission that their spouse is the one with faith) that has seemed so dangerous until now.

One of the two couples we are about to describe, Whit and Ruth Forbes, could not unite to accept that challenge. She cared about religion. He couldn't talk about the subject without becoming sarcastic. How would their children disentangle their disagreement? The other couple, Walt and Nell Kramer, began to grow together when their daughter expressed fears about the Jewish part of her identity. Their attempt to answer the five-year-old child's questions propelled them into a search that enriched their lives.

Ruth and Whit: "Is It Seder or Cider?"

Ruth and Whit Forbes, a Jewish woman, a lawyer, and her Catholic husband, an architect, never discussed their disagreement about the value of religion—or their religious differences—when they fell in love at Middlebury College. Those subjects never surfaced during the first winter of their marriage, which they spent as ski bums in Stowe, or during their years in graduate school.

They are bright, attractive young professionals whose ready wit, and interesting jobs have landed them in a milieu filled with Boston's most successful politicians, business people, and writers. They discussed religion once or twice when their daughters Claire and Wendy were born. But, with a fascinating social life and two small children, they barely had time to discuss *any* subject for long.

We had met the couple through mutual friends, and one day at lunch they talked to us about their religious backgrounds, and the identities they wanted for their children.

Whit, a tall, lean, well-coordinated man, sounds reverent only when he talks about his father, Austin Forbes, a psychologist who teaches behavioral science. Austin Forbes was born an Episcopalian and converted to Catholicism so that he could marry Whit's mother. His real faith, rationalism, assumed that the only truly religious act a person could perform was to ask another question, make another discovery.

When Whit was growing up, his father insisted that the family live in a middle class Catholic suburb "so that we wouldn't be tainted by the academic milieu." From Whit's point of view, that gave him an advantage over the other faculty children who lived in a predominantly Jewish academic neighborhood. Their parents "pressured them and pulled strings to get them into Ivy League colleges regardless of their merit. I think those kids had pretty miserable childhoods. I was a pretty happy-go-lucky kid. One nice thing about the crazy Catholic neighborhood we lived in was that all the families had lots of children. We could field a baseball team whenever we wanted to. I grew up playing sports all the time."

Most of Whit's friends went to Catholic church, "and my mother made an attempt to get us to go, too." But Austin Forbes sabotaged that through his studied indifference.

"I never saw my father go to church. How could I believe that there was a particular God who had ordered the universe when my father, this behavioral scientist, gave me such a rational upbringing? I couldn't take church seriously. My father got to stay home and read the newspapers and crack jokes about my mother and her religious superstitions while I had to truck off to this stupid church where the nuns would literally patrol the aisles, making sure that you kneeled. But my knees were always injured from sports. My clearest memory of church is sore knees. I quit going when I was twelve."

Whit described himself as a lazy, indifferent student. His parents didn't seem to care if he attended an Ivy League college. "They recognized that I wasn't all that academically driven, and that Middlebury would be a good college for me.

"Besides, in keeping with my recreational orientation, I only applied to schools where I could ski at least a hundred days a year."

Ruth Forbes, née Levy, was born in Fort Wayne, Indiana. When she was eleven, her father decided to sell the family furniture store. He went to the University of Illinois, earned a Ph.D. in sociology, and became a professor in Houston.

The family joined a Reform temple there. "The congregation was very wealthy," she recalled. "There were Cadillacs and diamonds everywhere you looked. But the rabbi made you forget that. He looked like what you thought Moses would look like—he had gray hair and a beard. Sometimes he came to Sunday school, and told us stories from the Bible in a way that brought them to life. He was a phenomenal speaker with a resonant voice. When he recited the *Shema* [the central statement of Jewish faith], his powerful voice almost made you weep.

"A lot of my friends feel culturally and ethnically Jewish, but not spiritually Jewish. It's the other way around for me. Because of that rabbi, I feel Jewish, in a religious sense."

But in Houston, she was socially uncomfortable as a Jew. In high school, "I began to realize that a lot of my Jewish friends had mothers who would not let them go out with non-Jewish boys, and that was where my problem began. There were very strong Jewish groups in those schools. So I was faced with a choice. I either joined the Jewish groups and had mostly Jewish friends or I became part of the in-crowd at high school—the football team, drill team, student council kids. I wanted a broad range of friends. So I chose the latter."

She hated the schism between the Jews and jocks. It convinced her to stay away from the University of Texas. "I would have had to pledge a Jewish sorority, or stick with the football crowd, and pledge some sorority whose meetings ended with a prayer in the name of Jesus Christ our Lord. I didn't think I'd be comfortable in either place."

Then, a cousin sent her a Middlebury College catalogue. When she decided the small New England college looked attractive, her father encouraged her to apply. She loved it from the moment she arrived.

"It was the first time I had lived around beautiful scenery. I got into hiking and backpacking. I took philosophy courses, and I'd sit around talking to people about writers like Herman Hesse. I never felt as if anyone was aware of who was Jewish and who was non-Jewish. I never went to temple, even for Rosh Hashanah and Yom Kippur."

After college, she and Whit spent a winter in Stowe, a ski resort, and were on the slopes every day. Since Ruth had described herself as "an overachiever, unlike Whit," that kind of life seemed out of character. So Rachel asked her if she liked to ski.

"I do now," she said.

"She has to," Whit said, with a slightly stinging chuckle. "It was clear that if Ruth and I were going to survive as a team, she was going to learn how to ski. That was the one value it was necessary for us to share. I wasn't going to give it up."

Though they never discussed religion, they were already aware of a disagreement over values. It cropped up when they began to discuss marriage.

"Ruth wanted to get married but I put my foot down there," Whit recalled. "I couldn't see the value of weddings. Who gives a damn whether we're married or not? I relented because Ruth had begun law school and we could only get a mortgage on a house if we were man and wife. But I didn't want a religious ceremony—or any ceremony at all. So we went to a judge, who performed the service, and then we threw a big party that weekend in Stowe."

Ruth wasn't satisfied. "My brother married a Jewish woman, and he had a beautiful wedding, under a *huppah* [a wedding canopy]," she said. "All the cousins came from Fort Wayne. None of them came to our wedding, partly because they didn't approve of intermarriage and partly because Stowe seemed so far from Indiana. Of course, my mom and dad were there—they love Whit and were thrilled by the wedding. But sometimes I wish I'd had a Jewish service that was as nice as my brother's."

Then she began to talk about her plans for Claire's religious training. "I thought I had discussed this with Whit . . . ."

"You didn't," he said. Then, looking at the couch where Rachel and I were sitting, he added, "You've precipitated our first religious discussion."

"Maybe," Ruth responded a little angrily. "But you know that I've been going to temple off and on all year after two of my friends died. I went on Yom Kippur too. I liked the rabbi. He gave a sermon about how Judaism had to be a more spiritual religion, and I agreed with that. I liked his liberal political views too."

Her four-year-old daughter Claire goes to preschool with a great many Jewish children. Last spring, she asked the question which forced Ruth to confront her feelings about transmitting Judaism.

"It was April, and she told me that a lot of kids in her class were talking about the cider their families were going to have. What she was hearing, of course, was talk about their families' seders. I got furious at myself. Why hadn't I taught her enough about Jewishness so that she could understand what they were talking about? I want my kids to be raised with some understanding of Judaism. I want them to go to a Jewish Sunday school. I mentioned that to Whit once, and he was worried about the money we'd have to pay for membership."

"Yeah," Whit said, "Ruth did tell me she wanted to join. Then she said there was a *fee*. My reaction was that Catholicism might have been a lot of bullshit, but at least it was free. And my second reaction was, couldn't my child find spiritual life in a condominium in Stowe at roughly the same cost."

Ruth was gentle but unyielding. "Well, I have such good memories of the rabbi in Houston, and I liked the rabbi here so much that I'm going to keep exploring the possibility."

Looking at Ruth, Whit said, "It's not that much of an issue. If you feel strongly about it, I don't care. I mean I know that with a father who doesn't participate, no child is going to get seriously involved. If I stay home reading the paper in the morning, I just assume my kids will react the way I did."

Then, more seriously, "I've seen the materialism at that temple. There are some values I don't think are particularly attractive. They're certainly not New England values."

Turning to us, he said, "You know, this *is* the first time Ruth and I have really discussed the subject, so it's a sort of introductory level. If we're talking about finding something spiritual, I can think of better ways than organized religion to do it."

"Oh, come on, Whit," Ruth said. "You're an agnostic. You don't care how I raise the girls religiously."

Whit had already said he wouldn't go to synagogue—even on the High Holidays. I wondered how he felt about a seder.

"I probably wouldn't participate. We've occasionally talked about going to a seder, but so far, we haven't made it to one."

Ruth said that she thought he'd be comfortable at one, "because any that we'd be invited to or would have would involve 99 percent couples who are half Jewish and half not."

"It would be a half-assed seder," Whit laughed. "But if it ever started to get serious religious overtones, I'd bow out. It would make me uncomfortable. I'd wonder why I was at something that meant so little to me."

Then Ruth said, "I could become somewhat religious, and my daughters could, too, without Whit's participation. At least, he wouldn't get upset."

"That's true. I'd just react with a kind of passive sarcasm, which is how I always try to beat Ruth down. I don't really have the conviction to go right at it. I just insult her over time."

Whit was still joking, but Ruth was becoming more worried, more serious. "You're *not* going to stand in the way of Claire's going to Sunday school, are you?"

"Well, if there's a major capital investment in this thing I'll argue with you. If you ever do it and it's no hindrance to me, that's fine. But if it ever takes my time, then it will become an issue."

"But if you can just do what you want to do on Sunday morning, and let's say I even taught a Sunday school class, you wouldn't really care, would you?"

"I'd find that very humorous."

"Well, I've thought about teaching a Sunday school class before," Ruth said.

"You have?" Whit asked incredulously. "Teaching a Sunday school class?"

"Yes. There are parts of my upbringing at that temple in Houston that I'm really grateful I had. I didn't think about them at Middlebury or at law school. But now, being a mother, I think about it more. I'd check out whatever Sunday school I sent Claire to. And if I thought there were some really bad teachers there, maybe I'd teach on Sunday morning. I'd want to make the school better."

"Well, if you did that my attitude would become more than just passive sarcasm. I'd try to sabotage you."

Whit had to go back to work. They walked to the door, hand in hand, and tried to heal their momentary lesion with an affectionate kiss. That night, they told each other, they would enjoy a long, leisurely dinner with a bottle of the finest wine Whit could find.

Walt and Nell: "Why Are People Always So Mean to the Jews?"

Walt Kramer is a Jew from Minneapolis. Nell Wilson, who was raised in Oregon, is the daughter of a white, Anglo-Saxon Protestant man and a Mexican woman who was born a Catholic.

When they were graduate students at Berkeley and Peace Corps volunteers in India, they were proud of the fact that they were an interfaith couple. They were people with roots in their pasts and tendrils of sympathy that extended through the world. They felt that as a couple with Jewish, Protestant, and Mexican Catholic roots, who had spent time in India and developed an affinity for the Hindu religion, they were a living tribute to integration. Then, when their daughter Vanessa was four, she asked a question that shattered their confidence in their decisions about their family's identity. They decided to reexplore their feelings in one of our workshops.

Nell and Walt had met in 1966, at a party Walt's Jewish fraternity in Berkeley had thrown for Nell's freshman dorm. "Their fantasy for the weekend was to get totally drunk and make love to all the shiksas," Nell recalled. "It was gross."

Walt wasn't at the party but "when my date took me upstairs to show me his room I saw him, with his blazing eyes. Walt was writing a paper, ignoring the rest of us. He seemed so striking, so aloof. I wished I was with him."

He wished he was with her. "She was dressed all in pink that night. I had never seen anybody before who dressed in pink."

"Pink was my favorite color," Nell said. "I had pink cut-offs and a pink fuzzy shirt and a pink bow and pink socks." Remembering the night, she dissolved in laughter.

"I felt that she was out to please," Walt continued. "To me, Jewish women were out to *be pleased*. She was the first gentile woman I'd ever dated, and she seemed more accepting than any woman I had met. I felt I didn't have to be careful to be smart or seem macho. Whatever I did was fine with her."

"You were right," she said. "I was in love with you, with those soulful Jewish eyes."

Unlike many of the couples we have interviewed, both Nell and Walt felt the other's background was attractive. Each was able to help the other appreciate their parents and their cultures.

Until Nell was eight, she lived in the Central Valley of California. She went to school with the children of migrant workers, and spent much of her spare time with her Mexican cousins. She was particularly close to her grandmother, a devout Catholic who believed in a gentle, loving Jesus.

But her mother—a descendant of Aztecs, beautiful, dark-skinned, with hair that flowed down to her waist—had married a tall, sandy-haired Protestant to escape her Hispanic background. She told Nell to keep her distance from her lively, cheerful relatives whom she always called "lowly Mexicans."

When Nell was eight her father, a former army officer, became an executive at Caterpillar Tractor, and the Wilson family moved to Oregon. Like her classmates, Nell loved hiking and canoeing. She joined the youth group of the Methodist church her Catholic mother had chosen for her. Still, she felt out of place.

"I was always aware I had a Mexican background and had been baptized a Catholic. I felt as if I were living a charade. I wanted to pick up the threads that were lost. I felt as if the heart and soul were gone from my mother—and from us. So, from when I was little, I was searching for what was hidden."

As a boy, Walt received almost as many mixed messages as Nell. His parents were part of Minneapolis' close-knit Jewish world, and his closest friends were the boys he had known in Hebrew school and grade school. But in ninth grade he was sent to a prep school, where he was the only Jew in his class. "All the kids in my school lived on the other side of town. I liked them, but I felt like a foreigner in their houses."

By the time he was seventeen, he began to feel that he didn't belong in Minneapolis' Jewish community either.

"I couldn't wait to get away from home. It seemed like such a conservative environment. All of my peers were going into their family's business. I didn't want any part of it. I didn't want to marry a Jewish woman and join the same country club and the same congregation as all my friends. I didn't want to see my life stretched out ahead of me, predictably."

He was just eighteen when he flew out to college at Berkeley, his American dream. "I didn't even know how to get to the campus from the airport. I hadn't bothered to get a room in a dorm. So I went to the Y. I wasn't afraid. I was exhilarated. I thought sex was going on everywhere. It was the West, and I was free. When I met Nell, she represented that freedom."

From Nell's perspective, Walt was so impulsively adventurous that he almost seemed like a knight. They met in May. That July, when Nell had a job at home in Portland, "Walt called me and said 'I'm coming up to Oregon tomorrow to see you.' It's about seven hundred miles. He drove all day. He picked me up at work, and we stayed out till midnight. I bought him two dozen doughnuts and he drove back to California. I said, 'This man's for me.' "

After Walt's graduation and Nell's sophomore year they decided to get married. Nell's parents called Walt a "cradle snatcher," and opposed the match so vehemently that Walt and Nell decided to elope. As a result, Walt didn't have to face the problem of finding a rabbi. He never told Nell his feelings about intermarrying. But, from his point of view, "I was thumbing my nose at Jewish rigidity—at the idea that Jews should only marry Jews. That seemed like a form of narrowness that was worth defying."

His parents did not seem upset by the marriage. After the couple eloped, the Kramers arranged an elaborate reception for them in Minneapolis. Walt endured it. Nell loved it.

"For years Walt's parents had been going to every bar mitzvah and Jewish wedding in town. This was a chance to reciprocate. I never saw such a roomful of people. It was an overwhelming experience for me. People were all talking and carrying on. They kept coming up to me and pinching me and saying how cute I was. Everyone was interested in me and very lively. Their liveliness made me feel at home."

Walt couldn't understand why Nell liked them so well. With fondness in her voice, Nell said, "You were so immersed in your parents' culture that you took what you had for granted. You learned to like your family through me."

Then, she added, "You did the same thing for me. You learned Spanish and told me I should be proud of my Mexican heritage. You helped me respect my past."

About a year after Walt and Nell were married, they decided to join the Peace Corps. Their experience with other volunteers taught Nell a new lesson about Walt's Jewish feelings, and hers. "When we were at Berkeley, all his friends were Jews from West L.A. But he was the only Jew in our Peace Corps group. I saw that he was different from the other volunteers. I realized that I liked most Jews more than I liked most other people."

Walt, more guarded, said, "Nell just made me realize that my problems with the other volunteers probably did have something to do with being Jewish. I think most people in our Peace Corps group felt that American culture and American language were superior and that Indian culture and Indian language were inferior. I never felt that I was an American like them. I thought the volunteers were bigoted against Indians in the same way as they were against Jews."

But neither Walt nor Nell connected those feelings to their own lives. They returned to America in 1972, and settled in New York, where Walt began to study for a Ph.D. in sociology. In 1979, Nell got pregnant.

"I was very cavalier about my children's religion," Walt said. "I thought we should give them some Christianity and some Judaism, and let them choose what they wanted."

"We were involved with Hinduism, anyway," Nell added. "We saw the integration of religions as positive. We used to go on a Hindu retreat for ten days every summer. I liked that. I was involved in meditation and there were a lot of Indians there. I was glad for the connection. We took our daughter Vanessa there until she was about three."

After Vanessa was born, they had their first battle over a religious symbol. "When Vanessa was two I wanted to have a Christmas tree," Nell said. "We had never had a tree before. It was very upsetting to Walt. We had a huge fight. I remember feeling very hurt, and thinking that Walt was very stubborn."

"But we had a tree," Walt interjected.

"Yeah, we had a tree, but it was so begrudging. Walt wouldn't touch it. He wouldn't put anything on it."

"I kept my back to it the whole season. I felt as if I was being very gallant to allow Nell to have it," he said somewhat remorsefully. "I thought I was being generous."

The next year Nell decided she could please Walt and enrich Vanessa's upbringing if the three of them celebrated Hanukkah, too. That decision ignited the time bomb that caused Walt and Nell to reexamine all their assumptions about their family's identities.

That December, Nell recalled, she was sitting on a chair, reading her daughter the Hanukkah story. When Nell told of the Syrian king Antiochus killing Jews who wouldn't bow down to statues of gods, Vanessa asked her, "Mommy, why are people always so mean to the Jews?"

"I felt very clutched," she said. "I knew that as a gentile I was coming from a different place than her. But I also knew that I didn't want her to grow up feeling persecuted. I wanted her to take pleasure in the Jewish part of her identity," she said. "But I didn't know how. I didn't like the way I choked and stumbled over what I said to her. When Walt came home, I told him what happened."

Walt and Nell had built up so much trust during their courtship and their two years in the Peace Corps that they were able to face the implications of Vanessa's remark instead of arguing over its meaning. "Everyone we talked to thought her question was connected to the fact that we were an interfaith couple," Nell said. "We had never thought about that. We didn't know how to handle the problem. But we knew we couldn't do it by ourselves. That was why we enrolled in your workshop."

In the course of the sessions, they both realized that Nell felt at home in Jewish culture while Walt felt very uncomfortable bringing Christian culture into his home. That summer they decided to spend time in Israel with one of Walt's best friends from childhood, who had become an observant Jew.

Within a year they discovered that they liked the ritual of lighting Friday night candles. They decided to enroll Vanessa in a Hebrew school and they became friends with the parents they met there. Now that Judaism was no longer the religion of Walt's bourgeois childhood, he discovered meaning in solemn holidays like Yom Kippur and joyous ones like Simchat Torah. If anything, Nell liked those occasions even more than her husband.

Their conflict deepened their understanding of each other. It allowed them to discover new meaning in a Jewish way of life.

A Parent Dies

Often, the death of a parent can rekindle religious sparks. That happened to our friend Bliss Geiger, a Methodist from Kansas, who married James Geiger, a Jew from New York. We had met them when we were in the Peace Corps, and had stayed in close touch with them as he got his Ph.D. in English and she got hers in Spanish. Now they're both full professors at New York area universities. The few nights we have dinner alone with them each year are a special time for intimate conversation.

They have a very happy marriage, with plenty of friends and stimulating intellectual work. They adore their daughters, Samantha and

Melissa, who play the violin and the piano respectively with extraordinary skill.

But even though Bliss seldom spoke about it, she had become nostalgic for her childhood Christianity when she had children, and she wished she could teach her daughters her faith. James was an ethnically identified Jew, who didn't like to discuss religion. He didn't want to send the girls to Hebrew school but he couldn't imagine them receiving Christian instruction. They had been married for fifteen years, and adhered to their agreement to raise their daughters as humanists, with neither Judaism nor Christianity.

Still, sometimes, when Bliss tucked the girls into bed, she would recite the Twenty-third Psalm or the Lord's Prayer. She never told James for fear that he'd regard that act as a transgression of their agreement to raise their children without religion.

Bliss's father died when she was approaching forty and the girls were in their teens. When we visited the Geigers in the Berkshires that summer, she seemed drawn and depressed. Her calm, warm smile was still there; so was the slightly naïve charm with which she disarms the academic friends she and James share. But when she talked about her father's funeral she dwelt lovingly on details like the Methodist hymns her father had loved, and the eulogy her father's best friend had given. Sometimes she seemed to drift into psychological spaces where no one could accompany her. Plainly, she was mourning a man of faith. "I wish now I had some of that faith for myself and my girls."

It was a wistful thought, not a demand. For she loved her life and her marriage, and would never consider returning to the simpler world her father had inhabited. Nevertheless, his death had left her feeling lonely. "James has never understood where I'm coming from. I wish Samantha and Melissa understood how my father raised me to see the world. It helped him so much when he was dying. He was so much at peace.

"Even though they're teenagers I would like them to go to Sunday school. It might comfort them in the way it comforted my father. But James would feel betrayed if I suddenly decided to introduce them to Christianity. When I got married I agreed with James that religion was outmoded superstition. But now that my father is gone I regret the decision. I feel as if there's a hole in all of our hearts."

* * *

The idea that time bombs can exist in interfaith relationships is a frightening one. How can a couple defuse them? And once that is accomplished, how can they map the geography of their lives together so that they don't wind up on an island that is too small to sustain their spiritual longings?

Over the past six years we have developed a set of exercises to help people explore those questions as thoroughly as possible. Some couples do them at home, but we have found they're more effective in a workshop setting. There, each couple has acknowledged that religion and ethnicity matter to them and that they are willing to spend time sharing their concerns with others. They discover that they are not living in a private world of neurotic fights over Christmas trees, or seders where they feel unwelcome, or over in-laws who resent them. In the workshops, as they hear other couples describe their fights and feelings, they begin to perceive themselves in a fresh way.

6
The Workshops

Our workshops at Manhattan's 92nd Street YMHA last two hours apiece and now continue over a six-week cycle. We conduct them in a classroom, with a blackboard, chalk, paper, and an occasional mimeographed article as teaching aids. Some of the people who come are married. Some are not. Sometimes only four couples enroll. Sometimes there are as many as twelve.

Some of the Jews come from thoroughly assimilated backgrounds; others, proud of their ethnic identities, were raised in left-wing families who never set foot in a synagogue as a matter of principle. But most describe their religious affiliations as an important part of their childhoods. About half of them had Orthodox or Conservative parents, who lit candles on Friday nights, went to synagogue with some frequency, and heeded the dietary laws. Most of the rest come from Reform backgrounds where they received a Jewish education until their bar or bat mitzva.

About 60 percent of the Christians are Protestants. Most were regular church-goers when they were younger. About 40 percent are Catholics, and about half of them attended parochial school at some point in their lives.

The Jews and Christians who come to the workshops range across a broad occupational spectrum. They are editors and writers; stewardesses and physical therapists; doctors, nurses, lawyers, and bankers; management consultants and labor organizers, psychologists and college professors; foundation officials, department store executives, people who work in film or television, in the fashion industry or advertising agencies.

Some come because they have read about the workshop in a YMHA brochure and thought it sounded intersting. Others are referred to us by rabbis, ministers, and priests. One Yeshiva-trained woman got an anonymous ticket to the workshop in the mail: later, she learned that her father had sent it. A Catholic from a Chicago suburb heard about the workshop from his mother, who is getting a Ph.D. in religion.

Sometimes, gentiles pressure their Jewish lovers to come: they hope the workshop will help the Jew define his or her hostility to Christmas or explain the reason raising children who identify as Jews seems so important. Sometimes Jews will pressure their Christian mates to come, hoping to resolve similar tensions. Finally, to an increasing degree, Jewish-Christian couples enroll in the workshops so that they can understand each other better and think about the future more realistically. In the spring of 1987, about half the people in our group of ten couples told us that their friends and office mates, who were also in interfaith relationships, would ask them, eagerly, to describe each week's session. Their participation in the workshops made them the objects of flattering curiosity.

The workshops are intended to help people develop a vocabulary of ideas and experiences that will allow them to understand the tensions they experience (or fear they will experience) as interfaith couples. We have developed a set of written and verbal exercises to furnish perspective on questions like these:

Why are many Jews unsettled by the prospect of a Christmas tree, or by the sight of a cross in church? Why does the thought of an uncircumcised child make so many of them feel like traitors?

Why do many Christians feel rage at the thought of not celebrating Christmas? Why does the thought of an unbaptized child fill some with fear?

Are these feelings that are subject to negotiations? Or do they reflect such deep tribal or religious roots that any compromise will later cause regrets?

What happy memories do the Christian and Jew have of the childhood moments when religion and family intersected? Does one or the other possess an enduring faith, or a sense of loyalty to a people or a tradition? Do they want to transmit those feelings to their children?

To put it more broadly, is faith a form of psychological dross that should disappear in the melting pot of romance? Or is it gold that should never be surrendered in the bargains couples make to keep their marriages alive?

Our workshops themselves are often emotional roller coasters. At the outset we tell the group that the weeks ahead may be very difficult ones. They probably won't experience their most tumultuous moments in the group. Instead, they'll argue in the car going home or in a restaurant or bar. We suggest they chart their emotional journeys in a journal, and describe them in the next workshop session, when we ask for feedback from the week before.

We urge them to remember that even when the workshop seems most difficult, it's important that they remain honest with one another. Over six years, we have seen that guided discussions and exercises can help many couples defuse time bombs, break out of spiritual gridlock, and reach some kind of resolution. The roller coaster can return them to firmer ground.

"What Brought You Two Here?"

Most interfaith couples who come to our workshops think that their conflicts are neurotic, not normal. They often feel self-loathing for what they regard as their own bigoted feelings. Jews feel guilt if they can't bring themselves to compromise during the December dilemma or if they insist on raising their children as Jews. They often wish they could shake their residual fear of persecution instead of inflicting it on a spouse. They may have heard the injunction, "Scratch a gentile and you find an anti-semite": and wonder whether those words apply to their mate.

For their part, some gentiles feel anguish at their unbidden feeling that these Jews who have suffered so much now seem like nationalistic, intolerant people. Some feel confused and abandoned when a warmhearted spouse suddenly displays inexplicable tribal loyalties. Others wonder why their popular, successful Jewish mate is so pessimistic about the future. It is as if a dark cloud always hovers over life.

But it's hard to discuss these feelings. They are anxieties without names. As couples cross the hurdle of loneliness, they realize they are not unique. They are part of a growing community of Americans who share such problems.

We begin the first session of every workshop by asking people why they have come. What is their background? How did they fall in love? When and how do their conflicts present themselves?

As they tell their stories, the mood in the room changes from one of tension to one of relief. Sometimes people express feelings so powerful that others burst out in a laugh of recognition. People whoop with surprise when they recognize that others share the feelings they had thought were their own idiosyncrasies. They burst into anger at mates, parents, or in-laws who seem rejecting. Tears flow as a gentile describes exclusion from a Jewish family, or a Jew describes persistent discomfort in Christian America. There are brooding silences. There are moments of intense confusion. As these moods flash by, each couple is building the foundation for the solutions they'll reach. And it's clear they'll reach very different solutions.

At the end of one introductory session Rona, a Jewish woman who had been fighting interminably with Paul, her Italian-Catholic fiancé, described her feelings when she heard other couples talk. "I realized that everyone here is engaged in the same struggle as we are. It isn't just a tug of war beween the two of us. It is more like an earthquake. Seeing intermarriage as a broader issue makes me feel less threatened. There's no right or wrong. Each couple has to find their own solution."

"I feel the same way as you do," a Jewish man responded. "Before I came here I thought this was just one more thing I was being stubborn about. Now I know I'm not the only one who feels that way. I wonder if that knowledge will help me in the future."

"Maybe not," his Protestant fiancée answered, "but I think it helps us now. Before tonight I thought that I couldn't negotiate with you because you were Jewish and Jews are stubborn. I couldn't understand what else was behind our arguments. Now, I'm beginning to see that, from your point of view, stubbornness has roots in history. I didn't even know about that before. At least we can talk sensibly now.' '

What Do You Think of Your People?

To move toward a resolution couples need to understand the sub-
text to their romance. Few Jewish-Christian couples just happen to
fall in love. For most, their mutual attraction was spurred by many
things. Often they love the otherness of their mate. Often they ro-
manticize the otherness, and denigrate the familiar. Their attraction
overlies tangled feelings about their own backgrounds.

Often, a Jew can love Judaism—or a Protestant or Catholic can love
their church—and still feel stifled by the thought of marrying someone who grew up in the same cultural milieu. Some lovers conceal
those feelings from one another. Very often, they conceal them from
themselves. It never occurs to them that when they fall in love they
are transforming negative stereotypes of people who are similar to
themselves into an idealized stereotype of people who are different.
But when a time bomb goes off, it is often because one spouse ceases
to see the other as a romanticized alternative to a past that seemed
confining. That can be an emotionally shattering experience. It's
alluring to court an image. It's difficult to create a life with a person
whose beliefs and behavior differ from your own.

One workshop goal is to help people free themselves from the
prisons of their fantasies and from their negative self-images. It helps
them to understand whether generic reasons form part of their attraction to each other. We begin to explore that question by provok-
ing a discussion of the participants' positive and negative stereotypes.

To open the session we ask Jews to list the first five words or
phrases that come to mind when they think about Jews of the opposite sex. Then we ask gentiles to think about gentiles and do the same.
Finally, we ask Jews to express the thoughts that come to mind when
they think about gentiles, and gentiles to do the same with Jews.

This exercise is usually easier for Jews than gentiles. They are used
to seeing a division in the world between Jews and non-Jews. And
they tend to express their feelings quickly. After all, whatever they
think of each other, they feel comfortable talking about their people.
It's as if they're describing their family.

Usually, gentiles respond more haltingly to the question. When
they try to list qualities in each other they don't have a single category
in mind. The word gentile is a catch-all, since it can include someone
whose primary self-identification is as an Italian Catholic, a California

Methodist, a New Englander, a Southerner, or simply an American. The assertion that "I'm a Presbyterian" doesn't carry the same cultural weight as the phrase "I'm a Jew." WASPs may be a group to the world, but not to each other. Even Catholics with strong feelings about the Church tend to make a clearer distinction between religion, on the one hand, and ethnicity and birthplace, on the other, than Jews do. If Jews seem to be describing family, gentiles seem to be thinking of neighbors down the block.

We've chosen the responses of three Jewish-Catholic and three Jewish-Protestant couples from one of our workshops to show the typical range of images. This tiny sample encapsulates patterns of feelings we've heard in all the cities where we've conducted workshops.

Here, first, is what the Jewish women said about Jewish men: "Mama's boy, balding and pot-bellied, lawyers and doctors from Long Island, not found at a state university," said one. "Brainy, scrawny, and thin, unathletic, very devoted to wives and mothers alike, non-alcoholic, able to get a good job," said another. "Neurotic, insecure, caring, loud, warm" were the associations of the third.

To the Jewish men, Jewish women were "Possessive, materialistic, domineering, intelligent, with a strong sense of family"; or "Mothering, intrusive, overbearing"; or "Talkative, materialistic, concerned with looks, status, success-oriented."

The Catholics and Protestants in the group complained that the category of gentile was too diffuse for them. Still, their replies had common themes.

One Protestant man distinguished between Catholic and Protestant women. From his perspective, Protestants were "correct, uptight, emotionless, private, upper class." Catholics were "obedient to a blind faith, ethnic, and religious." Another Protestant said that it was impossible to generalize about gentile women except that "They were traditional with respect to sex roles," which was a problem from his point of view.

Catholic men were equally judgmental. To them, Catholic women were "guilt-ridden, motherly, repressed"; or "dull, polite, pretending to be dumb, conventional, repressed."

One Catholic woman saw Catholic men as "confused, accepting, quiet except when drunk, loving."

A Protestant woman stereotyped Protestant men as "Country club, drinking, bridge-playing, middle class, Republicans."

In contrast, these Jews and gentiles saw one another through the romantic haze of an unfamiliar, half-forbidden culture, as positive stereotypes.

A Protestant man: Jewish women were "dark-haired and olive-skinned," "hip," "urbane,"—and "overbearing."

To one Catholic woman, Jewish men were "smart, talkative, argumentative, critical, loyal," and to another they were "Ambitious, bright, good providers." A Protestant woman saw them as "sensitive, loving, caring, successful, intellectual."

By contrast, one Jewish woman saw Protestant men as "good-looking, athletic, fun, caring, loving but not overbearing." Another saw them as "Generous, unable to articulate feelings, undemanding."

A Jewish man found gentile women attractive because they were "Blond, adventurous, cold, risk-taking." Another found them "Non-domineering, less emotional, quieter, more supportive."

Most Jews and gentiles in our workshops take the traits which Jews or gentiles of the opposite sex define as liabilities and turn them into assets. Here, for example, is how a Protestant man perceived the qualities that Jewish men call "talkative, demanding": "I love to listen to Amy. Her intensity fascinates me. She's always questioning things inside herself, and she won't let me hide my feelings from her."

Here is how a Jewish woman interpreted the quality that Protestants call "cold." "I always think I'm wearing my heart on my sleeve, and that makes me dull and vulnerable. I love his aloofness. I think his silences contain secrets, and a masterful ability to do anything he wants."

Plainly, this exercise distills the emotional reasons that opposites attract. We are going to show that by making one workshop into a script, which threads throughout the chapter:

Dramatis personae:

MARTY LEVINSON—a lawyer, whose excellent Jewish education and intense ethnic pride are disguised by his offhand, humorously self-deprecating manner of speech. He does not know if he can marry his fiancée, CHRIS JOHNSON, a Presbyterian born in Steubenville, Ohio, if she doesn't convert. She is the only child of a broken family, and wants to share religion with her husband and children, but feels that the Introduction to Judaism course she once took was dull and that Marty is too ambivalent about his Jewishness to make Judaism attractive to her. Recently, she has been attending a Unitarian church because she likes the sense of community it provides. That terrifies Marty, who wants his children to be raised as Jews.

AVIVA WEINER, a children's book editor, is a Hebrew school principal's daughter from St. Louis, who remained a Sabbath observer throughout college. Her parents have said they will never speak to her again if she marries her Episcopalian fiancé, TIM EVANS, an editor and writer. He refuses to convert simply to please Aviva's parents.

BARRY GLASS, a Reform Jew from Buffalo, is a quick-witted, blunt-spoken surgeon who met his wife MARIE on a ski trip to Vail. She is a lapsed Catholic from Providence, Rhode Island, who now works as an interior decorator. He insisted that their two children be raised as Jews, and Marie agreed even though she had no idea of what that meant. Now she feels that her marriage to Barry, whom she adores, has cut her off from her past. Barry thinks that she is sabotaging his efforts to pass on his tradition.

SHEILA STEINER is a Conservative Jew from Brooklyn whose agnostic fiancé, BRAD MARSHFIELD, an affable man, has so little use for organized religion that he can't even understand the terms of the arguments that consume the other couples. Why would Sheila care if they had a Christmas tree? Why would she want him to share in Jewish rituals with her? Brad also resents the exclusiveness he's sensed in many Jews, including Sheila's parents. When Sheila talks about raising their children as Jews, Brad says that he'd be upset since he would feel left out. A self-contained man, Brad rarely talked during the sessions.

At the beginning of the second workshop session, the couples discussed their backgrounds and the reasons they were attracted to each other.

MARTY: When I was a teenager, I went to a Jewish summer camp and I loved it. I still remember my bar mitzvah day as one of the happiest in my life. But then my parents sent me to a Protestant boarding school and I got embarrassed about going to synagogue. I guess that lasted. I like to read about Judaism but I feel ill-at-ease in religious services. I think I have my most intense religious experiences when I'm outdoors.

I love to ski and hike, and I love the outdoors. I never met a Jewish woman who felt the same way. I guess I think they're like my mother's friends—at the country club all the time. I met Chris when I was bird watching, and then we went camping in the Adirondacks together. She seemed tough and competent and supportive. Until then I didn't believe those three qualities went together in a woman.

But I feel very conflicted. Since I was a child I've been obsessed with Israel and the Holocaust. In a way, I see them both as signs of God's personal relationship with the Jews. I want to marry Chris, but I don't want to contribute to the complete assimilation of the Jewish people.

CHRIS: I'd never thought much about Jews as a group before I met Marty, although I knew a few in Steubenville. For some reason, the first time we met I began to tell him about my family. My parents got divorced when I was nine. We didn't belong to a church. We moved around a lot. So I've always felt a little lost in America. When I talked about those things he seemed really warm and interested. I felt close to him. We talked like friends. It was the first relationship I'd had with a man that didn't start out as something coquettish or full of sexual tensions. He seemed to care about me. I wasn't used to men who cared about women that much.

But now that I know Marty better I've gotten a little more wary. I don't see why *my* being in his life means assimilation. I'm not asking him to change. He wants *me* to convert—he's asking me to change. It seems like a double standard.

AVIVA: Half my father's family was killed in the Holocaust and he never seemed to get over it. During the holidays, dinner table conversation was permeated by a grim sense of Jewish nationalism—not by fun or by faith. We always discussed the Holocaust and intermarriage. My Hebrew high school emphasized restrictions: you shouldn't marry anyone who wasn't Jewish, you had to keep kosher, you had to join Hillel when you went to college. I was proud of being Jewish and I loved my parents. But I saw my family's Judaism as a kind of jail.

And what made being Jewish even harder for me was that I always felt pure and virginal because I was the Hebrew school principal's daughter. I love books and poetry and folk music, but I was always afraid that I'd be the "Shirley" that Herman Wouk writes about in *Marjorie Morningstar*, "Shirleys" marry nerdy Jewish accountants or lawyers. They live in Scarsdale with a two-car garage and kids in

Hebrew school. I can see the Shirley in myself. That's why I get so terrified when Tim and I fight. I'm scared he'll leave me and I'll marry a nerd.

TIM: My parents are both Episcopalians who got divorced when I was fifteen. I remember my house as a silent, tense place. Maybe that's why I see non-Jewish women as cold. I like dark women. I think Jewish women are particularly sensual and sexually interesting. I never understand what Aviva's talking about when she calls herself a nerd. But I wish she and her parents would relax and enjoy life instead of trying to bend it to what they'd call their sense of history and I'd call their rigid will.

BARRY: My grandfather was a Talmudic scholar, but my mother was ashamed of it. She and my father joined a Reform temple and always made fun of Orthodox Jews. I was the one who insisted I should have a bar mitzvah. My parents seemed to look down on the Jews who joined Hadassah or the UJA instead of raising money for museums or liberal political candidates. I always thought I should marry a stylish non-Jew, and Marie was perfect for me. She's warm, she understands so many important things about me and she's always sympathetic when I have pressure at work. She has taste, she's not religious, we love the same music and movies and concerts. But I live with a chronic sorrow that she won't understand some of the things that matter most to me because she's not Jewish.

MARIE: I came from a working class Catholic family in Providence. My house was full of crosses and statues of the Virgin Mary. When I was in high school, my friends and I fasted from midnight every Saturday until Communion on Sunday morning. I believed it all back then, but when I went off to study at the Rhode Island School of Design, I lost interest. My parents are both dead now. I haven't been back in church since their funerals.

Look, you all see what a handsome guy Barry is. I fell in love with his black curly hair and his smile and his sense of adventure. It didn't hurt that he had just become a doctor and drove an MG. It seemed as if we'd both work hard and when we were off, our life would be a vacation. I never imagined that anyone would fight over religion. I still don't really understand it. But we fight all the time.

SHEILA: I've never been able to date Jewish men. Maybe it's because I'm a feminist, but I find them arrogant and selfish and uninterested in my needs. I'm haunted by the Holocaust too, but it makes me

feel that if there were anti-Semitism in America a gentile could protect me better than a Jew. Brad's last name is Marshfield. Frankly, I
like the name Sheila Marshfield. It makes me American. But I still feel
very Jewish."

What Are Your Cultural and Religious Assumptions?

The combination of positive and negative stereotypes has helped
draw many couples together. But how can they then work out the
differences they are left with? How can they probe for the cultural
values they seldom discuss but which are the real fuse of the time
bombs in a marriage? As the workshops progress, we ask each group
to do three written exercises that uncover those feelings.

Holiday Seasons

The conflict over Christmas often begins during courtship, and
becomes the central symbol of the tension between Jews and gentiles.
In our workshops, we try to explore that tension—and the conflicts
surrounding Jewish holidays—to unearth people's hidden assumptions about their own and the other's cultures. We ask the couples to
write down the words that come to mind when they think of Christmas and Passover. Then we ask them to discuss the feelings the
exercise elicited.

We choose Christmas and Passover because they are holidays
where religion and family overlap. They summon powerful childhood
memories. We seldom ask about Easter and Yom Kippur because
those holidays are based in houses of worship and derive much of
their meaning from an individual's religious feelings, which many in
the workshops have rejected.

In general, we find that Christmas reminds Jews that America is a
Christian culture. Because the holiday is so highly commercialized,
they feel like exiles in their own country during much of December.
Passover is only important to gentiles when they begin to date Jews.
Many of them enjoy the holiday celebration—that is, if their partner's
family is willing to welcome them. But other gentiles feel like outsid-

ers during the seder. They don't understand the rituals or the Hebrew, and feel hurt if their Jewish partner (who might not know much
about the holiday either) doesn't explain what is going on. Even when
the Jewish family means well, the gentile partner can feel ignorant
during an impassioned argument over Israel or a discussion of Soviet
Jews or a spate of long-standing family jokes that depend on some
Yiddish word, or scrap of Jewish knowledge, for their meaning.

Sometimes the words that come to mind when gentiles think about
Passover are completely happy, homey ones: "My girlfriend, her
family, big dinner, freedom, wine for Elijah." Other times they are
value-free lists of a few familiar items: "seder, unleavened bread,
horseradish, friends."

But often you see the gentile's confusion and loneliness. To one
Protestant seders meant "motion, prayer, meaninglessness"; to another, "separation from my family, newness, shyness, his and hardly
mine."

Still another, who saw Christmas as "fairy tales made real, laughter,
sleigh bells, will there be a new puppy?" said Passover meant "Hebrew, which only a few people know," "feeling removed," "trying to
be part of things (not too successfully)."

Occasionally, gentiles leave a seder feeling as if they will always be
outsiders in a Jewish family. They don't know whom to blame for
their sense of disappointment and rejection. Within days, those feelings can flare into fights.

Nevertheless, the discussions of Christmas are more impassioned
than those about Passover. They usually begin with the specific detail
of the tree, which turns out to be an important psychological symbol.
Often the groups spend a great deal of time arguing about the meaning of the tree itself. Devout Christians and most Jews insist that it has
a religious meaning. Agnostic gentiles see the tree as a secular symbol that evokes a happy family time, an American object whose feeling tone is closer to a Thanksgiving turkey than a cross. Both Jews
and gentiles wonder whether Jews are being neurotically intransigent
when they refuse to have a tree in the house or whether they are
making a principled assertion of religious rights. Is compromise possible?

For some couples it's easy—the Jews seem genuinely fond of
Christmas. The words they use to describe it are "light, love, warmth,
goodwill, brotherhood, presents, joy."

Other couples have a harder time—the Jews are ambivalent. One woman wrote that Christmas meant "trees, singing songs and leaving out religious words, pleasure and guilt, loneliness, conflict, giving, romantic, alienation, shame, wanting to share it with my fiancé but feeling uncomfortable."

Still other Jews want no compromise—they feel a puzzled rage. One man felt so strongly about Christmas that he wrote an essay. He began by saying it was a time of "fun" and "gifts," a time when "Christians are in a good mood—they act more loving, the way they should all the time." Then his wounded feelings took over: he had a "heightened feeling of being an outsider," and felt the season was "oppressive—it's everywhere. So much Jesus! Christmas was a crisis for me as a child. I wanted so much to be a part of it. I felt guilty for feeling that way and finally decided it couldn't be something for me. It was a time of very great pressure."

A Jewish woman used one word. While Passover meant "tradition, leadership, strength of character, passage of time, spiritual bonding," Christmas meant only "outside."

At first the discussion is essentially an argument over the definition of a tree. Does it symbolize the birth of Jesus or is it a happy childhood memory? Then it becomes an argument over power. On a personal level, the debate over the tree can be a weapon in a marital skirmish: a way of establishing whose will is dominant. On a sociological level, it becomes a way for some Jews to explain the sense of oppression they have always felt in America—and for some gentiles to pinpoint what they think is narrow-minded rigidity among Jews. Often we intervene to point out that there are theological issues at stake as well.

The next act of the "workshop drama" shows how discussions of Christmas and Passover can lead to argument, insight, and greater understanding. Marty and Chris, Aviva and Tim, Barry and Marie, and Sheila and Brad began to talk about the holidays.

MARTY: I see Christmas as a Christian holiday I don't relate to. I don't find having Christmas trees acceptable in my home, but I kind of like to see them elsewhere. They bring back pleasant memories of celebrating Christmas in school and they make me think a lot about Jesus in history. I wonder who he was historically. What was the fight between Jews and Christians really about?

CHRIS: (reading her list of words about Christmas): Pine trees, smell, warmth, food, gifts, feeling cozy, feeling stuffed, sitting on floor, being warm when it's cold outside. It was the one holiday in the year when I really liked my family. I can't get Marty to understand what that meant to me.

AVIVA: When I began to date Tim, I insisted that we'd never have a tree in our house. So we go to his family's house. I feel uncomfortable there. I always get gifts from his family. I never got one I liked. I still feel strange when they wish me a Merry Christmas. I freak out when we go to midnight Mass. We always have a terrible argument when we come back home.

TIM: For me, Christmas is presents, waking up early, choir, snow, my grandmother, my family gathering and trimming the tree. I feel like Chris does. It's not a religious holiday for me, but it was the one time of year my family was happy. I can't make Aviva see that I identify Christmas with good feelings, not with God. I don't get to say whether we light Hanukkah candles at home—Aviva *insists* on doing that—but she begins to cry if I talk about bringing a Christmas tree into the apartment. That really makes me mad.

BARRY: I'm like Aviva. Christmas is not my holiday. From childhood on I knew that Santa Claus would never visit me because I'm Jewish. I look at Christmas trees and I feel there is something foreign about them.

MARIE: Barry's feeling is unacceptable to me. My parents are dead, and I'd like to visit my brothers and sisters. But Barry won't take our son and daughter to visit them on Christmas Day. There's nowhere I can go to celebrate Christmas. But I need it to bring back my youth. It's not enough to trim the neighbor's tree or see everyone on the street being happy. I need to experience the holiday. I want my kids to know the warmth I felt as a child.

I don't feel warmth at Passover. I do it and it's fine but I don't feel any warmth. I haven't converted, but everything we have in our house is Jewish. All our family holidays are with Barry's family. I feel deprived.

BARRY: I know how Marie feels. We always fight in December. I dread Christmas. Now we go on vacations to avoid dealing with the tree.

CHRIS: All the Jews are saying they can't celebrate Christmas. Is it the corollary that Christians can't celebrate Passover?

BARRY: I just can't see Christmas as a non-religious holiday. Besides, it's not part of me.

CHRIS: That's what I mean. Passover is clearly not part of me but I go to Marty's parents' house and I struggle. I'm even getting to like it and feel accepted. Two years ago a friend of Marty's was translating the Hebrew for me. That made me feel self-conscious and different. But last year I could read a little Hebrew and I felt better. At seders, that sort of thing is important because a gentile who wants to get something out of the night has to put in a lot of work. Is there any way a Jew can do that at Christmas?

MARTY: It's not equivalent. Chris, there's something you don't understand. The Christmas tree really does symbolize a Christian household. You look in the window and see this *monstrous* tree and lights. You see all those lights blinking on and you know what kind of home it is. That's not so bad if you want to live in a Christian home. But even though I'm willing to visit your parents at Christmastime, I can't have a Christian home myself. I feel as if I'd be betraying my past. I know you think I want to have my cake and eat it, too, but I don't know what else to do.

MARIE: In the couples here there are *two* entities, a Jew *and* a non-Jew. Who says we have to have Jewish homes? Why should it all go to one side? Why are we talking about a Jewish home unless one party has agreed to convert? Nobody here has decided to do that.

Barry always says I promised to raise our kids as Jews, and that's true. But I also insisted that I wanted them to know about my heritage, too. Without a tree, there is nothing of my heritage in the house. I feel invisible in my own family.

TIM (encouraged by Marie): We've never had a tree, and we have always gone to my mother's house. But I don't have the feeling of give and take. That's what makes me angry. That's when I feel we should break up instead of going around and around in the same fight over this one issue.

CHRIS: I have the feeling that ultimately if Marty and I are going to work out as a couple I'm going to have to give up things that are important to me. That makes me pretty sad.

It seems that when you're with a Jewish partner, these things aren't really negotiable. You can talk about it, you can live with different things for fifteen years, but eventually you'll have to give them up. I'm sure I'll give up my tree. That bothers me. It seems based on the premise that Jews have been oppressed throughout history. In order to make up for that the Jewish family has to be strong. So whoever gets connected with a Jewish person has to give up things they love.

SHEILA (who'd been silent for much of the session): That isn't always true. I've accepted the idea that as long as I'm with Brad, I'm going to have to give in on Christmas. We're going to celebrate it. I feel as if I'm giving up something. I used to *love* being a Jew on Christmas. I'd have the day off and go skiing or do something that had no relationship to Christmas. It was sort of a rebellious feeling: Here I am in a Christian society and I don't have to have anything to do with Christmas. Now, if we have the tree in our home, I'll feel it as an alien presence. If we have children I don't know what I'll say to them about it. So far it's pretty theoretical and it doesn't seem like the worst obstacle to love. But it's not *nothing*.

CHRIS: I'm feeling very upset. How far do you have to go if you marry a Jew? How deprived have Jews been? How many compromises does that mean I'm going to have to make? I'm not really talking about Christmas trees even though I'm scared that Marty will never let me have one. They don't even matter to me for now. I'd rather go home to Steubenville for the holidays than stay in New York. But what about things that *are* important to me? How can Marty and I make compromises on subjects that are so emotional? They're emotional for everyone here. Just listen to the strength of the feelings that are coming out in this discussion. All the Jewish people here seem so threatened by Christmas. It's as if trees are going to fall on their heads or Santa Claus is going to race over them in sleighs.

I have not heard any of the Jews talk about the oppression they have faced, and yet that's the basis for asking all of the gentiles here to give so much up.

MARTY: Oppressed? I don't think that's the right word. I think Jews have a sense of history. Maybe we look at history too much. But when I think about Christmas I don't see a tree in America. I see it in an historical context. I can see a period when Jews were oppressed and I can see a period when we were a kingdom. I can see the Holocaust and I can see Israel. It's a complicated history and I have a complicated reaction to it. Even though I'm marrying you I don't want to forget any of it. I realize that it's putting us both in a difficult situation, but I can't react any other way.

SHEILA: Chris, we Jews have a lot to lose. We're marrying Chris-

tians, but we all seem to feel that if we don't keep the faith somehow
we're going to lose this link that's been going on for thousands of
years. I don't feel oppressed, but I hate the idea of losing that link. It's
like a light going out. I think that's why we ask for so much. That's my
problem. I'm going to marry Brad, who has no use for Judaism at all,
and I'm going to raise kids who celebrate Christmas. But you know
what? That's going to make me put more energy into other Jewish
things, like Passover and the Holy Days. I can't bear to be the last link
in the chain."

The Cross

Virtually every Jew who comes to our workshops describes a
Thanksgiving, Christmas, or Easter visit to a partner's family which
included a disconcerting hour or two in church. Even gentiles who
consider themselves agnostics are surprised at the depths of the Jews'
feelings. Those who are religious Christians feel very hurt. Why
should a Jew feel repelled in a place that seems so benign?

Jews often react strongly to the cross. They seldom know there is a
difference between a Protestant cross and a Catholic crucifix (a cross
with the figure of a crucified Jesus on it)—a distinction which almost
all gentiles take for granted.

This gap illustrates the asymmetry between Judaism and Christianity. It is hard for Christians or even agnostic gentiles to find an
analogy that helps them understand how Jews feel, since there is no
object in synagogue (or in the Jewish religion) that fills Catholics or
Protestants with the feelings that consume most Jews when they see
the cross. They have no idea how fresh in the memories of most Jews
is Christian anti-Semitism.

So we ask couples to write down the first words that come to mind
when they think of the cross. Jews and gentiles alike are often shocked
by the differences this exercise reveals.

Here are some words and phrases gentiles have written down. It's
important to realize that even Catholics and Protestants who resent
their religious educations, or who never had one and have always
been agnostics, perceive the cross as a legitimate religious symbol.

They might have ceased to believe in its meaning, but it's still part of their ancestral legacy.

Some reverent responses: "Christ, crucifixion, salvation"; or "Sacrifice, beauty, selfless love, salvation, reverence, nails, pain, gray skies, a hill at Calvary, sorrow, weeping, thunderbolts"; or "Christ died for us, death—pain, guilt of sin, sacrifice and pride."

Some agnostics speak: "I don't believe Jesus was the Messiah, and I feel hypocritical kneeling in front of the cross. But when I see a crucifix in church I look at the face, the blood, the thorns, how thin he looks, the ribs. Ouch—it seems incredibly painful." Another sees the cross as a "symbol of the Church—animate representation of concepts that are intangible in history. Makes one think of what one was taught the cross represents." A third notes, "On a 'religious' level, I don't feel much. It was never a big thing in my church. We were taught that Christ carried the cross and died on it to salve our sins. But nobody kneels in my church. Nobody gives the sign of the cross. So it does not carry positive or negative feelings for me."

Here are some of the words, phrases, and sentences Jews have written down. The most benign Jewish responses are more troubled than the harshest gentile ones:

"Christ, Catholic Mass, fear and guilt if asked to kneel before it"; and, "Plus sign, crucifix, symbol of Christianity, piety, phony piety"; or, "Sacrifice, forgiveness, repentance, adulation, idolatry, mythology, forgiveness."

"A *specific* image of God. Mysticism. Makes me feel little and scared."

"Uncomfortable, negative because it symbolizes dying for sins. Sinning is a negative aspect of religion."

"Unattractive, gory symbol for a religion. Seems so negative, focusing on pain, sacrifice, suffering."

"I feel that the cross has almost a mystical power. It seems to make people accept what they are told rather than question or think logically and rationally."

"A 'flagrant' showing of Christianity, a statement of Christianity as a powerful religion, not a set of 'principles.' Ku Klux Klan. Cross burning."

And, angriest of all was the comment of a Jewish man whose lapsed Catholic wife was about to have a baby:

"HARSH, STAY BACK—AS IN DEVIL (the sign is used to ward off

vampires), like a dagger killing." Then, on the right side of the page, this person drew a cross with a point for a tip—a cross that looked like a dagger, with three drops of blood dripping off it.

The discussion that follows this exercise can be even more pained than the Christmas-Passover session. In one of our largest, most polarized groups almost all the gentiles perceived the Jews' responses as another sign of their clannishness. "You seem to me like a wall of people," said a New York-born Catholic who was married to a Jew from Philadelphia. "When I'm around Jews, I feel like a persecuted minority." "I was just amazed at all the hostility," said a woman from rural Pennsylvania who was raised as a Mennonite but now describes herself as an agnostic. "None of the Jews here seem able to tolerate religious differences." Her husband, who was born into a very prosperous, very assimilated Jewish family, agreed. "I'm not used to Jews victimizing other people."

It wasn't victimization. The exercise had unleashed a powerful tribal memory. But the words Jews used to describe the cross enraged most Christians. "I've been married to you for three years and I didn't realize you had such disrespectful feelings about my religion," a Methodist woman said to her Jewish husband. An Irish-Catholic woman whose wide smile disguised her obvious anger looked at the blackboard where we had written the words and said, "reverent is the only positive one I see." Then she turned to her husband. "I've always wondered why you don't kneel when you come to church with me, but you've never explained the reason. Now that I understand it I don't know what to do about our differences."

There were gentiles who understood how Jews felt. "You have to realize that we Christians can go anywhere in America wearing a cross," said the Protestant from Minnesota. "No one would talk to a Jew who wore a yarmulke in my hometown. Someone might even beat him up."

"Besides," added a lapsed Catholic from California, "I went to parochial school and when I see the cross I don't hate it but I see how a Jew would fear it."

"I don't care," said a man whose uncle was a priest. "It's horrible to hear those feelings about my religion. It's as if every Jew in this room only sees stereotypes like the Ku Klux Klan when they look at the cross." Then, turning to his fiancée, a medical student from Long

Island, he said, "You're always complaining that Christians don't know *your* history. This is a sign that you don't know *ours.*"

It was a perilous moment for a lot of relationships. The Jews tried to explain their reactions. "I'm acting out of my history," said one. "It's as if I had an ancestral memory of the Crusades."

"I'm the person who wrote down Ku Klux Klan," said a woman from Long Island. "All I could see was cross burnings in the South. I didn't mean to offend anyone here, but that's what the word brought into my mind."

"And I'm really afraid of evangelical Christians, and it makes me mad that they're always trying to convert us. Why can't they just respect us for who we are?" said the medical student. "I know you're more generous than I am," she said, touching her fiancé's hand. "You wear a yarmulke in my synagogue and I can't kneel in your church. But I really can't. All I hear is those voices on the radio, telling me that I'm a non-believer and I'll go to hell."

"Listen, none of the Jews here are acting out of a fantasy," said a banker who had been born into a left-wing family. "Jews have been persecuted for centuries by people who carried crosses." Then he looked at the gentiles in the room, one after the other, and said, "Maybe we have to know your history. But you still have a lot to learn about ours."

That session ended with the recognition that most of the Jews and most of the gentiles in the room were as ignorant about each other's ancestral backgrounds—and each other's theologies—as they were unaware of each other's feelings. Some would remain that way. There were eleven couples in that workshop, and after it was over, three of them broke up. But most loved each other too much to let the wounds that were opened remain unhealed. During the next two weeks, they asked us for reading lists. For them, the traumatic exercise had inspired an energetic effort to learn each other's religious languages.

What Will Your Family's Spiritual Life Be?

When a couple finds the language that defines differences they've never before articulated, they still have to focus on the decisions

they'll make in the future. That is very hard for any couple. So we ask
them to do an exercise in which they leap forward in time.

We ask them first to write down for themselves, then to discuss with
the group, the answers to several questions. If they're not married, do
they want a rabbi, a minister, or a judge to perform the ceremony?
If they haven't had children, what sort of birthing ceremony do
they plan to arrange? Will the baby be baptized or christened, or will
he have a brit or will she have a baby-naming ceremony in synagogue? How will the gentile feel at a brit? How will the Jew feel at a
baptism? How will they feel if they decide to stay away from religion
altogether?

Does raising a child as a Jew or a Christian involve more than
visiting parents or relatives for the major holidays? If so, what does it
involve? Study at home? A more formal religious education? If so,
where? At a church or at a synagogue? If that decision is made, will
both parents participate in it? And what kind of coming of age does
each parent envisage? A bar mitzvah? A confirmation in church?

Suppose they chose not to give the children a religious education.
How will they feel at secular moments that resonate with ethnic
overtones? How will the Jewish parent feel if the child, watching a
film on the Holocaust, refers to Jews as "those people," not "our
people"? What if the child brings home an anti-Semitic joke from
school without quite realizing that it refers to her? How will the
Christian parent feel if the child chooses to identify with Jewish history, as a Jew? How will the parents react if a child asks to go to
religious school with a friend?

How do couples want their children to feel at holiday times? What
do they want to communicate to their spouses and offspring about a
transcendant force in the universe? About life after death? What
heritage do they want their children to pass on to their grandchildren?

Finally, we ask them to take the most difficult psychological step a
person can—to imagine death: their partner's, their own. Have they
discussed their feelings about the Jewish tradition of shiva—mourning for seven days after a person is buried—or about Catholic wakes,
Protestant funerals? Where can they be buried together? Do they
want somebody to say kaddish for them, or to pray for them on All
Souls' Day? Who will do that?

Obviously, some of these subjects are easier to discuss than others, some are more urgent than others. These discussions can become very passionate.

Here is another episode from the workshop drama. During the past week, Barry and Marie had been arguing bitterly about her indifference to Judaism. Did it mean she was indifferent to him? Tim felt more rage than ever that Aviva's parents demanded he convert, and would refuse to see him until he agreed to do so. Aviva, caught in the middle, felt that she'd have to sacrifice her Jewish self—the source of her pride—or the gentile man who made her feel like a sensual, lively woman. Marty and Chris never argued at such a high-pitched scale, but Chris was quietly seething at what she regarded as Marty's ambivalence and insensitivity, and Marty, who usually masked his feelings with jokes, was inwardly very tense about Chris's involvement in the Unitarian Church. Sheila hadn't yet convinced Brad that he should take her worries seriously.

Barry and Marie had children. The other three couples were still wondering whether—and how—to get married. They were all amazed that the issue of religion had become so important to them.

CHRIS: When I was growing up in Steubenville, it never occurred to me that religion would become an issue when I got married. I just wasn't prepared for the conflicts Marty and I have had or that I've heard about here. I knew that it mattered to other generations, but not to mine. But it does make sense as something to struggle with. It's not as if Marty and I don't like the same art and decided to go to different museums. It raises fundamental questions about who we are and how we raise our children. I have to hand it to Marty. He saw those problems before I did. He made me see the importance of taking the conversion class.

That class made me realize that I wanted to believe in something that was bigger than myself and to share it with my family. I want Marty and me to have a sense of wholeness: to be part of a community, not out on some fringe.

When I began the conversion class, I assumed that I would become a Jew. I couldn't figure out why I was getting so angry. Then I realized that I felt caught in a web of pressure. Even though they didn't say anything, I felt like Marty and his family were hovering over me, waiting for the day I'd say I'll convert. They expected me to feel at home in a Jewish cultural milieu, and were hurt when I said I still felt like an outsider. But I did. I do. It's a long way from Steubenville to synagogue—or even a Woody Allen movie, or this Y. I haven't rejected Judaism. I'm just waiting to see if I'm more at home with the religion and with the people. I hope that Judaism will make me feel as satisfied and optimistic as the Unitarian Church does.

And, Marty, even though you say you don't like Unitarianism you haven't helped me be a Jew. Last Rosh Hashanah, just after I finished the class, I fully expected we'd go to synagogue together. You even took the day off from work and went to temple yourself. But you went without me.

MARTY: I thought it would be hot and crowded and that you would be bored. I didn't want a Jewish ceremony to turn you off.

CHRIS: You told me that, but it made me mad. It was as if you had all the information about Judaism and you were going to keep it to yourself. You were going to define what I would like and what I wouldn't like, as if I were a child. But I'd just taken the conversion class. I knew about Rosh Hashanah. If you didn't think I'd like going to services at one of the holiest days of the Jewish year, then why should I convert? I still haven't figured out whether you're more ambivalent about Judaism than you've let on, or whether you want to be an insider in a world that rejects your shiksa wife. Maybe you think that if I become a Jew, you'll be less special.

BARRY: Well, I know that Marie wants to be an outsider in my Jewish world. That's what she said last week and it really upset me.

My mother lives in New York now and she's very sick. On Friday night I went to the hospital to visit her and then I went to services at temple. Marie offered to go with me and normally I would have thought it was very nice. But, after last week's session, I felt differently. I said, if you have mixed feelings about Judaism, and all this seems hokey to you, why come along? She went—she really wanted me to feel less depressed about my mother—but I had trouble paying attention at services when I realized that the person sitting next to me thought it was a bunch of baloney.

MARIE: Look, Barry, you're being dishonest. You knew who I was when we got married. You knew that I was born a Catholic, and I don't go to church because I don't like religion. When we got married I said I'd help you raise the kids as Jews but I wouldn't become a Jew, and I wouldn't like it if the kids were separated from me by something as formal as a conversion. How could I have known how serious the choice was and how much conversion meant? I know about Catholicism. Where I come from, the church converts people all the time. Priests are much more open to newcomers than rabbis are.

You knew the rules. I didn't. If you didn't want to do it my way you shouldn't have married me. But that's all in the past. Why should I lie to you now and say that I feel Jewish? You don't just want me to go to synagogue. You want me to convert. Suppose I did? I wouldn't be any more Jewish than I am now. Not emotionally. It would be a joke. It is anyway. It's a joke on us for getting into this position.

CHRIS: Marie, I don't have your strong feelings. Actually, they scare me because I don't want to fight with Marty the way you're fighting with Barry. I want us to be unified about religion *and* I want to be true to myself.

But I don't even know what to do about a wedding. Where should we get married? I checked out City Hall the other day, but it seems too bureaucratic and sleazy for our wedding. I'd like a Unitarian minister and a rabbi to perform the service, but Marty is against that . . .

MARTY: I don't want my parents to see me married by a Christian.

CHRIS: Well, that's our sticking point. Every time I come up with a solution that makes sense to me, Marty says it will hurt him or someone close to him.

AVIVA: I have terrible trouble thinking about our wedding, too. When I was a girl, I used to go to Orthodox weddings with my father. His Hebrew school students would invite him. I loved them. They were some of the happiest times of my childhood. There was such energy in all the singing and the dancing. If I marry Tim, my family won't come. I feel like that old Groucho Marx joke. I wouldn't want to be married by a rabbi who would marry me.

CHRIS: Marty said the same thing and I felt offended. It was like he was saying any rabbi who'd marry us would be like a doctor who performed an illegal abortion.

AVIVA: Well, my point isn't really about the character of the rabbi. I'm not saying the rabbi would be sleazy. I'm just saying that the ceremony would be kind of wan. I'd rather be married by a justice of the peace than have a watered-down Jewish wedding.

SHEILA: When Brad and I first got engaged, I went to a woman rabbi to see if she would marry us. She said she doesn't conduct intermarriages because when you conduct a Jewish wedding you ask the couple to abide by the laws of Moses and the Jewish people. How can a non-Jew say yes? Brad certainly couldn't.

I agreed with her. But I cried because it felt like such a terrible rejection.

MARIE: Barry wanted a Jewish wedding so we found a rabbi. It didn't make any sense to me. In a way, I felt I was never really married. At least, I always pictured my wedding in a church. I just didn't know any of the Jewish traditions.

But I found the brit of our son David much harder. I'd never even heard of a brit before and I didn't really know what it meant until the guests came and the man who performed it got out his scissors and put the baby down on a white cloth. It was terrible. I couldn't believe that someone was cutting off a part of my son's flesh and all the Jews were making a party. It seemed barbaric.

SHEILA: I think I'd feel the same way. I went to a brit last year and I really felt for the baby. Maybe this isn't a difference between Jews and gentiles. Maybe it's a difference between women and men.

BARRY: It *is* a very primitive ritual, but I got completely caught up in it. I saw my son David entering into the covenant. I saw myself making a commitment. It was difficult to watch what was happening to him, but I loved feeling part of the oldest Jewish ceremony there is. It was one of the most important religious experiences of my life.

TIM: had been quiet throughout the session, but one could see anger dart across his well-sculpted face when Aviva expressed contempt and disappointment for the secular wedding they would have. Now he seized on the brit to express his feelings: "In my experience with Aviva, everything about Judaism is backwards. When you marry a Jew you're supposed to convert right away instead of growing into it gradually, which is the normal way of developing. When a boy is born he has to go through a ceremony that symbolizes he'll be a Jewish man. He doesn't do it. It's done to him. I think he should be able to grow into his Jewish manhood.

AVIVA: Tim, you know I agree with you about conversion, but I think what you say about a brit is crazy. You're being glib and trivializing a ceremony just because you're angry at my parents and me. I suppose the brit is pagan in its origins, but it has become a family's way of saying that a child will be raised in a Jewish home. For myself I feel the same way about it as I do about a Jewish wedding. It's sort of silly to marry someone who isn't Jewish and then say my child is going to be Jewish and have a brit. I love you and I'd rather marry you than sacrifice you for a set of ceremonies. But those ceremonies have a lot of meaning for me. That's why I feel so sad.

SHEILA: At least you can talk about this openly. If Brad and I have children I want to raise them as Jews, but how can I do that when Brad won't support me? Whenever I say I want them to have a Jewish education he gets furious. He says he doesn't want to feel like an outsider in his own family.

TIM: Sheila, if Brad doesn't want Jewish children why should he agree to give them a Jewish education? In this workshop, there's not a single Jew who is emotionally prepared to work out a fifty-fifty split with their partner. Aviva wants a Jewish wedding, but won't accept a Reform rabbi. Barry, you won't let Marie have a Christmas tree even though it's the only form of contact she has with her past. Marty, you want Chris to convert but you won't even take her to synagogue with you. Aviva's parents won't come to our wedding unless I decide to become a Jew.

At my worst moments, I look around at all of you and I think who *are* these people with their *ceaseless* list of demands? They're taking advantage of my good nature. I don't want my children to be the battleground for these fights.

MARIE: But, Tim, your children will be. David has already said to me, "Daddy is Jewish and I'm Jewish, and you're not. Why aren't you?"

I'll tell you the truth. I sound angry, but I'm also very frightened and confused. I love Barry very much, but I can't understand why being Jewish is so important to him. You know why I was reluctant to go to synagogue last Friday? Because if Barry gets in the habit of going with David and our baby daughter Jessica, I'll feel left out, just like Brad. One of the Jewish children in David's preschool class told him that his family made the *ha motzi*—blessed the bread—every Friday night. I didn't even know what the *ha motzi* was. I'm afraid that if David does things like that I'll lose him.

BARRY: I'm going to tell you a brutal truth. It makes me feel good that David wants to make the *ha motzi*. I want him to think of himself as a Jew and when he grows up I want him to feel a communality with other Jews. The terrible thing is that he'll have to reject part of Marie to do that.

MARIE: But, Barry, you don't see that the joke is on you—and, in a cruel way, on him. He hasn't converted. Half of the Jewish world won't even think of him as Jewish, because I'm not Jewish.

BARRY: But he'll think of himself as a Jew. Then he'll convert.

SHEILA: This is so silly. Barry, I should have married you . . . but I couldn't have. I've always had gentile boyfriends. I'm always going on personal campaigns to date Jewish men, but when I do I can feel all my anger rising. It's as if they mirror the worst parts of myself. But I still want Jewish children . . .

According to Jewish law, my kids will be legally Jewish, but they won't think of themselves as being Jewish. Or maybe they'll be like the daughter of a friend of mine, who said, "Mommy, I know you want me to be Jewish but I'm really half Christian because I am half of Daddy, too." I have a hard time facing the possibility that my children will say that.

But all week I've been trying to think of the reasons I would like Brad to convert. They all have to do with Jewish survival. I really love being Jewish, but I can't explain my feelings in a way that makes them sound like more than habit.

CHRIS: I can't tell how much of this workshop is about religion and how much is about power in marriage. Barry, are you really saying that you want your kids to be like you, or that you want them to be Jews? Tim, when you ask "Who are these people with their ceaseless list of demands" are you listening to the concessions Aviva's already made, or trying to take her away from her family completely? I don't know what Marty and I are really saying to each other when we argue about Christmas trees or my conversion, or why Brad resists the very small things Sheila asks for.

But I do know that, in our relationship, no other subject can make us get so emotional. Even if we use religion as a power trip we're talking about something real. So what I'm taking away from this discussion is that it's hard for an interfaith couple to disagree about conversion or a Jewish education without fighting. And it's hard to raise children in one religion without the other partner feeling like an outsider.

But you have to feel good about yourself to give the argument much meaning. Marty, Barry feels good about being Jewish. You don't seem to feel that way. I'm not like Marie or Brad. I'm open to conversion. But why should I be a Jew when you're not even proud enough of your faith to take me to temple on one of the holiest days of the year? Marty, you want to transmit something to our kids that you don't really want for me or for yourself. That's not a very convincing argument. If you want me to convert you're going to have to do better than that.

Religion: I Felt As If I Was Moving History Forward

The early workshop sessions usually enable couples to articulate their differences. Then, we encourage them to remember their own happy religious experiences so that they can think constructively about building a spiritual future together. We ask them to recall the positive experiences they would like to recapture and transmit, and to think of how they could do that.

Sometimes they focus on memories of moments when they felt special—on the bar mitzvah day, the First Communion, the confirmation, when the small universe of their family and friends seemed to revolve around them.

Barry recalled his bar mitzvah. "My parents had made a conscious effort to shut us off from my grandparents' Orthodox way of life. But when I was twelve I wanted to have a bar mitzvah. So I asked my mother to find a Hebrew teacher. She seemed to feel that I was wasting her time and her money.

"But I'll never forget standing at the altar on my bar mitzvah day. I was able to recite some of the Torah portion as well as the haftarah, [reading from the prophets]. I looked down at my mother when I was finished and she was crying. That day, I felt as if I had made a Jew out of her. I felt as if I was moving history forward. I would love my son and daughter to feel the same way."

Tim, who had felt estranged from his family as a teenager, recalled the quality of his childhood Sunday mornings when his parents would awaken him and his three siblings, fix them pancakes and bacon for breakfast, then pile them into a car and take them to a nearby Episcopalian church. He sang in the choir, which made him feel special. But he particularly loved the rhythm of Sunday lunch, when his grandparents, aunts, and cousins would come over to the house for the huge meal his mother would cook. "Those meals embodied everything I rejected later on. Nobody talked about anything but the weather, football, and dull details of work. But when I was a boy I loved the hum of all that small talk.

"I think of that feeling as spiritual. It was inside me, not embodied in any religious ritual. I don't know how to recapture it or transmit it."

"Religion," said Aviva, "was as much a part of my life as having meals or getting dressed. On Friday night we lit candles and had chicken. I knew that on Saturday my father and brother would go to synagogue while my mother and I would set the table and talk. At twelve-thirty, we'd have a big meal and take a nap and then go for a walk. Those Shabbats never had the spiritual qualities Tim is looking for. When I was a teenager they felt confining. But when I was a girl they were a symbol of safety. That's what I want for my kids."

Although Marie renounced her Catholicism long before she met Barry, she talked about her childhood holidays with great nostalgia.

During the week before Easter, her mother, who came from a Polish-Catholic family, would use wax and dyes to make intricately colored Easter eggs. On Good Friday, Marie, her mother, and all their friends would go to church. They fasted between noon and three. When they got home, her mother would make a special sausage and braided bread and put them in an Easter basket. She and Marie would take the food and the eggs to be blessed by the priest on the midnight before Easter. Then they'd come home and join all their cousins in a special Easter eve meal.

"I've forgotten how to dye the eggs and cook the sausage. My mother died before I was curious enough to ask her how to do it. I'd love to pass the tradition on, but Barry would never let me do those things with our kids. Anyway, without church the tradition is a little hollow and I have no desire to take our children to church. I guess it's a happy memory that's just gone."

Sheila's sorrow pierced her reminiscence. "My family wasn't very religious or very close. We never observed Shabbat or went to synagogue on the holidays. But on Passover I used to help my mother and grandmother polish the plates. Each plate had a story. My grandmother knew them all. My mother knew some of them. I didn't know any of them. I guess if I marry Brad there won't be much reason to learn. Unless I'm able to imbue my children with a strong sense of Jewish tradition, the stories won't make much sense to them."

In all of our workshops, these memories seemed to intensify the desire of each couple to resolve their conflicts. For religion and ethnic identity no longer represented an ill-defined source of marital tension. Rather, it seemed to promise something firm and stable that had almost been swallowed up in the all-consuming cosmopolitan present. People could not re-create the specific religious and ethnic experiences they had loved back home. But wasn't there still a way to give their offspring spiritual stability?

By the last session of the workshop, most couples have begun to understand their attraction to one another—and to their own ethnic pasts—well enough to start resolving that question. We've kept in touch with many of them, and seen that many take further steps. Some take classes. Some find welcoming synagogues. A few find churches.

People in some groups stay involved with each other. They are able to provide one another with the emotional support and the rudiments of a religious community that had been lacking in their lives.

Some Resolutions

There are no guaranteed outcomes from the workshops. But we have noticed some clear patterns. After almost every workshop, one or two people convert to Judaism. Usually, several couples decide to raise their children as Jews but postpone the question of conversion. Others decide that the steps necessary to resolve their dilemma would threaten their marriage: they make a conscious decision to give their marriage priority over religion. Occasionally, the Jew decides to acquiesce to a partner's desire to raise Christian children. Sometimes religious Jews and religious Christians decide they'll maintain a two-faith home in spite of the risks involved.

Almost invariably, some of the couples break up. Some decide that religion was a smokescreen, a way of keeping distance from one another and ignoring the real problems in their relationships. Others separate because they can't resolve their religious differences. When that happens, the Jew often gets more involved in Judaism, the Christian in some form of Christianity. But, over six years, we've seen several couples in which the gentile who breaks up with the Jew still decides to become a Jew. No Jews in our workshops have decided to become Christians.

The workshop with Marty and Chris and Tim and Aviva provided a stable context for an array of solutions. For they formed one of the groups that decided to deal with the tensions they shared by continuing to meet. Sometimes they discussed their problems. Sometimes they celebrated Hanukkah or Passover together. They attended each other's weddings and their children's birthing ceremonies. Sometimes they forgot about religion and just went out to the movies or shared a Chinese meal. They continued to give each other emotional support even though each of the couples found a different resolution to their problems.

Marty and Chris began serious negotiations in the month after the workshop ended. Then, Marty decided to take the issue of the wedding in hand. He found a rabbi he trusted who was willing to perform the ceremony and welcome Chris into his synagogue.

Marty had been listening very carefully to the discussion of the December dilemma. After he and Chris were married he suggested that they invite her mother to New York at Christmas. They would have a tree and he would help her decorate it. Chris heard his offer as an eloquent statement that he cared more about her feelings than an abstract principle. It helped her feel that he really loved her. That was a filament of the emotional bond she needed in order to think seriously about converting.

Marty hadn't yet gotten over his discomfort in synagogue. In that respect, he wasn't much of a religious inspiration. But Chris, who felt that her family would only be complete if they shared a religious life, knew that someday he might regain the enthusiasm he had for Judaism when he was a teenager and that he would never share her interest in the Unitarian Church. Now that she trusted him, she felt that she could take one step along his path.

When she became pregnant she agreed to convert the baby to Judaism. She also decided to attend a class called "Having a Jewish Baby" at a synagogue near their apartment, and discovered that the women—who knew she wasn't Jewish—accepted her completely.

These women displayed an eagerness to raise their children as Jews which provided some of the inspiration Chris had wanted to get from Marty. As she attended the classes she realized that she wanted to be a member of a community like theirs that took such pleasure in the

Sabbath and the holidays and in each other's presence. So, before the baby was born, *she* decided to convert. The baby was a boy, and she and Marty both looked shaken but happy at the brit. Tim and Aviva and Sheila and Brad were there, and the excitement of the ceremony helped counteract the image left by Marie's bitter tale of her son's brit.

Marty still doesn't like to spend more than a few hours in synagogue, even on the High Holy Days, and that worries Chris a little. For even though she's now legally Jewish, the spiritual transition is slow. But there is a tender, caressing quality in their marriage that was absent during the workshop. It suggests that one day, Chris and Marty will look back on the Christmas tree they once fought over as a transitional object that allowed them to gain the mutual respect they needed to enrich their spiritual life. For all of Chris's baffled anger and Marty's ambivalence, they are now sharing the journey they both wanted to make.

During the last session of the workshop, Tim and Aviva had a dialogue that proved prophetic. It began when Aviva added one of her sad teenage memories of Jewish rituals to her happier childhood ones. She came from the kind of observant family that started cleaning the house for Passover right after Purim. But one year, at the seder table, "my father announced that he didn't believe in divine revelation. We were all taken aback. From then on, Passover seemed to be about Jews and history and oppression. We kept all the laws, but it became a nationalist holiday, not a religious one. That was what Judaism was to us."

She used that memory to describe the complex attitudes she had developed about ethnicity and religion since she fell in love with Tim. "Of course, I want to marry him. It would be crazy to give him up. But there are times I feel like I can't go through with the wedding. It's hard to articulate why. Sometimes it's the Holocaust—the 6 million— the idea that we're all that is left. How can I break the chain?"

But then, the Hebrew school principal's daughter, who surely knows more about Judaism than 90 percent of the Jews in her generation, began to sound bewildered. "I feel that in some ways I'm struggling with religious questions now more than I ever have before. I have to because of Tim. He's looking for some sense of spiritual meaning in Judaism. I was never given that. My commitment is to Jews as an extended family. Like it or not, it's part of my skin."

Tim was trying to come to terms with that feeling. "I want to find some sort of archetype, some sort of spiritual image, that Aviva and I can hook into," he said. "But I feel like Aviva doesn't understand what it means to convert. She wants to satisfy her ethnic feelings, and I have to figure out a spiritual-religious way to do the same thing. We're not exactly talking the same language."

They continued to live together for nearly two years after the workshop. It was an eventful time. First, Aviva's parents agreed that they would attend the wedding even if Tim didn't convert. That frightened Tim. Since his parents were divorced and his siblings were scattered he worried that he would be swallowed up by Aviva's family. As a result, he kept insisting that he wanted to search for his Protestant roots. But at the same time he was taking an intense class in Judaism where he discovered, to his surprise, that he was attracted by the religion. He began to edit an article by a Hassidic Jew, and felt a surge of enthusiasm when he visited the writer at home. So, sometimes, he toyed with the idea of becoming an observant Jew.

Paradoxically, that terrified Aviva, who wanted the Orthodox wedding she had dreamed of, but still feared that a kosher home, Sabbath observance, and Hebrew school for her children would make her into a Shirley, a nerd. She was afraid that if Tim became an observant Jew she would feel imprisoned. She realized that she really wanted to marry someone who saw Jews as a tribe, not Judaism as a spiritually based system of laws.

After a while, she and Tim both decided that the issue of his conversion, which seemed to prolong their courtship, was really an excuse to avoid commitment. Was it possible to love one another as deeply as they did and still be fundamentally incompatible? Was their difference over religion—over the *way to be religious*, not Judaism—a reflection of a deeper difference between them? A year later they decided it was. They broke up.

Barry and Marie were both relieved when the workshop ended. For they loved each other much more deeply than their fights suggested. Before the workshop, the subject of religion had been a small blemish on a happy marriage, which flared into a boil each December. By the fourth session, it consumed them and threatened to provide grounds for a divorce that neither of them wanted. They were terrified by the anger that emerged.

In the end, their anger showed them the depths of their loyalty to each other. It unearthed the choice they had been reluctant to face.

They realized that, in spite of Marie's nostalgia for a Christmas tree, Catholicism meant much less to her than Judaism did to Barry. Since she didn't want to convert, they had two choices. They could either preserve their marriage by choosing to ignore religion, or by deciding that since Barry was the partner who cared about religion his feelings should prevail. After much discussion, they agreed to satisfy Marie's feelings about Christmas by paying an annual Yuletide visit to a sister of hers who lived in Boston. Barry would have to accept the emotional discomfort of a tree.

Then they decided that Barry should satisfy his powerful desire to transmit Judaism to his children by reading books to them and taking them to services at least once a month. Later they would enroll them in Hebrew school. They both worried that those decisions could create the distance between Marie and her children that she had feared throughout the workshop. But it was the best solution they could find.

They also realized that their problem stemmed from unexpected professional tensions. After all, when they'd met at Vail, they were both free spirits for once in their lives. Now their work as professional people and parents consumed most of their energy. When they fought in the workshops they were as weary as two heavyweights going into the fifteenth round. They needed more time with each other and with their children. So they decided to create a life together, outside religion, by buying a home in the country and making it a retreat for their family.

At first, they thought of their decisions as compromises. But how else could they resolve the tension that was at the core of their marriage? They were lucky they were wealthy enough to afford the solution they reached. At least, Marie had Christmas, Barry was able to raise the kids as Jews, and they had a pleasant place to enjoy themselves and forget about the one fundamental difference between them. When they defined their solution that way, they realized that they'd each gained more than they had lost by facing a problem that once seemed intractable.

Ironically, Sheila's solution lay in the group itself. For even though Brad didn't like Judaism, he did like the couples in the workshop. Sometimes Sheila went to synagogue with Barry or with Marty and

Chris. She and Brad celebrated Passover and Hanukkah with the other couples they'd met in the workshop. On those nights, when people were being Jews instead of discussing the tensions between spouses, her face glowed. She loved the rituals that bored Brad.

Two years after the workshop ended, eighteen months after she and Brad were married, she became pregnant. Suddenly, all the questions that had troubled her in the workshop were real. How could she raise a Jewish child in a non-Jewish home? She decided that when her child got old enough she would send it to the same religious school that Marty and Chris chose for their son. Since Brad liked Marty and Chris, he didn't perceive that decision as one that would make him feel excluded. It was a flawed solution, and when one remembered Sheila's face at a seder one realized that a time bomb might still be ticking in her marriage. Nevertheless, the workshop had allowed Sheila to find a group of friends who could help her try to solve the conflict between love of a man and love of tradition. It buffered her loneliness by furnishing her with a community of people who shared some of her problems and who cared about her.

7

Stepping-Stones to a Family Faith

Workshops provide an effective framework for consciousness-raising. But what happens next? How do couples find stepping-stones toward a family faith?

Those who have made up their minds about the general direction they want to take need to learn to be comfortable in the spiritual home they have chosen. That means acquiring information, and sharing experiences with people in a religious or ethnic community.

Others still need time to decide what the choice of religious direction will mean to them, practically and emotionally. They are travelers who have to discover whether they will feel at ease in a religious culture. Some will love Judaism, some will love Christianity, some will feel out of place in both. But however they come to feel, they have to live at the frontiers of their emotions while they are exploring.

We offer suggestions, but with diffidence. For one thing, we know much more about the Jewish world than the Christian one. Besides, we realize that the possibilities for exploration are limitless and we've only provided a short guide. But we hope these suggestions will prompt people to keep searching, and that their search will bring them as much pleasure and interest as we have found in ours.

The journey to a spiritual life can begin in small ways: with an exciting book, a discussion with a loved one about God or prayer, a visit to a needy person, an experience of inexplicable awe or terrible grief. It can help a couple to find good teachers. It can take them to a warm community in which experiences, feelings, and ideas become part of an integrated spiritual sensibility. At occasional moments, it can enable people to experience the Divine.

One couple we met began their journey with dessert. Sarah, a Jew, and Tom, her agnostic Protestant husband, decided after their second child was born that they would like to develop some rituals to enrich the fabric of their family life. They agreed they'd try to do that in a Jewish framework, since Sarah cared more strongly about her heritage than Tom did about his. They decided to begin by doing something special on Friday nights. But lighting the Sabbath candles seemed too religious. They wanted to adopt a more secular ceremony.

Normally they served fruit after dinner, so that first year they decided to celebrate the Sabbath with their children by having a special treat for dessert. Soon they began reading their children Jewish story books after dessert. Then they bought Jewish books for themselves so that they could discover what some of the deeper meanings of Shabbat were. They took an adult education course at a nearby synagogue, and joined it when the next High Holy Days came around. After their third child was born they decided to name her in the synagogue. Tom then decided to convert to Judaism. Sarah spent two years studying for her bat mitzvah, which she celebrated on her thirty-fifth birthday. The process took them ten years, and they moved together, one step at a time, never knowing what would happen next.

Of course, the experience of searching for a spiritual path causes some couples to encounter the deep differences in one another. Therefore, the voyagers should try to be as sensitive to each other's feelings as they are honest about their own. They should seek out other Jewish-Christian couples who are involved in similar explorations and discuss their reactions with understanding peers. If lovers find themselves fighting instead of growing, they should seek help from a trained therapist or spiritual counselor.

The prospect of making some kind of choice can be threatening to one member of the couple. What if the choice is for the mate's religion? In the workshop we described earlier, Brad Marshfield told

Sheila Steiner that if they raised their children as Jews, he would feel left out of the family. He thought he had everything to lose and nothing to gain and Sheila acquiesced to his fear.

But his fear didn't seem to be based on religion. If transmitting his Christian faith had been an important priority to him he *would* have lost a lot: the sacrifice would have been considerable, as it is for many Christians, like Lars Swenson and Bliss Geiger, who defer to their spouse's ethnic Judaism and give up the practice of their faith.

Peter Davidson, a Jew, a politically liberal foundation executive who finds the idea of "the chosen people" too limiting for his universalist ideals, didn't want his Catholic wife Susie to make that sacrifice. He listened with careful sympathy when she said she believed their children should feel rooted in a single religion. Though Peter didn't want to convert, he realized that Susie's Catholicism was more important to her than Judaism would ever be to him. He felt it would be unjust to let his unresolved ethnic feelings prevent her from raising their child in the faith that gave her life great meaning. He decided to transmit his values to their church-going children through his obvious love for them, through sports, through their studies, and later, he hoped, through the political ideas that nourish him.

It is helpful for couples who are caught up in the struggle over faith to remember that religion is only one of the ingredients in a family's life. Every family develops its own private culture—the jokes, stories, songs, and myths that can make a long car ride or a nostalgic midnight conversation such a memorable experience. Each parent serves as a role model for the children, shaping their attitudes toward others. A strong, close ethical family is likely to create children who become ethical, caring adults. People certainly don't have to be religious to be good parents or to pass humane values on to their children. The parent whose religion is not practiced can still play a starring role in the overall family drama.

Couples can often work out creative ways of negotiating about religion. One woman who was born in France agreed to study basic Judaism with the possibility of conversion when her fiancé offered to study French so he could communicate with her parents. Another man took a women's studies course when his feminist wife began to study the New Testament. Another man offered to clean the house on Sundays if his wife, a doctor, would come to synagogue with him on Saturdays.

Since we feel that many couples do want to reach some agreement about religion, we offer some ideas for ways that people can acquire religious information and experience.

Find Your Own Berlitz

Once, during a workshop session when people were discussing the images they associated with Christmas and Passover, with Christianity and Judaism, we listed the terms that had to be explained. The Jews and gentiles, who were intimately acquainted with each other's psychological, sexual, and professional histories knew little about the belief systems they were negotiating. Even for couples who had been married for years, it was often true that the Jews had very little information about Christianity and gentiles knew very little about Judaism. None of the Jews had read the New Testament. Even though many Christians had read the Old Testament, they had done so in the context of their own religion. None had read it as the Jewish Bible, with Jewish commentaries.

Most Jews knew what events Christmas and Easter celebrate. But very few could describe what Advent or Lent represented, or what a sacrament was. Some didn't know what event was commemorated on Good Friday.

Most Christians knew some of the Passover story from religious school. But as they talked about the holiday, it became clear that few of them knew why matzoh is served and bread avoided during the Passover week, or what ideas and teachings are embodied in the holiday. They knew that Jews give presents and light candles on Hanukkah, but were unsure of what the holiday celebrates. The word mitzvah (commandment) was alien to most of them, except as it is used in bar mitzvah.

Few of the participants knew a lot about their own religions either. For the most part, their church or Hebrew school education had ended when they were teenagers. Though they were arguing about religious identity, few could describe what religious beliefs they really held. Soon it was clear that virtually everyone involved needed to acquire a more sophisticated, adult's understanding of the different faiths if their decisions were to be relevant to their present lives.

For adults, there are now lively, interesting guides to Jewish and Christian life, including *The Jewish Catalogue,* an exuberantly written, well-organized three-volume *Whole Earth Catalogue* of the religion, *The Catholic Fact Book,* and *A New Dictionary for Episcopalians,* which is designed to break down the barrier between old-timers and newcomers in the church. We have listed some of these books in the Appendix.

We suggest that people amplify our suggestions by asking friends for the names of books they have found important, and by going to Jewish or Christian bookstores in their cities and asking the salespeople to suggest interesting introductory literature.

These books may not provoke intense discussions, but they provide the vocabulary necessary to transform an argument over residual tribal feelings into an examination of religious ideas.

If you have children, you can begin to learn by reading to or with them. Look for books that contain Bible stories, but make sure that the illustrations are of high quality. Look also for history books, for books that make the holidays seem interesting and warm, for books that have girls as well as boys in active roles. There are well-written books about God, prayer, birth, and death designed to appeal to a child's imagination, and to answer the questions which most children ask.

Use Books as Vicarious Experiences

Another place to begin is with fiction. Once I asked Rachel to read Ludwig Lewisohn's *The Island Within,* a novel in which an intermarried German Jew decides that assimilation is a psychologically depleting lie and that he has to live a Jewish life. I felt that Lewisohn had shown the confusion and uncertainty that must have affected my mother's outwardly assimilated German-Jewish family, and that his protagonist expressed my feeling that I had to recover my religious legacy in order to feel at peace with myself. I showed her passages in which Lewisohn conveyed attitudes I had always held but never articulated. She felt the book helped her understand me better.

A Catholic friend showed us that sometimes novels can define disagreements that couples express through barbed remarks but never explore.

Although she was no longer religious, she had strong, positive memories of the church and the parish she knew as a child. Sometimes she took Communion because the act reminded her of a happy past. When she did so, her Jewish boyfriend would joke that she was acting like a "cannibal." Of course, she was hurt. She wanted to show him what it was like to be part of a people who saw the bread and wine as the body and blood of Christ, and help him understand her attraction to Catholic life.

To explain her feelings, she asked him to read Mary Gordon's *The Company of Women* and James Carroll's *The Prince of Peace*. Even though she thought Andrew Greeley's novels were a little simplistic and sensationalized, she decided they provided a view of why the Catholic Church and Catholic culture retained the loyalty of people who had ideological reasons to be disaffected. Those books about parish life and the priesthood provided a context for her childhood memories. They helped her describe the serene joy she'd felt as a girl who took parish life for granted: who loved to run in and out of church on All Souls' Day so that her "Hail Marys" and "Our Fathers" would rescue the souls of her loved ones from purgatory; who still felt a surge of pleasure as she recalled the way the world seemed to brighten during the forty Lenten mornings when her family attended daily Mass, and how the world exploded with light on Easter Sunday.

She regarded herself as a guilt-ridden person, but believed that the Catholic sense of guilt and of sin could be seen as a virtue. She used Isabel, the main character of Mary Gordon's *Final Payments*, as a vehicle for conveying that feeling to her lover.

As they discussed the books, he realized that her lasting attraction for Catholic culture and the Catholic faith was more than a spasm of emotion on a saint's day or on Easter, as he had assumed during the first year they were courting. Her past was in her pores.

It wasn't in his. He couldn't imagine raising children who believed in the power of prayer to save souls from purgatory, or in original sin. The books helped them realize that their marriage would be a religious truce at best. If they had children, it could become all-out war.

It was just as well that happened. How could the couple have maintained civility in their marriage when the man used such cruel language about a ritual that was so important to his mate?

Use the Media as a Barometer for Your Feelings

Almost every week, the newspapers and television contain several stories concerning American Jews and Israelis. The media also devote extensive coverage to the Catholic church and to the influence of Christianity on politics. Do Jews and Christians pay attention to all those stories, or just the ones that connect to their cultures? How do they react to the news? The answer can be a clue that the partners view reality through different cultural lenses. It can show that they're unable to communicate about an aspect of life that is crucial to one or both of them. Or it can indicate that they have the self-confidence and flexibility people need to arrive at a shared faith.

Suppose Israel invades Lebanon, or clashes with Arabs on the West Bank. Suppose a newspaper publishes a piece about Israel's efforts to absorb Ethiopian Jews. Suppose the same issue of the New York *Times* contains one article about some Jews involved in financial scandals and another about a Jewish millionaire who gave a large sum of money to provide incentives for underprivileged high school students to go to college.

Does the Jew react with a passion—a love or an anger or a sense of personal responsibility that the gentile regards as an obsession with Jewish issues? Does the gentile blame Jews (or Israel) for each controversy? Does he or she notice the positive articles as well as the negative ones? Does the gentile understand that there is not a unified Jewish position toward American or Middle Eastern politics?

Does the Jew resent it if the gentile criticizes Israel in terms that would be acceptable coming from another Jew? Does the gentile feel free to express such criticisms?

In the past few years, the Catholic Church, as a force in politics, has been in the media almost as much as Israel. Does a Jew who is married to a Catholic care about the debate over liberation theology, or the rights of a person who dissents from the Vatican's position on sexual issues to teach at a Catholic university, speak in a church, play an important role in a parish? Has the Jew noticed the liberal positions the American Church has taken on disarmament and economics? Or does he equate all Catholics with the Pope, stereotyping Catholics as he would hate to have Catholics stereotype Jews?

Does the Catholic understand why the Jew is still angry because of the Vatican's silence during the Holocaust? Does he or she understand why the Jew is upset because the Vatican refuses to recognize Israel?

There is a constant debate between fundamentalist Christians like Jerry Falwell and Pat Robertson and spokespersons from the more liberal Christian denominations. Does the Jew who is married to a Protestant read the newspaper through a cultural lens that sees all churchgoers as fundamentalists who want to reintroduce school prayer? How does the Jew feel about the fact that these same fundamentalist churches support Israel while the more liberal ones are often sympathetic to the Palestinians?

Feminism is another area of religious life which generates interesting articles. Women are not only seeking ordination as rabbis, cantors, priests, and ministers, but they are also reshaping traditional liturgy to create images of the Divine which are not masculine, or patriarchal. The challenges to tradition that women are raising provoke important and fascinating debates. Often they spark interest in religious questions in people who would ordinarily pay no attention to talk of God or prayer.

Of course, there are many Jews and Christians who follow these stories for their own sakes, not because they arouse specific cultural feelings. But there are many more for whom they represent a barometer of religious and ethnic emotions.

In many cases, the stories in the media will provide a mirror that helps couples examine attitudes they can't quite define in themselves.

Attend Lectures About Religion

Sometimes it helps to attend lectures or courses in a church or a synagogue before attending formal services. For although these lectures occur in religious spaces, there is no formal prayer. They can provide a relatively low-key way to acquire information and explore feelings.

In one of our workshops, a Jewish man kept insisting that his Presbyterian wife convert. She couldn't see any reason to do so since he wasn't a practicing Jew and thought that Jewish texts were boring.

We suggested that they go to a midweek lecture in a Manhattan synagogue where a particularly interesting rabbi was speaking about

Noah. The lecture was in the synagogue sanctuary. Since the ark that held the Torah scroll was in the room, the men had to wear yarmulkes.

The woman had only been in synagogue when she visited her in-laws on the Holidays. She had been unable to follow the Hebrew prayers.

The synagogue was crowded. When the rabbi began to talk, she was astonished that he could take a brief biblical story and conclude that Noah was less virtuous than Abraham because he had failed to challenge the Almighty on behalf of the human race as Abraham did when the Lord decided to destroy Sodom. She had not heard a Presbyterian minister give so much thought to an Old Testament figure.

But then the rabbi said that just as Noah had been corrupted by the evil ways of the people of his generation so Jews are being corrupted by America's gentile environment. That remark offended her. She thought she would like to become part of a religious culture that discussed the Bible so interestingly, but not if the price was the idea that gentiles could corrupt Jews.

Her husband had an important experience there, too. He was not accustomed to wearing a yarmulke, and took it off his head as soon as they got outdoors. "You always say you're so proud of being Jewish," his wife said. "Why don't you wear the yarmulke on the street?"

"Because I might run into someone I know."

"So what?"

After a moment's pause he said, "I guess I would be embarrassed."

As soon as those words were out of his mouth, he had to reexamine them. What did they indicate about his sense of identity? How could he ask her to take on a new faith when he was ashamed to wear one of its most familiar symbols on his head? The experience helped him see that the issue between them wasn't only her indecision about conversion. It was his attitude toward himself as a Jew.

They talked about the substance of the lecture and their reaction to the synagogue itself for hours after they got home. Like most such discussions, it was inconclusive. But it was based on an adult experience, not the memory of childhood feelings. It allowed them to move past a theoretical argument over conversion into a realistic discussion of the ways they would have to change, and the kind of open-minded

community they would have to find, if they were really going to live as
Jews.

Talk with Friends About Their Religion

Virtually everyone has religious friends who enjoy discussing the
intricacies of Judaism, Catholicism, and Protestantism with outsiders.
One can learn an immense amount by asking them to describe their
religion's ideas and practices.

Sympathetic questions—about dietary laws and confession—about
how Jews and Christians define good deeds—about their respective
beliefs in what happens after death—often yield informative answers.

Sometimes such questions lead to new experiences. A Jew might
invite a couple to eat in a *sukkah,* the leafy wood-framed booths where
Jews enjoy pleasant meals during the week-long autumn harvest festival. A Catholic might encourage them to spend time at a church-
sponsored shelter soup kitchen, and accompany them to an upbeat
folk Mass. A Protestant might invite them to a concert of choir music
which they will both enjoy.

Such friends can help an anxious couple take a few first steps on the
pathway toward a shared faith.

Ask Older People About Their Experiences

When a Jew and Christian marry, their grandparents are often
reluctant to talk about their religions. Many, who have strong feelings, are worried that they may seem intrusive if they express them.
But once they are asked, fascinating memories of synagogues,
churches, and parish life often flood out. Many love to tell stories
about the neighborhoods they lived in when they were young. Their
words can deepen each partner's sense of the other's ethnic history.

If no grandparents are nearby, it can be useful to make friends with
older people who live in one's neighborhood, or to contact one of the
many agencies that arrange for young people to call on senior citizens
every week. Such people can become surrogate members of an extended family.

A relationship with an aging Holocaust survivor gave Rachel a sense of having Jewish roots after she converted. By then, she'd studied enough Hebrew and Bible so that prayer and texts had taken on great meaning for her. She had lived on the Upper West Side for long enough that she felt part of the Jewish community. But everyone else could talk about their *bubbe* or *zayde*, a grandmother or grandfather, who had transmitted the husk of Old World Jewish feeling. Rachel's grandparents, all dead, were New England Protestants.

Shortly after she converted she became Program Director of our synagogue, Ansche Chesed. She became particularly close to Eugene Klein, a Hungarian bachelor who had vowed that if he survived the Holocaust he would devote the rest of his life to preserving Judaism. He saw Ansche Chesed as his family.

He came to the synagogue every day, and shared an office with Rachel. He'd often reminisce about his childhood in Budapest, his years in the concentration camps, his first days in America. When she told him she was beginning piano lessons, he gave her a recording of Bartok he had bought on his last visit home to Budapest. He would call her on Sunday nights to make sure she was all right, and she'd visit him if he was sick, and send him postcards when we were on vacation. He was her surrogate *zayde*, her personal link to the Jewish past. She was his link to the American present. We visited him in the hospital the week before he died. Rachel keeps his picture on the wall of her office.

Take a Vacation in Israel

If you can afford a trip to Israel, it can provide an immense amount of factual and emotional information. For you're visiting in a country run by Jews, at the confluence of Judaism and Christianity and Islam.

Just wander through Jerusalem. Go to the Western Wall and talk to the men and women who pray there; visit Yad Vashem, the museum of the Holocaust; walk over to the excavation of the city where King David lived; spend time with Israeli soldiers, with the Ethiopian Jews who have recently arrived in the country and the North African Jews who comprise its majority. Talk with everyone you meet.

Look out over Calvary, the scene of Jesus' crucifixion. Drive to

Bethlehem where he was born, and Nazareth where he lived. Bring a New Testament to the Galilee, where he delivered the Beatitudes.

Learn about these places and their history. Most likely, you'll have a succession of different, powerful responses to them. Heed them and discuss them. They may yield the religious language of your heart.

Think About Your Home as a Stage Set for a Faith

If religion is a drama that has been imprinted in a Jew or Christian at a young age, then the home is the living theater in which the play is acted, and the most modest words and objects of faith and culture are part of the script and scenery that convey the powerful tale.

What do you want the stage to look like? Can you agree on the props? One way to answer that question is to look around both sets of parents' houses and pretend they are your own. If the parents are religious, they'll have many objects in common—and many that are strikingly different.

Suppose the Jew comes from a fairly observant family. There will be a mezzuzah on the door. Sabbath candlesticks and Hanukkah menorahs will be displayed in the house. Somewhere there will be a box of Passover Haggadahs that are hauled out for every seder. Somewhere, there may be a box for *tzedakah,* charity. The bookshelves are almost sure to contain Jewish fiction and non-fiction, a translation of the Torah. There may be Jewish magazines like *Moment* or *Commentary* or *Hadassah,* and the hometown Jewish newspaper. There are likely to be photographs of Israel or woodcuts of Eastern European Jews on the wall, and pictures of bar mitzvahs and Jewish weddings among the family memorabilia.

Suppose the Catholic comes from a religious family, with one or more crucifixes on a wall, an Advent calendar in December, and the palms from Palm Sunday displayed before Easter. There may be a special box—perhaps a replica of a bishop's miter—where the family collects money for charity. On the bookshelf, there will almost certainly be a Bible. There will be magazines like *Commonweal* or *U.S. Catholic* and photographs of weddings and First Communions.

Protestant households may have religious art, Bibles and prayer books, a charity collection box. The crèche that goes under the

Christmas tree is in the closet, near the angel that sits on top of it. There may be Tasha Tudor's wonderfully illustrated books of Easter and Christmas stories, which the children love to read. There will be photographs of the baby's christening, a church wedding.

Do you want the menorah or the crèche to symbolize your winter holiday, the book of Easter stories or the Haggadah to suggest your springtime celebration, dinner on Friday night or Sunday noon to convey your idea of precious weekly time? Do you want a mezzuzah on the door or a cross on the wall or neither? When you're forty-five, do you want pictures of your children's bar mitzvah or confirmation? Do you want to base your religious tale on the King James Bible or the Torah?

Or do you want a household whose stage contains no religious props—whose decor is composed of antiques, or photographs of nature, or tapestries from South America, or pop art or modern furniture. Are you telling solely a secular tale?

These possessions and photographs all suggest different dramas. Is there one that makes you feel comfortable, another that makes you feel awkward and out of place?

These questions are worth asking in a household where the furnishings echo the answers. In that setting, you can come close to feeling your future. You can choose your script before it chooses you.

Explore Religious Services

It is important for a couple to think carefully about this step, and to be patient as they take it. It can, of course, be meaningless. But it can also be highly charged. It is very important for people to remember that churches and synagogues vary greatly. If one seems dull or oppressive, or chauvinistic, try another.

Remember that religious feelings in intermarriages are asymmetrical. Crosses and crucifixes do make many Jews uncomfortable. Many can't sing hymns in praise of Jesus. Often, if the service involves Communion, the Jew who goes with his Christian spouse feels very lonely and self-conscious remaining in a pew, but finds it impossible to go up to the altar.

Christians feel like outsiders in synagogue. That feeling can be terrifying. They wonder: How will I ever find meaning in this unfamiliar ritual? Is everyone looking at me, thinking I'm a *goy*? Will they ever accept me? Can I ever feel like part of them?

They should remember that the Jew they married may feel like an outsider, too, since many have forgotten the Hebrew prayers and the order of the service. The Jew wonders: does my spouse think I'm a fool because I don't know what's going on? Does the congregant beside me notice that I'm on the wrong page in the prayer book? Am I being judged because I haven't been to services in years? Am I being judged because I didn't marry a Jew?

In every city there are synagogues whose rabbis and congregants understand that most gentiles and many Jews who come to services for the first time feel as if they are on foreign soil and that the process of acculturation is a difficult one. They have created beginners' services for people who are unfamiliar with Jewish ritual and prayer, where Jews and Christians can ask the questions they wonder about during ordinary services. Many synagogues now have support groups designed to help people who are thinking of converting or people who have converted sort out their complicated reactions to being newly Jewish. They try to create an environment that makes newcomers feel welcome.

In such places, Christians may feel welcome—but not at home. They may feel that Jesus is missing or that Hebrew prayers will never comfort them, and long for the King James translation of the psalms they have been reciting. They may miss the hymns that were so inspiring in church.

Couples can discover whether those are fleeting fears or bedrock emotions only if they go to a variety of services in a variety of settings. For, plainly, the way Jews feel about church and the way Christians feel about synagogue is the heart of the religious conflict in an intermarriage. The couple have to confront it openly and discuss it honestly, and do so as soon as possible.

Study!!!

The only way of putting the conflict in a context where it can be discussed is to study the two religions and cultures. For most of the arguments we've heard in our workshops and interviews take place in a vacuum of information. Unless you know the history of the concepts and symbols that trouble you, you are debating stereotypes, not history or theology.

Look to local colleges, to church and synagogue adult education programs, to Jewish Community Centers and YM/YWCA's for course listings. Get on the mailing lists of the interesting institutions in your community. Look for film series and concerts as well.

You might argue when you begin to read religious texts or ethnic history or novels or sociology. But you often find yourselves talking to each other with mounting intellectual excitement. This is particularly true when you have the stimulation of a good teacher and interested classmates.

When a couple breaks out of spiritual gridlock into an emotional clearing where they can learn together they are almost certain to transform the differences that frightened them into a challenge that excites them. They will embark on a project that enriches their lives.

8

Some Resolutions

In this chapter, we are going to describe four couples who used the act of deciding on a religious life as a way to strengthen each other and their marriages. Their decisions differ from one another, but their stories have a crucial element in common. They involve people who approached their situations with sensitivity and a commitment to finding a solution instead of avoiding a problem. They were willing to work and learn together. Each spouse had an ability to anticipate the other's spiritual longings.

Brenda Goldman, a religious Christian, was aware of the fact that her secular Jewish husband Frank didn't want to be the last link in a Jewish chain. Though she could not give up her Christianity, she realized she cared more about having religious children than she cared about the religion of her children. Now the Goldmans have a Jewish household while Brenda remains a regular churchgoer.

Ned Rosenbaum and Mary Helene Pottker Rosenbaum have such deep love for each other, and for religious ideas and religious worship, that they have performed an emotional and intellectual feat that is nearly impossible. They have created an authentic two-faith home.

Linda Frank, a Congregationalist by birth, was acutely aware that her husband Paul, a disaffiliated Jew, was ill-at-ease in any church setting whose language and iconography so much as hinted at a belief in the divinity of Jesus. In turn, Paul knew that Linda would never be happy as a Jew and that she had loved the comfort of the church in which she was raised. When they experienced a tragedy in their life, they both found a home in the Unitarian Church.

Ed Jamison, who was a religious Christian throughout high school, sensed that his wife, Rebecca Weiderman Jamison, the daughter of Holocaust survivors, would need to reassert her connection to the Jewish people at some point in their marriage. When she did, after a long detour, she took pains to see that Ed found a conversion course that would satisfy his intense curiosity about religion, and a synagogue where he would be welcomed. She made sure that he took enough time to grow into Judaism at his own pace. She wanted the religion to suit his spiritual needs, not her emotional ones. Each loved the other enough to nurture a carefully thought out growth into Judaism.

These three couples share an intimate vocabulary which contains respect for faith, for history, and for tradition. For them, one aspect of love is the ability to see their spouse through his or her own spiritual eyes. They find new sources of strength in themselves and in each other. They find new possibilities in life itself.

Keeping the Faith in a Two-Faith Home

Many intermarried couples try to establish a two-faith household. Neither spouse wants to surrender a set of beliefs or of family traditions. Some couples celebrate two sets of holidays, but do not choose a religion for the family. Others do choose a single religion for the family, even though one spouse practices a different religion privately. Very few couples are able to create a genuinely bi-religious home.

Many couples try to resolve their differences by establishing what we call a bi-holiday home. They don't want to decide on one religion for the children, either because they are each genuinely fond of both traditions, or because one parent is unwilling to let the other dominate in this important area. They balance the two by celebrating the four most familiar holidays—by lighting the menorah, decorating the Christmas tree, having a seder, and hiding Easter eggs. They embellish these activities with special family traditions. They create wonderful celebrations. But these celebrations are just a glimpse of the fabrics of both religions. They don't teach much about Judaism or Christianity, or about identity and community.

Some children feel enriched by this variety. They love all the celebrations, all the family meals, the gifts, the relatives. Others wish they felt rooted in one religion. One teenager, whose own reading had caused her to conclude that a Jewish-Christian home obscures the difference between the way each religion approaches Jesus, reacted angrily when her parents objected to her plans to go to a Christian summer camp. She snapped at them, "The idea that I should be both Christian and Jewish was *your* agreement. But I believe in Jesus. I'm living *my* life."

Other couples who feel equally strongly about their respective religious backgrounds adopt a different solution. Neither parent is willing to convert to the other's religion, but both agree that the children need one religion and a unified identity. So they decide that the family will practice one of their religions, observing its holidays, attending services and religious school in its institutions. Meanwhile, the parent whose religion is not adopted by the family maintains his or her own identity by becoming personally involved with a church or a synagogue, with religiously affiliated social action programs, or with philanthropic organizations like the United Jewish Appeal, or Catholic Charities.

There is unity in the home, and a parent who cannot convert to a spouse's religion has not had to suppress a religious faith or sacrifice an ethnic commitment. Children in these homes grow up secure in one religion, but comfortable with the other.

Frank and Brenda Goldman have created a Jewish home for their two children. Friday night they light candles, eat Shabbat dinner, and go to services at their temple. Sunday mornings Brenda goes to services at her Episcopal church while Frank takes the children to Hebrew School. Every year the family spends Christmas Day with Brenda's sister and her children.

Frank and Brenda hadn't worked out this arrangement before they married. They met during an intense Colorado political campaign. He was a lawyer, she was a political science professor. Although she made it clear to him from the beginning that she was a practicing Christian, and he loved to tell her anecdotes about the working class Jewish neighborhood in the Bronx where he grew up, they never discussed what they would do about their future children's religious upbringing.

They had been married by a judge in the living room of the large adobe house that some close friends had built on their ranch outside Denver. Brenda's father, a retired professor of Bible, read a prayer and a blessing he had written. Frank broke a glass. Some guests shouted "congratulations." Others called out "mazel tov!"

Since Frank never went to synagogue, and did not object when Brenda bought a small Christmas tree for their first Christmas, she assumed that he did not care much about the family's religious orientation. Even after the children were born, he didn't seem to think much about it, although he brought home a menorah when their son Josh was old enough to help light the candles and listen to the Hanukkah story.

Often, on Sunday mornings, she'd take the children to church with her while Frank worked. She would leave them in the nursery room while she went to services. One afternoon, when their children were four and two, they drove past Brenda's church. Josh cried out, "Look, Daddy, there's my church!"

Frank was furious. Turning to Brenda, he said, "I never said you could make them Christians!"

"All I've done is leave them with the baby-sitter there," Brenda replied, "but you've known where I've been going, and you know how important church is to me! And what have you done to teach them about Judaism?"

They argued for several weeks. Brenda said that she wanted the children to have a serious religious education. She wanted them to believe in God, and she wanted the family to practice what the children learned in religious school.

Frank said he wanted the children to be Jewish, but he didn't want to go to synagogue, and he didn't know how to practice Judaism at home.

Brenda told him he was being stubborn and unreasonable.

Finally they negotiated an agreement. They were bargaining over the way they would organize the family's religious life, not trying to hammer out an agreement about their personal faiths. Brenda realized that she would be satisfied if the children were Jewish, as long as they were religious. She does not worry about the fate of their souls, for she cannot imagine an afterlife that is off-limits to Jews. But she insisted that Frank take responsibility for his Jewish feelings. She told him that if he wanted Jewish kids, he would have to find a synagogue with a good Hebrew school where she would be welcome. If he couldn't do that, she would enroll them in Sunday school in her church.

Frank agreed to look for a synagogue where he would feel at home. After talking with his friends, meeting with several rabbis, and attending Friday night services at three synagogues, he found one he liked. The rabbi had taken several liberal stands on community issues. The Hebrew school had an excellent reputation. Furthermore, the rabbi told him that the Board had just approved the formation of an Outreach committee which was making plans for making the synagogue a more welcoming place for interfaith couples.

Eight years later, Frank was on the board of the synagogue. The family had traveled to Israel together, and Josh had decided he wanted to have his bar mitzvah on Masada.

Brenda is on the board of her church, and has organized a weekly soup kitchen. Often Josh goes there to help set the tables. She is pleased that her children have a strong sense of their Jewish identity, and that they are familiar with Jewish prayer. She looks forward to Friday night dinners, and enjoys the services at the temple.

Her only regret about her family's religious life is that Jesus will never mean anything special to her children. She has always gained strength and peace from her personal relationship with Jesus, and she wishes that her children could share it. But, she feels, that is a small price to pay for a happy marriage and a warm, peaceful family life.

Ned Rosenbaum, an observant Jew, and his wife Mary Rosenbaum, a devout Catholic, have succeeded in permeating their homes and their children's lives with Judaism and Christianity. Their story shows the love and labor involved in establishing a bi-religious household in which everyone is as familiar with the two theological tongues as a Spanish speaker and an English speaker might be in a bilingual home.

Their home is an extension of the intellectual and spiritual life they have shared since the early 1960s when they met at the University of Chicago. Ever since their first date, they have been discussing religion with an unflagging fervor. Over time, they decided that since they were both monotheists they could each become immersed in the other's faith and practice and still preserve their belief that there are separate but equal pathways to God.

Now Ned is a professor of Jewish Studies at Dickinson College in Carlisle, Pennsylvania, and Mary is a professional copy editor. Their eldest child, Sarah, graduated from Bryn Mawr in 1985, and is doing research on geriatric neurological diseases at the National Institute of Mental Health in Washington, D.C. Will, their eldest boy, is a junior at Cornell with a double major in English and philosophy. Their youngest child, Rafi, is a junior at Carlisle High School.

For the past twenty-four years, they have organized much of their professional, intellectual, and social life around religion, the area of thought and action that brings them the most pleasure. They have each kept their faith in a two-faith home. But it has demanded an immense amount of flexibility, and intellectual curiosity. It has demanded more time than most people are willing to devote to theology.

At times each has had to anticipate the other's religious feelings. For example, at one point in their marriage, when Mary was becoming disaffected with the Catholic Church, Ned knew that if she stopped going to Mass she would surrender an important part of herself. He urged her to go to church regularly. For her part Mary always sensed when Ned was ready to take his next step into observant Judaism, and satisfied his needs with her actions. Unlike most couples we have interviewed, they were not threatened by their religious differences. They used them to help each other grow.

I visited them in early January. Their red brick Georgian home looked more like the kind of Princeton fraternity house one reads about in F. Scott Fitzgerald's novels than the setting for an unusual religious experiment.

The house was full since Sarah and Will were home for the Christmas break. (Rafi was at school). After I'd been with them for just an hour, I felt as if I'd entered a marathon seminar about faith. They were all acquainted with the works of theologians like St. Paul, Martin Buber, Thomas Aquinas, and Martin Luther; with the Gospels, the Torah, and the Talmud; the intricacies of *mitzvot* and the sacraments; the ideas of great Christian and Jewish novelists.

As we ate an Italian dairy lunch—a *tortallaci*, noodles stuffed with spinach—Ned and Mary described how they incorporated Judaism and Christianity into their daily life. At home, they observe Jewish

dietary laws and the Sabbath. They treat Christmas, Good Friday, and
Easter as Holy Days. For a while, they tried to go to synagogue and
church together every Saturday and Sunday, but that proved to be
too much. Now, on Saturdays, Ned leads services in Carlisle's small
synagogue. On Sundays, Mary is a lector at her Catholic church.

When Sarah and Will and Rafi were in grade school, Ned and Mary
said they could attend a Jewish religious program or a Catholic religious program but they had to stick with the one they chose until the
end of the year. Then they could switch. Over time, they hoped, the
kids would become native speakers in both theological languages. For
the moment, their children have reacted in very different ways. Sarah,
twenty-three, is an observant Jew. Will, nineteen, is a secular humanist, Rafi, still in high school, is interested in religion but hasn't made
any choices.

Their private rule was that both of them—and all of their children
—had to know enough about Judaism to explain the religion to a
Christian and enough about Christianity to explain it to a Jew. Inside
the household, any argument about faith was fair game as long as it
didn't descend to the level of name-calling.

As Ned and Mary talked, it was clear they were proud of their ability
to raise children who are religiously literate, and open-minded
enough to discuss the family's wide range of theologies without getting into a fight. But they were also aware of the psychological cost of
their commitment to a two-faith home.

Ned worried that some of his children whom he helped raise in two
faiths will be lost to the Jewish people. Mary understood that fear and
emphasized its importance to any gentile she met. Nevertheless, she
felt regret that so far she was the only Catholic in the family. She was
very close to Ned and her children, but she longed to feel their
emotional presence at moments that had spiritual meaning for her.
More importantly, she worried about her offsprings' souls.

After their own long, difficult journey, Ned and Mary have come to
believe at heart that intermarriage is a mistake. But, whatever their
reservations, their shared passion for ideas and religion has made
them and their children extraordinarily loving, interesting people.

Mary, brown-haired, opinionated, a geyser of enthusiastic laughter, expressed her thoughts through long, personal statements. Ned
had an academic's taste for epigrams. In that respect, as in so many
others, they complemented each other.

She was the child of a Christian intermarriage. Her father was a Lutheran who acquiesced to her mother's Catholic faith. His attitude toward the Church and the Church's attitude toward him affected Mary's ideas about religion and marriage. He was "a passive observer in our religious life who only came to Mass with us on Christmas and Easter," she recalled. Once, "when a nun told us that only Catholics went to heaven, I said 'Wait a minute.' I went home and asked my mother if Daddy was going to heaven. She called up the nun and raised hell. So I grew up with a consciousness that things weren't as neat a package as was being presented to me in the Catholic Church. And when I fell in love with Ned I knew I didn't want him to play the same role as my father had. I didn't want my husband to be an onlooker in a home that was dominated by my religion."

To do that, she had to make a religious Jew out of an atheist who barely knew anything about his background and was just becoming curious enough to read about it. Ned was a German Jew whose family had been in America for six generations. At home, in the suburb of Highland Park, Illinois, his parents celebrated Christmas and ignored all the Jewish holidays. "Until I was twelve years old I didn't know there were Jews and non-Jews," he recalled. He only got a religious education because a schoolmate of his, a Presbyterian, took him to his Sunday school for six years. "Of course, what they do in Protestant Sunday school is a lot of Old Testament history. I started getting interested in Judaism when I was seventeen."

But there was no reinforcement in his parents' house. His father was a fourth-generation Reform Jew, who thought that any step toward traditionalism was a betrayal of the family's heritage. His mother was the kind of German Jew who regarded the religion as a social liability. So neither parent objected when Ned decided to marry Mary. In fact, Ned recalled, "My mother thought the kids would be better off if they were raised as Catholics. She told me, 'There are more of them than there are of us.' "

He was a graduate student in American history when he met Mary. While they were first courting, Ned's roommate, a Protestant, urged him to audit a theology course that was being taught by the head of the University of Chicago Divinity School, and the ideas "just blew me away. I never realized religion was so interesting. Mary and I started arguing about it right away."

In those days, Ned felt "there was something Jewish hiding in me," but his curiosity about it was completely intellectual. He couldn't imagine himself as an observant Jew or as part of the Jewish people. He had no problem agreeing to be married by a priest in a Catholic church. "At the time Mary's religion mattered more to her than mine did to me, and I wanted her to do whatever was necessary to stay in good standing. In those days, I thought the Pope himself could not put impediments to my marriage."

"Now," he said ruefully, "I feel differently. Mary has made me so Jewish that I couldn't marry her if we met today."

That change was gradual. At first it displayed itself in Ned's academic interests, not in his daily life. "I was writing a thesis on the old *Vanity Fair* magazine, but I found that I had run out of steam in American history." In 1964, he decided to switch his field to Jewish Studies. His parents regarded the move as a return to the ghetto. "It was the best move I could have made. I tell my students that you can take all of American history and put it between Moses and David—and it disappears. In Jewish Studies there's so much to know that you never get bored."

In 1966, he transferred to Brandeis because they had one of the best Jewish Studies departments in America. But he hadn't thought of observing any of the Jewish laws he was studying.

"One Friday night," he recalled, "it was dark when I came home and Mary had lit Sabbath candles. I asked her why. She said, 'It is time to start.' "

She was eager to explain her reasons. "I always believed that it was necessary for Ned's psychic integrity and personal growth that he explore his Judaism as fully as possible. I never had any intention of converting, but I was convinced that the better Jew Ned was, the better person he would be."

Back then, she felt enthusiasm for Judaism's practice but was ignorant of Jewish law. "In those days, we lit Friday night candles and I baked challah. But we were still perfectly likely to have ham on Friday night. We didn't even know what prayers to say."

A decade later, Mary—who believes that Jews should be kosher, but that as a Catholic she has no reason to follow dietary laws—sensed a mood Ned hadn't articulated, and made their home kosher. "I get emanations from him when he wants to take a religious step," she said, "and since I'm the primary cook and housekeeper it seems that the burden of that step devolves on me."

When Mary decided to have her wedding ceremony in a church, the Chicago Archdiocese made the standard demand that she and Ned sign a paper promising that they would raise their children as Catholics.

"I asked the priest what that meant in terms of canon law," she said. "He told me it wasn't defined. We told him our plan to raise the children in both religions, and he said it was a perfectly terrible idea. He said that children are like plants in a garden, and that parents had to nurture them with one faith to be sure that they blossomed. I said that kids were unique. My approach was that if Catholicism is the Truth, then presenting it by precept and example will have the effect on the children that the Church wants. So there was a sense in which we were raising the children as Catholics. The priest had rigid ideas but he was a lovely man, and he let us sign the paper. That meant the children could be baptized."

Sarah and Will were both born in America, and were baptized in the Church. Ned didn't mind "because I regard baptism as something parents do to the child as protection."

"That's because you don't believe in the efficacy of the sacraments," Mary said, renewing a theological argument they've had for twenty-four years. "You don't believe that something happens at the moment of baptism that changes the baby spiritually. I do."

But it wasn't until the Rosenbaums were in Israel, in 1970, that she realized the strength of her Catholic faith. When Rafi was born in Hadassah Hospital in Jerusalem he was very ill. "When the doctors handed me the baby I had an emotional feeling that if he died unbaptized I'd never sleep soundly again. It surprised me because it's not anything I believe intellectually. The only thing that kept me from performing an emergency baptism was the counter-superstition that a desperate move like that would have meant he was dying."

Then she paused to review the kind of theological argument that has gone on in her mind. In retrospect, she wondered if "I would have fulfilled my responsibility as a Christian better if I had not had them baptized. I'm not sure you should baptize a baby unless you have a clear expectation that the adult will ratify the baptism. So far, none of my children has done that."

For a brief time, it seemed as if Sarah, now twenty-one, would adopt her mother's faith. She had been sitting in the living room as Ned and Mary talked. A little sadly, Mary reminded her, "When you

were eleven you wanted to be a Catholic and asked me to come to
First Confession with you. You didn't want to be alone in the confes-
sional with the priest."

"I still wouldn't," Sarah said with a laugh that sounded almost
exactly like her mother's.

Ned continued the narrative. "Shortly after that she started making
serious noises about being Jewish. Mary and I were surprised. We had
not foreseen that any of our children would make that choice when
they were so young. We told her to do a course of study and write
papers on Judaism for us."

Mary remembered that "Sarah pushed us for a couple of years to
have a conversion and a bat mitzvah. We wanted her to keep studying.
We felt it was too soon to make a choice like that. But when Sarah was
fourteen she said, 'I don't care whether or not I have a bat mitzvah. I
consider myself a Jewish person and I plan to live as one.' Those were
the magic words. All our resistance crumbled."

She began to study for conversion and a bat mitzvah with a Conservative rabbi in Harrisburg. "I remember the first day we took her
to his office," Mary said. "He brought up some question that got us
into a three-corner theological go-round. He withdrew and watched
us. Finally, he asked, 'Do you people do this often?' We said, 'All the
time.' He said, 'That's depressing.' But we told him that in a family
like ours you have to hammer through everything all the time."

Mary knows that Sarah's choice to be a Jew was far less of a problem
for her than the choice to be a Catholic would have been for Ned.

"We always stress that distinction when we encounter couples
where each partner continues in a different religion," she said.
"We've seen a lot of hostility and frustration arise because the Christian feels that he or she is making all the compromises. It just has to
be clear from the beginning that there is a real difference between a
Christian's child being Jewish and a Jew's child being Christian."

But Mary still felt a great deal of sorrow. "I look at my children now
and it seems as if none of them will be Catholics. That is an unresolved problem for me. Here is something that I believe in passion-
ately that I have not conveyed to my children in any way that seems to
have reality for them. So I have to consider whether I've done right by
them, by their souls. That's an ambiguity I have to live with. I can't
see any way out of it.

"That's one of the prices of this marriage. It would be true in spades for Ned if none of the kids became Jews."

"It would be worse," he said. "My relationships with the kids wouldn't change, but my feeling of having defaulted on my obligation to my people would always be on my mind."

Ned wasn't talking abstractly. He was thinking about his sons Rafi and Will.

When Will came downstairs for lunch, I asked him how he identified himself. "Not with either parent or even either religion. I think that being exposed to two religions has given me a good perspective on the subject, and I believe Judaism and Catholicism can both be worthwhile. At least my parents get a lot out of them. But I don't see myself subscribing to any specific religion ever."

Most fathers sound edgy and judgmental when they discuss the things that concern them most with their college-age sons, and Ned was no exception. "William seems to be a fairly happy humanist, but the ball game is going to change for him when he falls in love and the woman is something or nothing." Turning to him, Ned added, "Then the wind is going to fill your sails, and you're going to have to go off in some direction."

Ned's comment sounded autobiographical to me. But Will turned it into the basis of an argument. "I could definitely marry someone who had a strong religious belief as long as she's willing to accept the fact that I don't have one.

"I think that basically it all comes down to faith. The foundations of religion were laid down a long time ago and are poorly documented. So unless you have faith you can't really *prove* any religion."

"I don't agree with that, of course," Ned said. "I think you're putting the cart before the horse. I'm a card-carrying agnostic. I don't know that there's a God. But I'm a member of the Jewish people and their concerns are my concerns. My theology is almost irrelevant."

The argument between father and son was exactly the kind of discussion Ned and Mary had always encouraged. It was a discussion of the reasons a person makes a spiritual choice.

Leaning toward his father, Will said, "You're saying the same thing as I am except that you've chosen Jews as your community and I have not yet chosen a community. But you have to admit that you're not talking about God."

Ned's voice got a little more heated. For he was both an intellec-

tual, trained in the heady environment that had permeated the University of Chicago, and a Jewish father trying to convince a wayward
son of the value of historic continuity. He feared that the Rosenbaum
experiment in a bi-religious household had jeopardized Will's identity in the same way as Mary feared it had jeopardized his soul.

"I'm saying you don't have to make a theological choice before you
make a communal choice. You can be part of a community without
being dogmatic about the historical veracity of some event on which
the community has founded itself."

"This is a Rosenbaum family conversation," Mary said. "We argue
this way about everything. Our first real fight after we got married was
just before Sarah was born. It was over whether or not—*if* Sarah was a
girl—she would be allowed to date a boy who was riding a motorcycle
at the age of sixteen. Ned was the conservative."

"That wasn't so farfetched," Sarah laughed. "When I was sixteen
the first person I ever dated was talking about getting a motorcycle.
My first response was, 'Fine, I'm never getting on it.' "

"That's the real secret to successful parenthood," Mary said—"to
raise your kids to want to do the things you think they should do."

"That idea should work in religion as well," Ned said. "I feel that a
sound religious education is the best proof against things you don't
want to have happen. Obviously it's not prophylactic. But I'm
tempted to say it should be. Even in the case of a kid who flips out
religiously there's something that wasn't done right. In a Jewish
household, in a Catholic household, if the thing is done right you
have an overwhelming chance that the kid will grow up not only being
of that faith but enjoying it."

Now Ned the father was posing a fundamental challenge to the
gospel of pluralism he had tried to ingrain in his children.

Sounding shocked, Will said, "You're saying that the reason a
person becomes a Jew or a Catholic is almost certainly because his
parents made him that way. What you're saying, basically, is that
many or most people who are strongly religious and are the same
religion as their parents feel the way they do because of the way they
were raised. Truth doesn't play a role in your argument. But you and
Mom told us, in effect, 'These are *your* choices, never mind what we
believe.' I think you were right to do that. Aren't you contradicting
yourself now?"

Ned was, of course. Talking to Will, he questioned the decisions that had sounded so brave and promising so long ago. "If you come from a single-religion family and you want that religion to continue I think that you can have the result that you desire," he said wistfully.

Now Mary disagreed. "That's like saying if you toilet train your kids right then they'll never be neurotic. I don't think parents can be that farsighted. They can only point backward and say, 'Here's where we made a mistake.' We both know plenty of single-religion families who are perfectly loving and nice people who have had disasters with their kids."

Then, Mary said, "Ned and I have reversed roles. I would have taken his position twenty years ago."

"Well, you were right," Ned said with a wry laugh. "Why didn't you say it more loudly?"

As Ned and Mary talked, it was clear that their commitment to religion had made their complicated marriage unusually strong. The shared faith they called monotheism encompassed the practical details of raising a family. It helped furnish them the patience to be lifetime lovers who had the unusual ability to explore their diversity with each other and share it with the children they cherished. Even when there was tension between Ned and Will, or disagreement between Ned and Mary, their idle conversation was suffused with old jokes, loving memories, and a determination to listen to each other's ideas.

There was a wonderful sense of pride on Mary's face as she talked with Sarah and Will as intellectual equals. From her point of view, even Will's post-adolescent bout of defiant secular humanism was far more literate than the similar arguments she had heard from most of his contemporaries. When she disagreed with him, it was with loving respect.

Ned was wise enough to realize that his argument with Will was part of a psychological and theological dynamic that might last for years. His own experience had taught him that, most likely, his son's secret religious script would only surface once he was a husband who had to decide how to raise children.

As a father and as a Jew, Ned was proud of the fact that Sarah was still involved in Jewish studies, and once considered a career in the rabbinate. But one could see the anxiety that had darkened his face flicker again as Sarah described how she hoped to raise children.

These days, Ned was always worried about the long-term cost of his spiritual gamble. Should Sarah take a similar risk in her generation?

She thought so. She was glad her parents had exposed her to conflicting religious ideas. "What could be more exciting than these three-corner religious conversations we've had since I was four. It was a wonderful way to grow up. I would ask a question, then Mom would answer, then Dad would answer Mom's answer. Then Mom would answer, then Dad would answer. I'd walk away and be done, but two hours later they would still be there, talking about God. That's my image of love of each other and love of a Supreme Being.

"I think people who have parents who are both well educated and both devout in one faith miss something. They lack an empathy for other ways of believing. Most of the people I know in Carlisle are clones of their parents' beliefs. They might wonder whether or not there is a God, but they never stop to think about what God they believe in.

"I hope that when I get married I'll use my training in other religions to raise kids who know as much about Christianity as Judaism. I'll be loading the deck, of course, because I plan to live in a community that is much more Jewish than Carlisle. I'll be an observant Jew at home. But I still want my children to think about their choice before they commit themselves to live as Jews. Before they have a bar or bat mitzvah, I want them to be able to explain *why* they are Jewish. I would want them to be able to hold a conversation with a non-Jew about that person's religion before they make a formal choice. You can't choose if you don't know—or if all you know is Judaism."

"What you're saying is risky," Ned told his daughter. He was still musing about Will when he said, "Sometimes, now, I worry about the whole business of choice. I think maybe it's better for two apathetic Jews to marry each other and just keep this pilot light burning so that at some point it can take flame again. Clearly, I haven't done that. But sometimes I think it's best to create a sort of minimal Jewish consciousness—'I'm Jewish, my wife is Jewish'—because that guarantees us a future."

Then he paused a minute, thinking out the implications of that idea. When he resumed, it was clear that Ned the monotheist, who believed that Christians had as much claim to truth as Jews, was battling Ned the anxious father, who worried that each child who chose another religion endangered the survival of a people. "Sometimes I think people who are raised in Jewish communities must have gotten their idea of Christianity off a Cracker Jack box. I remember the third rabbi on Sarah's *bet din* [the religious court which asked her questions before approving her conversion]," he said with a laugh. "He wanted you to denounce Christianity as a religion that believed in superstitions and miracles. I shudder to think of the congregation that learned its theology from him."

Then Sarah said, "I've been teaching at a Hebrew school and those kids don't know anything about Christianity. They know about the streetlights at Christmastime, but sometimes, in class, I'll throw in a Christian phrase, and I'll have to explain it. Sometimes I have a temptation to teach them Christianity as well as Judaism."

As she said that, Ned looked at his daughter with a father's worried pride. "Your background has the virtue of its fault. It has given you two perspectives, which means that you're more comfortable in the world than a Christian or a Jew who was raised in a religious box. But if you really choose to live as a mainstream, affiliated Jew—or if Rafi or Will decide to live as traditional religious people—there might be a real problem. It's not at all clear that the world you want to live in will be comfortable with you."

A Unitarian Resolution

This is not an age when many Jews convert to mainstream Christianity, though scores of thousands do become involved with Eastern religions or sects like Jews for Jesus. There is no church forcing them to relinquish their faith. Conversion to Episcopalianism or Congregationalism doesn't bring social rewards as it did when Anne Lazarus became an Episcopalian. As a rule, even if a Jew finds churches aesthetically appealing, and feels that Christianity is universalistic and Judaism is too narrow, the act of being baptized or christened seems treasonous.

We have interviewed Jews who agreed that their spouses could raise the children as Christians. They make their sons or daughters pancakes before they drive them to Sunday school, and participate wholeheartedly in Christian holiday celebrations, sometimes because they enjoy them, sometimes because they want to preserve family harmony. As a rule, religion interests them less than sports or politics or literature or science: those pursuits are their links with their youngsters.

Some Jews in intermarriages become Unitarians. Since Unitarian ritual and liturgy are Protestant, while its theology rejects the idea of Jesus as the Messiah, it seems to represent a sort of spiritual common ground. Many Christians feel that Unitarianism is too rational and academic, bereft of mystery and passion. Many Jews ultimately feel it is too Christian. But if you visit a Unitarian church on a Sunday morning, you'll find scores of interfaith couples.

Paul Frank, fifty-three, a lawyer whose parents were non-practicing Jews from Queens, and his wife Linda, forty-five, whose family were enthusiastic Congregationalists in a small Connecticut town, have both been officers of All Soul's Unitarian Church in Manhattan.

The Franks, who share a need for a religious home, feel Unitarianism serves their family perfectly. Its liturgy harmonizes silent languages which would have clashed if Paul had wanted Linda to attend temple with him, or if Linda had insisted on expressing her Christian feelings in a more Christ-centered setting. More importantly, it contains a community that has helped them through times of great stress.

We talked one Thursday night, after Rachel and I had performed our weekly secular ritual of watching "The Cosby Show" and "Family Ties" with Lisa and Matt, and Linda and Paul had done the same with their thirteen-year-old son David.

Paul, who was born in Manhattan and raised in Forest Hills, Queens, describes his parents as highly assimilated Jews who rarely went to synagogue or had a seder, and who celebrated Christmas from the time he was in nursery school. His family moved to Forest Hills in 1941, when the neighborhood—now predominantly Jewish— was still half Jewish and half Christian. "Some of our Jewish neighbors objected to the fact that we had a Christmas tree on the sun porch. We moved it to the basement. My sister and I couldn't understand that."

In Forest Hills, Paul made Jewish friends and decided to go to Hebrew school with them so that he could have a bar mitzvah. As he recalled it, when he stood up in the Kew Gardens Reform synagogue, read his Torah portion, and gave a speech about what it meant for

Jewish boys to come of age, his entire family displayed immense pride in him.

At Columbia, where he went to college and law school from 1951–58, most of his friends were Jews. Like almost all his friends at college he rarely went to synagogue, even on the Holy Days. In those years, a love affair between a Jew and a gentile caused raised eyebrows. If his temperament had been slightly different, he would probably have married a Jewish woman whose loyalties flickered as faintly as his. But, he said, "I was a shy bashful fellow who rarely even went out on a date."

Linda's family settled in Avon, Connecticut, in 1943. When Linda was growing up, Avon's population was about three thousand. There were two Congregational churches and a Catholic church. She recalled the town as a quiet but wonderful place to grow up. "There weren't any movie theaters, only a bowling alley." In that environment, much of her life revolved around the church. "My whole family went every week, and my mother taught Sunday school. There was a husband and wife who were both ordained ministers there, and I grew up thinking I might want to be a minister, too. It was certainly a positive experience. I always knew that if I had children, I'd want the same for them."

Holidays, for her, were very special. "We always had a Christmas tree that my brother and I decorated with tinsel. There was a skating scene under the tree." It wasn't a secular Christmas since the family always went to church on Christmas Eve. They felt the same undiluted spiritual passion that night as they did at the Good Friday services and sunrise services at Easter that were so much a part of their lives.

Throughout high school, her parents kept track of the boys she dated. She thought they might have been uneasy if she had gone steady with one of the Catholic boys who lived in Avon. She didn't know any Jews, but "I expect that if I had dated one it would have been mentioned. As it happened, I went out with a Congregationalist."

In college she realized that she had internalized some of her parents' attitudes. "I met Paul through a roommate at college, and when I started dating him I could feel a very subtle displeasure from my mother and father. I think it is to their credit that they didn't make a big issue of it.

"They didn't have to. From my point of view, the fact that Paul was Jewish wasn't ideal." But, "I knew he had always had a Christmas tree so it was clear that he wasn't a religious Jew. If he had been, I'm not sure what would have happened. It would have been a trickier relationship."

As it was, she had to make an important compromise. "I had always imagined getting married in the picture postcard Congregational church where I was raised, but I didn't think that would be fair to Paul. It would have offended his family, just as my family would have been offended if we had been married in a synagogue. So we wound up in an ultra-modern Unitarian church in Hartford with a beautiful service that 'both sides' thought was very special."

Paul, who had been talking to David, turned to her and confessed that "When we got married I didn't appreciate how important it was for you to get married in the Congregational church you grew up in."

"How could you?" she asked affectionately. "You didn't have a frame of reference. I think you appreciate it now because our Unitarian church has become so important to us."

Linda always knew that she wanted the family to have one faith, and she wanted it to be Christian. That's why she had been relieved to hear about Paul's Christmas tree and realize he wasn't a religious Jew. "I could never have become Jewish," she said. "I don't feel comfortable with the religion. It is steeped in ceremony and tradition that I don't know. And I don't like the idea of 'the chosen people.' It's too exclusive for me." If Paul had experienced a surge of ethnic pride, and insisted that his children be raised as Jews, it would have disrupted their relationship.

Even though Linda knew that church should be an important part of their family life, it took years for her and Paul to join one. When they were first married, they made occasional visits to All Soul's or Downtown Community Church.

Then, a time bomb splintered their lives: their first baby died of a neurological disease. "He was cremated but we didn't have a service," Linda said. "That was a bad time. We weren't affiliated with a church or a minister we could turn to. I realize now how important that would have been to us."

They postponed finding a church until David was born. Then, Linda said, "Paul and I realized that if religion was going to be part of our family life, our child would have to go to Sunday school." But she was careful to heed Paul's religious feelings. For she knew that, assimilated as her husband seemed, a faith that professed the divinity of Jesus would offend him. "That's why we thought that starting out as Unitarians made sense. I knew that I would have to give up the idea of Jesus as divine, but that didn't matter very much to me. I believe it's the way we live our life that matters, not all the trimmings."

Paul was satisfied with that choice. "There's nothing in the service at All Soul's that disturbs me," he said. "The prayers and readings recognize that we have come from varied religious backgrounds. We talk about uniting for worship and service 'in the spirit of Jesus' and 'Jesus as a great teacher and moral leader.' But we don't see him as divine.

"I did have one problem. The church used to have a large, dominant cross and that made me uncomfortable. Then, when the cross was removed for the painting of the sanctuary, the congregation decided to study the question of appropriate religious symbolism. The congregation voted to use a chancel wall hanging, a string sculpture in which the cross is clear but not overwhelming. I knew they had done it right when I saw it and thought that it was still too much of a cross for me, but the little old lady sitting next to me asked where the cross was."

After Paul and Linda joined All Soul's, they discovered that their third child, Kate, was suffering from the same neurological degenerative disease that their first child had died from. "I don't believe in hellfire and damnation," Linda said, "but when I found out how sick Kate was I wondered what we had done wrong to have suffered that. I needed the comfort of people who cared, and our friends at church furnished that."

Paul and Linda were so grateful for that sense of community that they began to devote a substantial amount of time to the congregation. In 1984, Paul was elected its president. Linda now serves on the Board of Trustees and runs a soup kitchen at the church. Paul explained his commitment to the church with typical terseness. "You look around and see that each of us carries burdens and cares. We're here to help each other."

Possibly, if Paul had married a more conventionally devout Christian or Linda had wed a Jew with a concealed religious script, the death of one child and the terrible ailment of another would have caused searing conflicts. But Paul and Linda have weathered tragedies that tear many couples apart with astonishing calm. Now they and their son David derive immense comfort from the prospect of spending Sunday morning in the presence of loving friends and of a God they can all worship.

A Jew by Birth, Two Jews by Choice

Gentiles who feel pressure to convert to Judaism usually say that they haven't ruled out the prospect entirely. But, like Tim and Chris in our workshop, they want to feel as if they are making the decisions for themselves, not for a spouse or for an in-law. They want to be treated as individuals, with their own histories, their own accomplishments, their own values. They bridle when a rabbi, an in-law, a spouse make them feel that the only important question about them is whether they'll become Jews.

In those situations, it is important that the spouse or in-law who hopes the gentile will choose Judaism find a program of Jewish study that is intellectually stimulating and doesn't demand immediate conversion. It is important that the gentile is exposed to a ritual life with meaning, and a community of Jews which welcomes newcomers. For people are far more willing to choose Judaism if they see it as an attractive way of life than if conversion is only portrayed as an homage to the 6 million.

Ed Jamison, a psychologist, and Rebecca Weiderman, a social worker, were able to lead each other into Judaism after they were married. The road was almost as long for Rebecca, the daughter of Holocaust survivors, who once considered becoming a Christian, as for Ed, who was a religious Protestant until after he graduated from college.

Ed, a tall, well-built blond, a shot putter and a frat man in college, came from Philadelphia, Pennsylvania, where his family were members of the American Baptist Church, a smaller, more restrained, more politically liberal denomination than its Southern counterparts. The American Baptists are a missionary religion, and Ed's father, a doctor, spent several months as a physician in a mission hospital in Nigeria. His deeds impressed his son.

Until college, Ed had been involved in Christian youth groups, often as a leader. He had taken pleasure in going to church every Sunday, in saying grace before every meal. "We always had a lot of religious discussions about God and about a Christian life style," he recalled with some pride. "I had a very strong belief in God and I still do. Even when I was a very young child I thought seriously about going into the ministry."

He was baptized when he was twelve. "It was intense. The baptismal font was in the front of the sanctuary. We put on black robes and walked in, in front of the whole congregation. At twelve, I thought that lightning was going to strike me. That didn't happen, but I remember feeling that I was completely purified." That was just one of a series of powerful adolescent religious experiences. "I remember as a small child I sang 'Holy, Holy, Holy, Lord God Almighty,' and the adult choir was there and the children's choir, and the organ was playing. I felt filled with His spirit. I can remember when I went to church camp. We had services in the pine trees in an amphitheater. One midnight everybody made a little boat out of paper and put candles in it. It was a very moving experience."

When Ed was a senior in high school, he began to feel uneasy with the staid, well-groomed services at the First Baptist Church. But instead of staying at home on Sundays, "I developed an alternative service where we sang folk songs—sixties stuff. It gave me a chance to express something that was more meaningful to me."

Then, more reflectively, he added, "I think that religion has always been a holding ground for my passion. My family was very restrained. Church was one of the few places where I could express my intense feelings."

His Christian fervor stayed with him in college. But he didn't feel comfortable in the formal Baptist services. He couldn't find another church that appealed to him. "I felt I wanted to do something with my life that had meaning to me, and something which God wanted me to do." He tried to accomplish that by tutoring black inner city children.

If Ed grew up amid answers, Rebecca had many unformed questions. She was the daughter of Polish Jews who met in a displaced persons camp after the Holocaust. Her father, who had escaped the Nazis by fleeing to Russia, died of a heart attack when she was four. Her mother, the only one of eight children who survived the Holocaust, had been hidden by gentiles until the war ended.

After her husband's death, she wanted to forget all the nightmares she associated with Europe. She settled in an ethnically diverse neighborhood in Canarsie, where she joined an Orthodox synagogue, though she went there only on the High Holidays. She rarely talked about the Hitler years.

"She was trying to protect herself and protect me because the memories were too painful for her," Rebecca said. "I didn't know about the Holocaust until I was about twelve. Then we were watching a TV show about World War II and she told me a little about what happened to her. After that, I wondered about my family and about Jews. Once, after the 1967 war in Israel, my mother and I went to hear Golda Meir speak in Madison Square Garden. When she said 'never again' I remember having a really emotional reaction." But when her mother enrolled her in after-school Hebrew classes, Rebecca refused to go. "My experience was almost the reverse of Ed's," she said. "Judaism as a religion seemed flat. I did have a lot of Jewish friends, but they all had American-born parents. Besides, nobody talked about the Holocaust when I was growing up. I didn't hear it mentioned in synagogue, in Hebrew school, or even in my high school history courses. That increased my sense of isolation."

She spoke about her past in a calm, flat voice with a heartland accent. "In high school, they gave us speech lessons so that we wouldn't sound like New York Jews. People tell me that I sound like a Midwesterner. That's nice to hear because sometimes I feel hysterical and Jewish inside."

When Rebecca got to college she continued to feel estranged from the Jewish community. She helped organize a Women's Caucus and became involved in community service, but she was looking for a more spiritual way of expressing herself.

She had begun to attend Quaker meeting when she and Ed met in a psychology class. Then she began to date Ed and saw that he was expressing his faith by working with disadvantaged kids. She was impressed by his desire to be a minister, "though it accentuated the difference in our backgrounds. It seemed like it would be nice to be a Christian and have a strong belief in God. It seemed very optimistic. I liked the idea of doing good things and feeling I would be rewarded in the afterlife. I liked Christian altruism."

If she was attracted by Ed's religion, he was unusually skilled at understanding Rebecca's feelings as the child of a survivor. He perceived things about her that she didn't yet understand about herself.

"When we first got together, I always saw the pain she felt about the Holocaust, about the fact that I wasn't Jewish, about her mother's disapproval of me. I'd hardly ever heard anyone talk with that much feeling in my family."

Then he paused for a moment. "My understanding was that if I was going to be with Rebecca, I had to recognize the undeniable force of her background in the Holocaust. I realized that if I was going to marry her, I would have to respect that as deeply as I could. I certainly couldn't see her converting to Christianity, especially since I was beginning to doubt the religion anyway. And I saw that something about being Jewish was very important to her."

They decided to begin their married life by working overseas. "We were both interested in living in an underdeveloped country, and had applied to several programs, including the Peace Corps." Then Ed was awarded a Watson Fellowship to study child development in Africa. The program he had outlined involved living at the Baptist hospital where his father had worked years earlier.

"I liked the image of us as a young, dedicated American couple," Rebecca said, "though I did wonder what a Jewish girl from Brooklyn would be doing on a mission station in Africa. I wondered how I would handle it and whether I would convert to Christianity."

Ed was still looking for some way of expressing his religious feelings. He hoped he would find it in Africa. Instead, within a year, he became completely disaffected with Christianity.

The program was sponsored by the American Baptists. Shortly before Rebecca and Ed left America, she asked one of its administrators if he thought it would make any difference that she was Jewish. "The guy nearly fell over. We started to realize that we wouldn't fit in there."

Shortly after they arrived, Rebecca began to work with Africans and Peace Corps volunteers to develop a way of teaching farmers to immunize their chickens against Newcastle disease. She liked that work. But she was always uneasy at the missionary station, where she felt a relentless pressure to become a Christian.

"I remember one missionary talking about what a great place this is. 'We even have a Jewess here,' he said. Sometimes people were direct about urging me to convert. The idea was always in the air. It seemed as if the missionaries believed that one Jewish conversion is worth a lot of African ones."

That pressure changed her attitude about herself. "Before we got to Africa I had felt very Jewish but I didn't feel positive about being Jewish. That was why I wondered whether I'd convert to Christianity. But when I felt all the pressure from the missionaries, I realized that I wanted to remain a Jew. I had to ask what the religion meant to me, beyond the fact that my parents had survived Hitler. I wanted to find something more positive to hang onto."

During their year in Africa she began to read every book about Jews she could find in the library at the Baptist station. She read *The Source* and all of Chaim Potok's books. She decided she wanted to go to Israel on their way home from Africa.

Ed was surprised to discover how deeply he disagreed with the missionaries' attitude toward Rebecca and toward the Africans. "There wasn't enough acceptance or tolerance of differences. I couldn't buy the idea of making the natives into Christians. I was too interested in their culture."

To his chagrin, he realized that from childhood on he had held some of the same attitudes that the missionaries did. He wondered how they affected his feelings about Rebecca. "Even when I was most sensitive to her Judaism, there was always part of me that believed 'I have *the* way for everybody, and if you don't have it you'll burn in hell.' "

When Rebecca said she wanted to go to Israel, Ed realized he was eager to make the journey. After his experiences at the missionary station, he no longer identified himself as a Baptist. But he still believed in God.

In Israel, he discovered, "the history of Judaism began to appeal to me. The prayers go back so far that they almost have dust on them. I loved being in the country and seeing that."

In the year after Rebecca and Ed were married, their attitudes toward their respective religions had undergone a complete reversal. And, since they had both begun their marriage as spiritual seekers, they were eager to understand the nuances of each other's feelings.

Rebecca's were evolving quickly. In Africa she discovered that for her, "it was painful to be an interfaith couple." In Israel, she began to wonder "whether we would fit in anywhere. I remember being very melodramatic about it, like Romeo and Juliet," she said with a laugh.

She began to urge Ed to convert, but the idea didn't appeal to him. "I kept thinking that we could work things out without changing faiths. We were on a secular kibbutz most of the time, and they were so eager for us to stay there that they didn't make much of an issue of my religion," Ed said. He loved the place. "I had a great job there, working in a machine shop as a welder. I really got to know the five or six guys I worked with. I felt like I was part of things."

When the couple got back to America, they spent a year working in upstate New York. Rebecca decided to find soil in which the Jewish feelings they were both developing could grow. She tried to join a Reform temple. But "the rabbi was really cold. He basically said that we couldn't join because Ed wasn't Jewish. I didn't want to expose him to that kind of feeling. That was the last time we went there."

They moved to Boston the next year, where Rebecca went to social work school and Ed studied special education. Rebecca visited another Reform temple. "That rabbi's reaction was very different. He said, 'Why don't you join. Ed doesn't have to convert. We'll see how things go.' His attitude was very welcoming. We started going to services on the High Holidays."

But to Ed's disappointment, "It wasn't so different from Philadelphia's First Baptist Church. Services were a big, formal production." They decided to keep searching.

In Boston, Rebecca found a new way to get in touch with her untapped Jewish feelings. She joined One Generation After, an organization for children of Holocaust survivors. "It was the first time I had ever sat and talked with other people my age whose parents had been survivors, and it was a wonderful experience. We met for about four years. Those people were like kin. I had never felt so close to a group before."

But now that she had moved from the cosmopolitan world she had known in college through the missionary station to a primarily Jewish world, she "felt a little schizophrenic. I am so grateful that Ed was so supportive."

In fact, it was what he had expected to happen ever since he met Rebecca in college. Instead of recoiling in fear that she would vanish into a Jewish world, Ed "thought it was terrific, that Rebecca was finding Jews she could talk to. I knew, caring about her, that she had to do something with her experience."

Rebecca was still pushing Ed to convert. "I hated to pressure him and I tried not to. But I felt such tension in our relationship . . . I was afraid of losing him, and yet I had discovered just how much Jewishness was a part of me."

But much as he supported her discovery of her Jewishness, he couldn't become a Jew just to please her. "I needed a context to learn more," he said. "I could encourage Rebecca's search because I loved her, or work on the kibbutz because I felt accepted there, but I *am* a religious person and this was a big decision about God."

Instead of viewing his resistance as stubbornness, Rebecca decided to look for a place where they could both learn. "The Gerim Institute"—a Jewish studies course—seemed perfect to Rebecca "because you weren't supposed to know whether you wanted to convert or not."

But, Ed said, "it turned out that everyone in the course was planning to convert because they were getting married soon. I just wanted to learn. When it came to the end of the term, everyone but me converted. But for me, it felt like a giant leap and I hadn't built up enough of a foundation to take it. I took conversion very seriously. I felt enormous anxiety about it. Once I decided not to convert, I felt very comfortable. I was sure I had made the right decision."

Rebecca understood his reservations, especially because they couldn't find a Jewish group where they both felt at home. They went to synagogue at least once a month, but those that were informal and intense—like Havurat Shalom in Somerville—required too much Hebrew, and those that were comprehensible, like the Reform temples they visited, seemed flat.

Then, when Rebecca finished social work school in Boston, she got a hospital job in a Connecticut town while Ed studied for a Ph.D. in special education. They resumed their search.

Ed recalled that "We felt welcome in the Conservative synagogue from the first time we went there, during Simchat Torah [the celebration of the Giving of the Law, one of the most jubilant holidays of the Jewish year], and everyone was dancing with so much joy. We went there every Shabbat for months—it was wonderful. I remember one Saturday someone asked me to say the blessing over the Torah and I had to refuse because I wasn't Jewish. The next week he remembered my name and greeted me warmly. I was amazed that he was so friendly. I felt at home."

Now, he thinks that his stay in Israel and his weeks at the Gerim Institute gave him the confidence to feel comfortable in the synagogue. He is especially grateful to one of his teachers at Gerim who told him that if he was interested in becoming Jewish, he should adopt one form of observance at a time instead of trying to change his life overnight. That meant he didn't have to surrender the self he had always been in order to become a Jew.

Besides, Ed knew that Rebecca was searching with him. Unlike couples who use their religious differences as weapons in a warped version of "The Newlywed Game," the desire for faith was always part of their marriage. For example, instead of singling out unfriendly rabbis as if they were spokesmen for the entire community, as couples who feel ambivalent about commitment do, Ed and Rebecca befriended those who made Judaism attractive. They provided each other with inspirations, not obstacles.

"We were very fortunate to have tolerant families," Rebecca added. "They certainly had moments when they disapproved of the things we did. My mother regretted that I had married a non-Jew, but she got to know Ed and liked him as an individual. Ed's parents would have preferred that we join a Christian church. But they've accepted our Jewish life. In fact, when we stayed with them for a week over the Christmas holiday his mother carefully prepared meals that didn't mix meat and milk. She served a kosher turkey on Christmas Eve."

People who convert to Judaism often have more trouble getting accustomed to the culture they've joined than understanding theology or remembering niceties of Jewish law. Ed had time to acculturate to Judaism. He went to synagogue, and people thought he was Jewish. He and Rebecca began to follow the dietary laws. He took Jewish holidays off from work. Unlike Rebecca, who is more interested in the Jewish people than in Judaism as a religion, he found he was able to pray to a God who lived for him while he was in synagogue. Soon "I began to feel that I was Jewish." Then it seemed "ridiculous not to convert." He did convert, seven years after they were married.

He saw Judaism as a religion for adults. "The whole structure of Judaism makes more sense to me now than Christianity does. I feel as if it has more tolerance for everything. It doesn't have the same sense of sin. Rather, the belief is that if you did something wrong this time, you can try again next time. Everything, from sexuality to death, is discussed. Besides, I don't buy the myth of Christianity anymore. It doesn't respond to the feelings I have. Judaism contains the passion I tried to express in church.

"I love the age of it—the fact that these prayers have been going on for thousands of years and that everyone is doing the same thing at the same time. And I like the Hebrew. Part of the reason I get into the services is because of the age of Hebrew."

Sometimes, when he can't follow the Hebrew, he prays to God in somewhat the same manner he did as a boy in church, only he feels more comfortable with a synagogue as the house of the Lord. He knows that Rebecca, sitting beside him, feels she has found her community there, too.

He and Rebecca, who always shared an interest in faith and good works, were able to listen to each other's words and hear the silent languages behind them. They were able to lead each other home.

9

Advice from Some Children of Intermarriage

"I'm half Jewish and half nothing."
(four-year-old boy in an elevator, to his friend)

"What about our children? We're adults and we can maintain our separate identities, but what about them?" That question, more than any other, haunts the people who come to our workshops. Listen, as two of the more than sixty adult children of intermarriage we interviewed give their answers:

"When I go to a church or a synagogue I feel interested, but not connected to either religion. If you asked me what I am, I'd say I'm Jewish but I come from a mixed marriage and religiously I'm not Jewish at all. "At times, I feel as if I have a special outlook, a window into both worlds. But sometimes I get the sense that I have a foot in each territory and I'm not a citizen of either. The reward of not choosing between religions is that I can keep the freedom and flexibility I have now. The advantage of being Jewish is a sense of solidity and a resolution of a very big question in my life."

"All my life I've been aware of being half and half. I feel like I'm on the fringes of things in a lot of ways. I'm half Jewish, half Christian. I was raised a political radical, but I don't really have any politics. I don't have any geographic roots. I just feel there are a whole lot of ways I don't belong. I've wanted to know who I was ever since I was a teenager."

Whatever their age, whatever their gender or generation, most children of intermarriage sound variations of these themes. They are not talking about happiness. There is no evidence, in our interviews or in the few studies that have been done, that children of intermarriage are more or less cheerful, more or less content with their lives, more or less loving to spouses or children, more or less successful in their professions, than any other group of people. Many say that they feel unusually well equipped to move back and forth between two cultures.

Others experience a negative version of that same feeling. They say they feel like double agents, darting back and forth between enemy lines. The writer, director, and actor John Houseman (born in 1902) —the son of a British mother and an Alsatian Jewish father—summed up that feeling in the title of the first chapter of his best-selling theater memoir *Run-Through.* He called the chapter which described his childhood "The Education of a Chameleon."

Some people echo Mike Lerner's feeling that the cross and the star are at war inside him. Most of these people describe a lifelong sense of rootlessness, a lifelong need to resolve persistent questions about their identities.

The children of intermarriages we interviewed ranged in age from eighteen to forty-five. That means most of them were born between 1940 and 1970, in an era when intermarriage rates were relatively low, when there was much less conversion to Judaism than there is now, and when Jews, even those with a strong sense of ethnic pride, were more likely to let their children be raised as Christians or in religiously neutral households than their counterparts are today. They grew up in a time when synagogues were much more hostile to interfaith couples than they are now. As a group they were more estranged from Jewish life than many of their counterparts in this generation will be.

Many of the people we interviewed had never discussed how they felt about being the child of parents whose religious and ethnic differences were so marked. But as they talked, they almost invariably remembered a moment in their lives when they had felt a surge of strong emotion because of their dual heritage. Most had assumed those feelings represented an evanescent mood that no one else would understand. They seldom discussed them with lovers, friends, psychiatrists. They didn't see themselves as "children of intermarriage," as men and women who fit into a category.

When we interviewed them, they had no preconceptions of what they would say; we had no idea of what we would hear. Often, as they talked, confusions and angers that had been bottled up for years poured forth. The depths of their feelings surprised them and us. Their stories were long and complicated. Clearly the fact that one parent was Jewish and one was Christian was only one aspect of their childhood experience, one explanation for complicated attitudes about themselves, their place in the world, and their religious values.

Yet within their collective responses we found clear patterns. They described pitfalls that face any interfaith couple. They sounded warnings that we feel parents should hear.

At the end of our interviews, we asked them whether they wished their parents had done anything different about their religious upbringing. Of course, the answer varied from person to person. But both those who praised their parents and those who criticized them conveyed the same message. They valued clarity and a sense of security. They felt parents should choose a religious identity for their children and not leave it up to them to choose. Furthermore, they thought parents should furnish an environment in which the children would feel comfortable living with that identity.

They wanted roots in one of their parents' religions and cultures, but branches that extended to the other's. Indeed, many of the children we talked with were troubled that one parent had suppressed all traces of his or her own religious heritage and culture. In many cases, the children had felt compelled to follow the few clues they had found about this past and sought to re-create that hidden identity for themselves.

We have used our interviews with children of intermarriages to glean ideas about practical measures that parents can take to give their children a clearer sense of identity. We have taken excerpts from interviews to illustrate the need for those measures. While these excerpts do not show the complexity of each individual's experience, they are faithful to the sense conveyed by the interview as a whole. We have arranged them as a list of suggestions to help people who intermarry open up discussions of important life decisions.

Many of the items on this list apply to one-faith families, too, but very differently from the way they apply to people who intermarry. If parents have the same religious background they might disagree about the importance of their faith, but their children still perceive themselves as members of that faith.

If parents grew up in different branches of Judaism—if one parent is Reform and the other is Orthodox—they may disagree about the significance of dietary laws or the Sabbath—and a child might wonder whose lead to follow.

If they are from different denominations of Christianity—if one is a Catholic and the other is a Protestant—the child may be troubled by it, as Mary Rosenbaum was when she noticed that her Lutheran father "was a passive observer in our religious life who only came to Mass with us on Christmas and Easter."

But the problem for the children of Jews who marry Christians is much more complicated. When two Jews or two Christians marry, the children may wonder *how* to be a Jew or a Christian. But they don't wonder *whether* they are Jews or Christians.

We saw that clearly when we talked with our friend Fran, a Reform Jew, who had been arguing with her husband Dick, a Jewish socialist, about their son Eli's upcoming bar mitzvah. Fran, a synagogue-goer, saw the event as the glad day Eli would take his place in his people's tradition. Dick worried that he'd feel uncomfortable during the service, and that he'd experience Eli's religious rite of passage as a rejection of his secular tradition.

But Eli knew that his father was a Jew and wanted him to identify as one. He knew that, however much his parents might disagree about religion, they had no doubt that they were part of the same people and shared the same history.

Last year, when Eli chose to write a sixth-grade essay about ancient Israel, he approached Fran with a question which showed just how secure he was in his identity. "I don't know what to call the Jews in this paper," he said. "It sounds funny to say 'we' in my school, because most of the kids aren't Jewish. But I can't imagine calling the Jews 'they.' "

By contrast, we've heard most children of intermarriage whose parents have not made a choice of religious or ethnic identity for them describe the times they felt like outsiders in both the Jewish and Christian worlds. They could never answer the unspoken question: "who is we?"

We have become convinced that their parents have a special responsibility to enable them to answer that question. So we hope this list provides helpful suggestions for ways of doing so.

Think About Your Child's Jewish Status

This consideration is important for couples who decide to raise Jewish children. There are now two different working definitions of who is a Jew. According to *halakha* [Jewish law], a child of a Jewish mother and gentile father is a Jew by birth while the child of a Jewish father and gentile mother must be converted in order to be a Jew. The Orthodox and Conservative movements of Judaism adhere to that law. By contrast, Reform and Reconstructionist Jews assert that if either parent is a Jew the child is a Jew if he or she is raised as one.

The distinction, which is hotly debated among rabbis and Jewish leaders, is very hard for many gentiles to understand. If the gentile mother has any doubts about raising Jewish children in the first place, the thought that they might have to be converted adds to her fear of separation. Many couples, even those who have decided they want their children to be Jewish, are not willing to grant Jewish law authority over their lives.

On the other hand, children who have not been converted often describe the pain and anger they feel when they are told they can't celebrate a bar or bat mitzvah in a Conservative synagogue, or join an

Orthodox synagogue, or when the traditional Jew they love refuses to date them or marry them unless they become legally Jewish. We have met many people who have been angry at their parents for not making them halachically Jewish when they were young. They feel they would have been spared a lot of turmoil.

If the parents do decide to convert the children, they should arrange for the ceremony to take place when the children are young, rather than when they are old enough to feel that being required to convert separates them from their born-Jewish friends (many of whom may be less observant than they are).

The decision is full of emotional and legal complexities. It is a good idea to find rabbis you trust, and discuss the issues with them.

Think Carefully About the Neighborhood You'll Live In, and the School You Choose for Your Children

If you want to raise your children as Jews, don't move into a predominantly Catholic or Protestant neighborhood. If you want to raise your children as Christians, don't move into a predominantly Jewish community. If you want to raise them without any religious affiliation, don't move into an area that is primarily populated by religiously observant people. Otherwise, they will feel like outsiders among their friends.

In one of our workshops, Jed, a Jewish doctor, convinced his wife Lydia, an Italian-Catholic schoolteacher, to raise their children as Jews. But he didn't foresee what would happen when they moved into the Italian-Catholic neighborhood where her family lived.

"I feel swamped by all of Lydia's relatives," he said. "Sure, my son had a brit but since he goes to school with Catholics and always plays with his Italian cousins and grandparents, I don't think I can raise him as a Jew. I'll have to go my own way and hope that he follows." He sounded despairing as he talked.

The conflict between Jed's desire to have a Jewish son and Lydia's loyalty to her family and neighborhood has made their marriage so tense at times that the decision whether to eat bagels and lox or pasta and cheese can cause a fight.

* * *

It is hard to be the child of a Jewish-Protestant intermarriage when
you are supposed to be a white bread American in a discernibly
Jewish town.

"I felt like an outsider in Teaneck," said Ann Gordon, whose Jewish father and Protestant mother, the happily married owners of a
small business, were Unitarians. "Most of the kids in my high school
were Zionists. I never sympathized with them. I used to go to a lot of
temple activities, but I would have felt immoral if I had joined the
temple because I didn't feel Jewish. But I envied the Jews for having a
clear-cut heritage.

"Then I went to college in New England because I thought I would
feel more mainstream there. I put on preppie clothing and tried to be
like everyone else. But a lot of those kids seemed very superficial and
childish. They'd have keg parties and get rip-roaring drunk."

As a junior, she switched to an urban university, where she is
majoring in psychology, studying the psychological effects of being
raised as an ethnic minority. With anger, she asked, "Why didn't my
parents ever stop and think about how they were going to raise my
brother and me? I have to adapt to whomever I'm around. I wish my
parents had either given me a single heritage or prepared me to feel
like an outsider in a minority town. I feel like I'm a chameleon."

Clement Werner Kronfield, thirty-four, a successful advertising executive, was named for his Catholic mother's favorite Pope and his
Jewish father's cousin, a Holocaust victim.

His parents could make that compromise about his name because
they "thought of themselves as freethinkers. Their plan was to exclude all ethnic identity from our lives. They thought they were
superior to people who actually practiced a religion."

But they settled in the Bronx near Clement's Jewish grandparents,
and sent him to a predominantly Jewish public elementary school.
That was his problem.

"In our household, Jewish holidays were energetically *not* ob-
served. In those days, the schools were open on Rosh Hashanah and
Yom Kippur, and my parents would tell me I had to go. They said that
Judaism was not my religion. Atheism was."

Throughout grade school, he was one of two children at school on Yom Kippur. "My parents' intellectual positions were great, but for a grade school kid the pain of being different from everyone else in school is real. I was always an outsider."

As an adult, he says he has trouble making moral decisions. He thinks that failing is connected with the way his parents raised him. "It was half-assed. There was all this intellectual content in our house, but no spiritual content. Because there is no bedrock of decisiveness about religion in my background, I straddle all sorts of issues in my life. I think of myself as a person who is always vacillating about principles."

Be Aware of the Attitudes of Significant Relatives

Often grandparents, aunts, and uncles may be prejudiced against the person who has married their child or sibling, or may be troubled about their religion. Sometimes they see the grandchildren as their allies, and seek to communicate their biases, or to convert them to the religion which they believe is true. In the South we met many couples who were confused about how to handle relatives who were born-again Christians. They didn't want to prevent a child from seeing a grandparent. But how could they stop these fervent Christians from baptizing their youngsters in their eagerness to save them from going to hell? After long discussions in their workshops, several decided that they would invite their parents or siblings to come to their home to spend time with the children, but not let the children go off to visit them.

Some children of intermarriages recalled feeling wounded and jealous when they saw how obviously their Jewish grandparents favored their cousins who had two Jewish parents over them. The cousins would be invited for all the holidays, would get more presents, and would be hugged with much warmer embraces.

When one grandparent is anti-Semitic, and confides this to a grandchild, the child may become confused. On the one hand, he or she may be flattered to be included in a confidence, but may also feel angry at the insult, or guilty for having listened to it. John Levy is a college senior whose father is a Jewish lawyer and whose mother is an upper class Protestant artist. "My name represents my situation," he said, "since Levy is obviously Jewish but John is spelled in the Christian way."

He had inherited his mother's looks and grace, and that made his Protestant grandmother enormously proud. John had never forgotten the afternoon when he went to have tea with her and she assured him, "You're Jewish in name but WASP in character." During that moment of conspiratorial closeness, he remembered, "sort of agreeing, but feeling bad."

Now that he was in college he moved easily among the gentile elite that still discriminated against obviously ethnic Jews. He liked to be among patricians. He wondered whether he should feel that way. "Sometimes," he said, "I think about my grandmother's remark and feel like I was lucky. But sometimes I feel like sort of a traitor."

Keep Religious and Ethnic Slights out of Arguments

Is there any part of you that is sometimes tempted to couch marital arguments in ethnic terms? Don't do it!

Jill, a physical therapist whose mother had acceded to her father's wish that she be raised as a Jew, would sit at the dinner table in her family's elegant Miami dining room, watching in horror as her Methodist mother expressed rage at her Jewish husband for his infidelities by serving him pork, a food he had vowed never to eat. She told him it was veal.

Her mother was allowed to celebrate Christmas. "I used to love Christmas," Jill said. "We had a big tree, and presents, and eggnog. My sister and I would rip open the presents. They would say 'Love Mom and Dad.' But Dad never knew what they were. We would give him gifts but he would complain that they were never right. As the day wore on and my mother's relatives came over, my father would get grouchy and sullen. Soon he'd disappear."

Her father bought her a necklace with a diamond-studded star of David and she wore it every day for weeks. Then her mother demanded that she take it off. Shortly thereafter it disappeared from the house. "My mother and I went to a psychiatrist to try to work out our differences. She told him she didn't wear a cross, so why should I wear a star. Then she said she was just trying to protect me from anti-Semitism. I'm still very bitter about the incident."

Jan, a TV producer, remembered that his Swedish-Lutheran father would tease his Jewish mother whenever he had a run-in with an unpleasant Jewish merchant. He'd say "They should have killed more of you." She, in turn, would tell him that he had a *"goyisheh kop"* and that his "ancestors worshipped trees."

Jill, who sympathized with her father, became an observant Jew. Jan developed a prickly disdain for all religions, which, he insists, divide people.

Be Careful How You Teach About the Holocaust

Many parents try to create a child's Jewish identity with stories about the Holocaust. No one is served if Judaism is presented as a religion of fear: a passport to the gas ovens.

Some intermarried Jewish parents tell their children that Hitler would have considered them Jewish and killed them along with all the other Jews. The reminder is supposed to give them a sense of identity. Instead it terrifies them. They are not given any other pathway into Jewish life. With no sense of a large, vibrant Jewish community, with no larger frame of reference, they imagine the Holocaust as the terrifying sum of Jewish history, as the sole content of Judaism.

Felicia Hayden is a college student whose Jewish mother, a doctor, had married a well-traveled international lawyer. Her mother, who seldom talked about her own Jewish background, had sent Felicia to private boarding schools. But, at the same time as she coached Felicia to modulate her voice, use her hands properly, sit demurely at dinner or in chapel, she would remind her daughter that "If you had lived in Nazi Germany, Hitler would have taken you, too."

"Maybe she was trying to prepare me to deal with anti-Semitism,"

Felicia said. "But I think it was her way of retaining some Jewish contact with me.

"Now I have nightmares about terrible things happening to me. When I was a freshman I had a series of dreams about being tortured by the Nazis. One term I didn't do my schoolwork. When I was awake I worried that some terrible thing would happen. Sometimes at night I dreamed that my brother and I were being chased by the SS. I saved my brother but I was going to be sent to a concentration camp. Then I would wake up.

"At college people don't always know that I'm Jewish. I hear them make jokes about how they're going to collect money greedily, like the Jews. The Jews I know say I shouldn't be upset. I should laugh about it. But I can't. I always fear the worst. If the Jews are going to be rounded up again I'll be part of it. I associate being Jewish with something inside me I can't help. My identity. It's as if I was born with it and I'm going to be punished for it the rest of my life."

Don't Suppress a Parent's Past

If the parent whose faith isn't practiced suppresses his or her ethnic background, a child can spend much of a lifetime trying to unearth it. For children idolize their parents. They fantasize about them, trying to imagine their childhoods, seeking to reconstruct important personal facts or marital bargains that seem to have been hidden.

That happened to me. From my boyhood until the day my father died I was always aware of the fact that he had once been a Cohen and was now a Cowan, and that he had a father with a past that I wasn't permitted to know about. He and I had an unusually close relationship. We talked on the telephone several times a week, and met for lunch or supper at least once every two weeks. During the last ten years of his life, he was either bedridden or in the hospital for months at a stretch, and I visited him frequently. We always discussed political developments or trends in the arts, books he was reading, or stories I was writing. But, even though he knew how curious I was about his father, he would never describe him or discuss the Jewish aspect of his childhood.

I didn't try to provoke him to talk. I respected the fact that the mere mention of Jake Cohen's name caused him a great deal of pain. But within weeks of my father's death I set out to discover his hidden past. As I learned about it, I began to alter my picture of the Judaism my parents had transmitted to me. But I wasn't forced to choose one parent's faith or ethnicity over another's, as I might have been if my mother was a gentile and my father had concealed his history in order to placate her.

Lorrie White, twenty-eight, an Episcopalian minister, was raised in Cincinnati by a Jewish father who owned a dry goods store and a Methodist mother who had been born in an Appalachian coal camp. Though her parents celebrated Christmas and Easter and seldom went to synagogue, they agreed that Lorrie would receive a Jewish education. She wasn't unhappy about the decision. She had always had a taste for religion, and she liked her Hebrew school. But, as a child, she could never answer the nagging question that seemed to hang over her family in the same way as Jake Cohen's identity hung over mine. How could she—an only daughter—understand her mother, who escaped Appalachia by joining the Navy and studying nursing on a military scholarship? She seldom talked about her family or her childhood.

"I knew she'd been one of seven children in a tar-paper shack in a coal camp where her Christmas present each year would be one orange. I used to imagine her as a little raggedy kid looking sort of like a Holocaust victim." Why had her mother struggled so hard to lose her coal country accent? Had she disguised her faith, too? Had she married Lorrie's father for love or security? Why was she so guarded about the past? Why did her face light up on Christmas and Easter morning in a way that it never did on Jewish holidays? "Her presence confused me," Lorrie said. "I wanted to vault over those silences—which seemed like willed silences—and find her roots."

Lorrie's parents were upwardly mobile people who sent her to an Episcopalian private school, where she strove to emulate her classmates' calm grace. Culturally, it was the wrong place to preserve a Jewish identity. Religiously, the school left her in a limbo, where she remained for years.

She liked the mandatory chapel service, with its poetic English language and its subtle connection to her fantasy of her mother's background. But how could she express those feelings? She couldn't take daily Communion—the most obvious way to make a connection —since she was studying for confirmation at her Reform temple. Instead, she played guitar while her classmates knelt to receive the wine and wafer.

"I played songs like Judy Collins' 'Both Sides Now,' or sang lyrics like Gordon Lightfoot's 'I'm standing in the doorway with my hat held in my hand, not knowing where to sit, not knowing where to stand.' I was sending out messages, but nobody wanted to deal with them."

Her ambivalence was reinforced in Hebrew school. One morning, her class saw a movie about World War II called *Let My People Go.* The rabbi turned to her and asked, " 'Lorrie, you could have passed. Would you have died for your faith or run away from the Nazis to hide?' I sat there thinking, 'Why are you asking me that? I don't know the answer.' "

But she wanted to find out, and the search began to dominate her life.

For years, she had a recurrent nightmare. "In it, I'm always in a concentration camp but I don't belong there. There is barbed wire. It is dark. I'm hungry. I'm alone and scared. I want to run but I can't. I need my glasses but I can't find them. I don't have a name.

"That dream came to represent the central question of my life. Was I willing to die for my faith? What was my faith? Was I a Jew? Was I a Christian?"

Her classmates in Hebrew school reinforced her doubts about her identity. "They kept saying, 'You're not one of us because you go to an Episcopalian school and your mother's not a Jew.' Once I hit a guy in the nose because he said I wasn't a Jew." But she was beginning to have questions about the faith she was fighting for. "I kept wondering about Jesus. I'd say, 'How can we ignore a guy who turned history around?' Jesus did that in a more powerful way than Moses. But no one talked about him."

She was looking for her religious home—and her relationship to her parents' history. She thought she should be a Jew. "I kept telling myself I was a Jew, but I never felt that I fit."

She seemed like her mother's child, not her father's. "I always thought she gave up her history to accommodate us. But I wanted to understand her—the tensions she felt about leaving her heritage and her family."

She tried going to church. "One day I took Communion even though everyone knew I wasn't baptized. Suddenly, I felt connected to a community, to God, to myself. But I didn't want to be baptized because I had read that they baptized Jews right before they put them in the ovens.

"Then, finally, I came to a place in my mind where I said: 'I have to be baptized. This is where I belong. I don't understand why, but I do.' "

After a great deal of thought, she applied for admission to Union Theological Seminary and was accepted. She felt as though she were acting out her mother's wishes as well as her own. "Recently, I asked her if she believed in Jesus and she said she did. She said she didn't want to tell me when I was a kid because it would have confused me. But I knew it anyway. I think I've spent a lot of my life reclaiming the Christian, Appalachian side that she hid from me."

But Lorrie still felt ambivalent. "I keep thinking that I'm copping out on something crucial by being a Christian. Who am I to say that I believe in a religion that has killed Jews for thousands of years because they rejected it? As a minister, I think that one of my vocations is to build bridges between Christians and Jews and to help the children of intermarriages find themselves."

Peggy Shaw, thirty-two, a magazine editor who was raised in a Protestant suburb of Portland, Oregon, was always troubled by the cultural differences between her father, Benny, a New York Jewish intellectual who taught philosophy, and her mother, Stacey, a German-Lutheran housewife from Wisconsin.

Benny never talked about being Jewish. From his daughter's vantage point he was a brilliant, eccentric man, whose taste for strange foods, for exotic books, were peculiar to him, not rooted in his past. Nevertheless, he was the most distinctive presence in her American life.

Her parents had fallen in love in the classroom, where Benny, the professor, impressed Stacey with his brilliance and Stacey, the good student, awed him with her milk-fed American quality. But the White

Christmas marriage didn't work. Peggy's adolescence was a confusing, conflict-ridden time.

In her bearing, she was a blend of both parents: small, with dark curly hair, but so reserved and quiet I understood the intensity of feeling behind every word only after I'd been interviewing her for an hour.

Her father, who was now in his seventies, was a flamboyant man. "He loved conversation and he was always the life of the party. His voice used to get loud and he'd talk with his hands whenever he had an idea.

"My mother was a quiet person. She would never say anything when their friends were around. She built up a terrible resentment against him. But she could never say what she thought. So she'd just get very cold and snap at him, whether or not he said anything offensive. Then he would yell at her. I felt divided between the two of them."

Benny Shaw, who thought he had lost out on academic jobs because he was Jewish, had become very secretive about his religious identity. Though he gave a lot of money to Israel and drives for Soviet Jews, he always did so anonymously. At his suggestion, the Shaws were regular worshipers at the local Presbyterian church. He seemed to be happy that they celebrated Christmas and Easter.

Peggy, who thought of herself as a Christian, was haunted by the weird, Chagall-like presence that hovered over her outwardly normal family: "my father and his Jewishness." For his tastes made his presence seem discordant in the suburb where they lived. "He was nothing like the other fathers I knew. He was always reading a book. He didn't know how to mow the lawn. That was something my mother had against him. He didn't play sports or build things in the wood shop. It used to bother me that he was so different from the other men in our neighborhood."

From Peggy's point of view, his taste in food was even stranger than his physical incompetence. "He'd eat borscht. He'd put shmaltz on everything. He made matzoh brei and ate gefilte fish. He was always cutting up cucumber and putting sour cream on it. Nobody I knew ate that way. I hated looking in the refrigerator at all that stuff. But I always thought that's what older people from the East Coast ate. I didn't know it was Jewish."

Benny, who spent most of his time squirreled away in his book-lined study, had terrible insomnia, and he'd sip scotch until two or three in the morning, waiting for exhaustion to set in. When she was in high school, Peggy loved to sneak into the library and visit him. She'd always ask him about a book, or talk about a movie or a play she had seen. His mere presence gave her comfort. "I knew that if I couldn't sleep or I had a problem he would always be there to talk."

Her parents got divorced when she was sixteen. For years, she blamed Benny and his eccentric ways. How could her mother, who was so pretty, so nice, so eager to help out as home room mother or Girl Scout leader, disrupt a marriage? Now, though, she saw things more coolly. "The difference between my parents was just so great that they couldn't span it. People who are as different as they are should never get married."

For an hour, it was a curiously disjointed interview since Peggy was talking about childhood traumas in such matter-of-fact tones that I felt she could have been describing a third person. Then, as I was about to put my tape recorder away, her voice became passionate. Suddenly, it was as if, in talking to the machine, she was writing a verbal letter to Benny Shaw.

"Look," she said, "I'm furious at my father and I think the reason is that I love him so much. He didn't ever give me any idea of who he really was. He loved to let me into his library or his refrigerator, but he never gave me the key to his Jewish identity."

I began to identify with Benny Shaw in a way that startled me. Maybe because Peggy was a girl, an older version of a potential Lisa, I imagined Benny as an older version of a possible me. I saw him as a person who was in love with America and Stacey Shaw, the Midwestern farm girl. I imagined his book-lined study as the equivalent of my office, where I can spend days and nights at a time writing. I'm an insomniac who sometimes drinks to get to sleep: I could imagine those intimate hours Peggy described. I eat smelly foods, and Lisa and Matt criticize me for that.

What if Rachel hadn't been so attuned to the kids that she noticed their questions about their identity? What if, instead of the Upper West Side of New York, we had lived in Portland, Oregon, where the easiest way to unify a two-faith marriage was through a Christian church? Then I would have seemed to be a clumsy, bookish father, who ate strange foods and talked about everything but the subject that draped over the household: my Jewishness. Would I have blamed myself for feeling free to give money to Israel and Soviet Jews, but withholding Judaism from the children I adored? Would I have felt, at some tormented level, that I had relinquished Peggy to her mother—and to Stacey's Christianity?

I realized I still didn't quite understand her feelings about her father. I asked Peggy if she would let me role play her father while she acted as herself. She was eager to do that. As Peggy talked to Benny through me, I felt as if she were addressing thousands of Jews who intermarry and then suppress their true feelings.

"There's a big hole in my education," she began, speaking rapidly and angrily. "There's a hole in my personality—a hole in my sense of identity as a person because of the way you raised me. There was a Jew in the house, and you couldn't deny that. *You* were always there. But you never explained yourself."

It was easy to imagine how Benny would answer from his vantage point as a professor who thought he had been denied tenure because of his religion. "I thought you were safer thinking of yourself as a Christian than as a Jew. Besides, I didn't want religion to be another rift between me and your mother after all the fights we'd had."

"You didn't need to protect me like that," Peggy said. "Children are a lot smarter than their parents think. I knew there was tension between you and Mom. I know that you were different. I just wanted you to tell me why."

"Now you say you had a hole in your personality, but you seemed very happy in high school," I said.

"I wasn't happy," Peggy answered. "That was when I was most alone. I didn't fit in anywhere. I just felt confused, particularly after you and Mom got divorced. Everything was floating around when I was in high school. Nothing was permanent and solid and always there."

Peggy sounded self-pitying to me, so I said, sternly: "Look, all teenagers feel alone, especially if their parents get divorced. How did you feel especially alone?"

"Kids may feel alone in a certain social sense," Peggy said. "But I felt alone in a very basic family sense. I never felt I belonged anywhere. I didn't belong. You should have known that."

Belonged! That was Benny's dream for his child. "I would have been glad if you'd joined the Presbyterian church. The kids looked nice to me. They were blond. They were attractive. Their fathers could build houses. I couldn't do all the things the other men did. I liked herring, lox, and other foods that no one else ate. You thought it was disgusting. You don't know what an outsider I felt like. I wanted you to join the Presbyterian church."

"But I *couldn't* do it," Peggy insisted. "It wasn't in me. I may be my mother's daughter, but I'm also your daughter. Your tastes influenced me. Now I eat smelly foods too."

Then, Peggy spoke to me directly. "You sound like my dad. He would have been very happy if I had assimilated and joined the church. The kids at the Presbyterian church were blond and freckled, and they never spoke with their hands. But all I could feel in the Presbyterian church was," her face recoiled, "ick. It just wasn't me. I didn't like talking about Jesus Christ. I didn't like reading their prayers and singing their songs. I remember going out with them once and having a good time. Then we came back and one of the girls said, 'We had a good time because we're all good Christians.' I was ready to explode, but I didn't know what to say.

"I didn't know where I fit in. I just floated. There was something artificial and hidden about our family and it made me uncomfortable."

Now, I resumed the dialogue, playing Benny again. "How could I have made my Jewish identity clear to you? You were a teenage girl. What would I have said? Peggy, you know I'm Jewish and that means I'm different? I might have said something like that if you had told me about that feeling of floating. But I always thought you were happy."

"How could I have told you?" Peggy asked.

In college, Peggy became friendly with a group of Jewish students, and discovered that she felt more at home with them than she had with her neighbors in Oregon. She went to synagogue and liked Jewish ritual better than church ritual. When she fell in love with a Jewish man she decided to have a formal conversion. Although she had been on bad terms with her mother, "she was very supportive. I think she wanted to become a Jew when she married my father."

Now she's on excellent terms with Benny Shaw, but his first reaction was, "If you're going to convert, why don't you become a Catholic or a Protestant? Become anything but a Jew." Still, she said, "down deep I think he's pleased."

Make Religion a Life Style, Not a Label

If a religion is no more than a family label, it is not likely to mean much to children. If it seems to signal that one partner has won a marital struggle, that the other's identity has been ripped at the seams, it may provoke the kind of turmoil that Lorrie White and Peggy Shaw described.

It is prudent for parents to work out ways of embodying the religion of one without hiding the other's past. Those who choose to weave Judaism into their lives display tact and foresight if they visit the Christian in-laws at crucial moments of their religious and secular year. It is wise for those who choose Christianity to show the same respect for the Jewish side of the family. Most of all, it is important for the couple, as a unit, to remember that they are their children's primary role models. If they embody a grudging sense that one is acquiescing to the other, they convey a negative, hostile message to their children. If they display loving sensitivity to each other's spiritual sensibilities, they convey a positive, optimistic one.

Sue Stern, nineteen, was a college freshman and the daughter of a Jewish man and a Presbyterian woman who were both physics majors in college. After graduate school, they both got jobs at a Southern university.

They knew that when they moved South they would encounter many fundamentalist groups who would insist they join their church. In order to avoid that pressure, they decided to settle on a religion of their own before they left the North.

They joined the Unitarian Church and raised their children in it. As far as Sue could tell, they shared their religious faith in the same way as they shared their enthusiasm for science, for classical music, and for hiking. They transmitted a strong sense of security to her.

"I think my parents have one of the most beautiful relationships I've ever seen. I really admire them. What they have taught us children is to love and respect all people, and to think that they all have the right to believe as they wish."

She was strongly in favor of intermarriage. "Once two fundamentalist Christians in my high school class told me that they had gone to a Baptist convention where they stood up and accepted Jesus and

promised not to date non-Christians. When I asked them why, they
said, 'Because interdating could lead to intermarriage and that would
cause problems.'

"I said, 'Well, it caused me.' "

Phil Rossi, a graduate business student, is the son of a Bronx-born
Italian man, a certified public accountant, and a Bronx-born Russian-
Jewish woman, a financial manager. The couple met on a blind date in
college.

From the moment they began to court, Phil's father Mario made it
clear that his children had to be raised as Catholics. That was fine with
his fiancée Marcia, who seldom went to synagogue anyway. Even
though Marcia's parents refused to attend the wedding because it was
in a church, they quickly became close to their grandchildren. Now,
Phil unabashedly calls his Jewish grandmother "my best friend."

Phil accompanied his father to church every Sunday. He went to
catechism class and discovered that he was very religious. "I wasn't
forced to pray, but I did pray. I felt that I could talk to God any minute
of the day. He was my constant companion."

But Phil was also aware of his mother's religion. He went to his
grandmother's house for Hanukkah and Passover, and occasionally
accompanied her to synagogue on the High Holy Days. Though he
thought of himself as a Catholic, "who experienced the birth of Christ
every Christmas," his love of his mother's family convinced him that
"people should not use religion to set up barriers. Nothing in the
world is important enough to set up barriers between people."

Now that he had been through college and was enrolled at business
school he had begun to feel that "the Catholic hierarchy tries to run
your life. I've decided not to say that I'm a Catholic, but to call myself
a Christian. In another five years, when I have time, I want to study
Judaism to see if that makes sense to me."

He was a religious explorer who felt safe in his spiritual skin. He
thought that, as the child of an intermarriage, his security stemmed
from the fact that he was raised with one religion. "It would have
been terrible if I'd been raised with neither religion or if I'd been
expected to make the choice between Judaism and Catholicism.

"As a kid, all my questions were answered. Now that I'm an adult,
of course, I have plenty of questions. But if my parents hadn't given

me a foundation, those questions would engulf me. Every kid views his parents as somewhat omnipotent. If they hadn't been able to provide me with coherent answers I would have felt overwhelmed. I would have thought: if my parents couldn't deal with religion together, then how can I deal with it on my own?"

Lisa Cowan is our daughter. In 1986, she entered college. When we asked if we could interview her for the book, she laughed and said, "I don't really think of myself as the child of people with two religious backgrounds."

But then she recalled that she did have one worry when she was younger—that Rachel's parents would feel rejected. She described the episode that assuaged that fear.

"Remember when we were visiting Maggie [Rachel's mother] one Easter when it was also Passover? We brought along enough matzohs for all of us, but it was before we had completely given up eating bread during Passover. Maggie brought out a plate of warm hot cross buns for breakfast. Mom picked one up. She said, 'This is my heritage!' I remember the pride on her face when she said it. I'm not sure whether she ate the bun, but I was glad to see her show pride in her past. I didn't like the feeling that she had turned her back on her family."

"Does my conversion ever trouble you?" Rachel asked.

"No! Judaism seems so normal to me that I don't quite understand people who belong to another religion. But then I think, what if Matt became a Buddhist? What if he stopped doing all the things we've been doing since we were little? No matter how much he explained it —or it helped him grow—I'd still think it was strange. So I was glad when Mom did something to show her parents that she was still proud of them and what they gave her."

When Lisa was in high school, she seldom came to synagogue with us except on the High Holy Days. But lighting candles on Friday night was special. That was a religious experience for her.

"Well, maybe not religious exactly. I don't know if I believe in God. But it was the purest form of family time I've ever known. It had a quality of . . . wholeness, which is the same kind of feeling I get when I'm in direct communication with nature or feel in communication with myself."

Then she laughed a little self-consciously. "I hate to put these things into words. It sounds so totally corny. But when I feel it, I know it."

The sense of family tradition was important to her. "This year, when I stayed at school during Yom Kippur I went to services. It's not that I like being in synagogue that much. But I feel like I'm linked to my family."

Although she is an agnostic, she made it clear that the religion her parents chose gives her a sense of place and of internal order.

"I was a little disappointed when we stopped celebrating Christmas. Who wouldn't be? I loved all the excitement. But now I think it would be wrong to have a Christmas tree. I don't mean morally wrong. It would just feel wrong. It's the same thing during Passover. I don't eat *chametz*. [leavened foods]. It's a tradition I care about. It wouldn't feel right to eat bread. It would be like eating pork."

Toward the end of the interview, we told her that a great many children of intermarried couples resent their parents' thoughtlessness or indecisiveness. If she could give us retroactive advice about her religious upbringing, what would she say?

She began to laugh. "I don't know. I can't think of anything. You're both such different people, but you share the same values. Even though you had different religions when I was born, I don't feel like the child of an intermarriage. Judaism is a part of me."

Coda

Most intermarried parents who choose to make religion a way of life and not a label begin by doing so for their children. But in fact they are untying a knot at the core of their marriage. For even if the child ultimately rejects their way of life—as some will—the husband and wife have resolved their own dilemma.

They have transformed the problem of an intermarriage into the opportunity to fashion a faith they can share for a lifetime.

10
A Personal
Afterword

When we began to research this book, in 1981, we were living at the crossroads of the secular America we have always loved and the traditional Jewish community that was our new home. Since then, we have become increasingly immersed in the Jewish world. *An Orphan in History* has allowed me to meet thousands of Jews in America. I feel as if I have become part of a large, warm, contentious family that extends from Maine to Oregon. Rachel has fallen so deeply in love with Jewish life and Jewish teachings that she has become a rabbinical student. I've never seen her so excited as she is by what she's learning.

But we are still part of the secular world we come from. That is why our work with interfaith couples engages us so deeply. The fact that people from so many different backgrounds can explore their religious and ethnic feelings so freely is a tribute to the American openness we were both raised to treasure. The discussions always teach us something new about America, religion, and ourselves.

In a room at the 92nd Street YMHA, a young man talks lovingly about his grandfather, the Yiddish-speaking anarchist who became an Orthodox Jew. Then his Polish-Catholic fiancée describes the coal mining town where her grandfather organized labor unions. They don't know whether to raise their children as Catholics, Jews, or political radicals. A European-born Jew describes the anti-Semitism he experienced as a boy at Christmas and then listens to his Protestant wife talk about the church whose activities were at the core of her family's social and religious life. She is pregnant. How can the couple combine such different histories, such different memories, in the two-faith home they plan to establish? A former minister reveals the betrayal he feels because his secular Jewish wife, who married him in a church, has suddenly come to feel that she is making an unacceptable compromise of her Jewishness when she and their 7 year old daughter attend Sunday services with him. Is there a way they can ease that tension?

Whenever such couples talk, the part of both of us that loves American diversity longs to tell them that they'll have no trouble blending powerful ethnic and religious feelings in the same household. But we've heard too many people express the pain these important differences have caused them to offer an easy assurance.

So we try to help the couples define and translate the differences between them, and identify the values and experiences they are most eager to pass on. The workshops, which can be painful, become optimistic experiences as Christians and Jews cease to dismiss their families' religious and ethnic history as cultural baggage and realize that, for them, religion is part of the fabric of life, not a scene to be glimpsed on Yom Kippur or Easter Sunday and forgotten for the rest of the year.

Then, couples stop dwelling on their disagreements and begin to think about creating a spiritual life out of the problems that brought them to the workshop. Is there any way they can use their memories of their childhood faiths, and their longing for something transcendent in their adult lives, to fashion a religious culture that will nourish them? Can they do it together? When those questions emerge, we are never sure where they will lead. Will the Jews become more Jewish, the Christians more Christian? Will couples find a religion they can share, or discover that their different faiths divide them after all? Or will they decide that the secular values and interests that attract them to each other are more important than their religious feelings? It is painful and thrilling to watch people work out their own decisions. As we do so, we feel like neutral mediators whose job is to help each person in the workshop discover where his or her deepest loyalties lie.

But we are also committed Jews. So it is especially satisfying to us when Jews discover the depth of their loyalty to Judaism. We remember our own experiences as they begin to translate their irreducible core of Jewish feeling into a desire to live a Jewish life. We feel a special responsibility to help these couples find ways to enter the Jewish community. But the connection is hard to make. Often the couples feel as wary as we once did of synagogues and mainstream Jews.

In the end, both the interfaith couples who are thinking about living as Jews and the Jewish community which wants to prevent assimilation have to take risks. Both groups have to face their own fears.

Couples who intermarry should not blame each other or their parents or in-laws or clergy for their problems. They are adults. They entered into the marriage consciously. They have to take the responsibility of confronting their differences and resolving them. If they don't, they run the risk that a time bomb will explode later on in their marriage. They risk depriving their children of a clear sense of identity—and depriving themselves of an experience with tradition and the transcendent.

The Jewish community should open the door for them. One way to do that is to expand the programs it has already devised to help them, allocating more money for Introduction to Judaism courses or weekend retreats where couples can learn the pleasures of the Sabbath and of studying Jewish texts.

But the programs the Jewish community creates for interfaith couples aren't as important as the attitude it adopts toward them. As a whole the Jewish community has not yet decided whether to treat interfaith couples as problems or people: as pariahs or as men and women who are not yet committed Jews.

Often the Jews in interfaith relationships hope to learn more about Jewishness but hesitate to become more involved in mainstream Jewish life for fear that other Jews will make them feel like traitors for intermarrying. Often the gentiles hear words like shiksa, shaygetz, or goy and feel wary or hurt. Those words reflect an attitude which make many gentiles hesitate to convert. They doubt that they'll ever be accepted as authentic Jews. But we have seen time and again that when they are welcomed into a community they become enthusiastic participants. Indeed rabbis in cities across America have told us that converts are playing vital leadership roles in their synagogues.

If interfaith couples are invited into the Jewish community they may well join. If they're told their love is heresy they'll probably flee.

Our own histories remind us of how important patience and openness can be. What would the Paul and Rachel Cowan who are writing this book have said to themselves, the young couple who fell in love en route to Chicago twenty-four years ago?

What if our current selves had been guests at our own wedding? Would we have despaired because the butternut tree wasn't a huppah and a minister was reciting the vows? Would we have thought the isolated act of breaking a glass revealed an ignorance of Jewish tradition—not a flicker of the loyalty that would later burst into consciousness?

What if my current self had heard me telling the sociologist who interviewed me in 1970 that there was no need to worry about intermarriage? What if Rachel the rabbinical student had been in the audience at the Dialogue in Israel, listening to the brash young American Jew say that "for people like me, Jewish feeling is going to have to be translated; it's going to have to be taken out of the synagogue." Would we have dismissed those naïve youngsters as people who were lost to Judaism forever?

We like to hope that we would have talked to them gently, saying: At the important moments in your life you'll be grateful for this sturdy religion, the wise ideas and the brave history it embodies, the quiet times it allows for prayer, the joyous moments it lets you burst into song and dance. Saying: You'll be very busy soon. You'll want the warmth and joy of family time. You'll see it at its purest in the Sabbath candles. Saying: You can live out your passion for social justice. That passion is at Judaism's core. Saying: You'll find an exhilarating comfort in the musty old chapel at Congregation Ansche Chesed, filled with people who are thrilled when your children are born, when you get a new job; who visit you when you're sick or comfort you when you're bereaved. Saying: A congregation of Jews that reads from the Torah every Saturday, that includes babies and grandparents, the memories of Holocaust survivors and the enthusiasm of converts, will show you that you need not live and die on your own island of time. You are part of an extended family whose memories stretch back past Mount Sinai. Saying: You won't believe us. The place we're talking about is still too far from your experience to sound appealing. But come some Saturday morning. Don't expect a sudden surge of faith. That seldom happens. Faith unfolds slowly, unexpectedly, at routine moments, in the midst of plain deeds. It helps you pause lovingly over life; see hope in the future; see what is holy in ordinary things.

There is a midrash, an ancient Jewish story, which, we find, lends a religious interpretation to the practical work we do. According to the midrash, God offered the Torah to all the peoples of the world. Everyone rejected it until God came to the Jews at Mount Sinai. They finally agreed to accept it. In every nation, there had been a majority who rejected the Torah and a minority that wanted it. Among the Jews, the situation was reversed. Most said yes to the Almighty's promise of a special mission. But some said no.

From that perspective, part of Jewish history has been a process of those souls who had wanted the Torah finding their way back to Mount Sinai. We hope our work helps that process along.

Appendix

Recommended Reading

We have chosen books that we hope will get you started in your explorations and studies. The Christian books have been recommended by knowledgeable friends who themselves have made journeys into Christian thought and practice. The Jewish books are ones that we have come to appreciate in our own studies, or that people in our workshops have found helpful. We also include books about Jewish-Christian dialogue. Look for them in a library or bookstore and begin with a few that interest you especially.

Christian Books

Mere Christianity. C. S. Lewis. Macmillan, 1964.

On Being Christian. Hans Küng. In libraries, out of print.

Reaching Out: The Three Movements of the Spiritual Life. Henri J. Nouwen. Doubleday, 1985. Paper.

He Is Risen. Thomas Merton. Argus Communications, 1975.

The Seven Story Mountain. Thomas Merton. Harcourt, Brace, Jovanavich, 1948.

Turning: Reflections on the Experience of Conversion. Emilie Griffin. Doubleday, 1982.

Waiting for God. Simone Weil. Harper & Row, 1951.

Returning: A Spiritual Journey. Dan Wakefield. Doubleday, 1988.

The Catholic Fact Book. Thomas More, 1986.

New Jerusalem Bible. Doubleday, 1985.

Practical Guides:

A Handbook of Christian Theology. Arthur A. Cohen and Marvin Halverson, eds. Abingdon Press, 1984. (Essays about Protestant thinking.)

A Concise Guide to the Catholic Church II. Felician A. Foy and Rose Avato. Our
   Sunday Visitor Publishing, 1986.
A New Dictionary for Episcopalians. Harper & Row, 1985.

Jewish Books

Basic Theology:
Basic Judaism. Milton Steinberg. Harcourt Brace, 1975.
This Is My God. Herman Wouk. Doubleday, 1979.

Bible Study:
The Torah: A Modern Commentary. Union of American Hebrew Congregations,
   1981. (This book contains the Five books of Moses in Hebrew and
   English, with notes and comments gleaned from a wide variety of
   sources.)
The Enjoyment of Scripture. Samuel Sandmel. Oxford University Press, 1978.
Back to the Sources: Reading the Classic Jewish Texts. Barry W. Holtz, ed. Summit
   Books, 1984.

How-to Books:
The Jewish Catalogs (3 Volumes). Richard Siegel, Michael Strassfeld, Sharon
   Strassfeld. Jewish Publication Society, 1980.
The Shabbat Seder. Federation of Jewish Mens Clubs, 1986. (Conservative
   perspective.)
Gates of the House. Central Conference of American Rabbis, 1977. (Reform
   perspective.)
How to Run a Traditional Jewish Household. Blu Greenberg. Simon and Schuster,
   1984. (Orthodox perspective.)

Guides:
The Book of Jewish Books, A Reader's Guide to Judaism. Ruth S. Frank and William
   Wollheim. Harper & Row, 1986.
To Pray as a Jew: A Guide to the Prayer Book and Synagogue Service. Hayim Halevy
   Donin. Basic Books, 1980. (Orthodox perspective.)
To Be a Jew: A Guide to Jewish Observance in Contemporary Life. Hayim Halevy
   Donin. Basic Books, 1972. (Orthodox perspective.)
Gates of Mitzvah: A Guide to the Jewish Life Cycle. Simeon J. Maslin, ed. Central
   Conference of American Rabbis, 1979. (Reform perspective.)

The Jewish Holidays, A Guide and Commentary. Michael Strassfeld. Harper & Row, 1985.

The Complete Family Guide to Jewish Holidays. Dalia Hardoff Renberg. Adama Books, 1985. (Many activities for children.)

The Book of Modern Jewish Etiquette. Helen Latner. Schocken Books, 1981.

The Jewish Holiday Kitchen. Joan Nathan. Schocken Books, 1979.

Conversion:

Choosing Judaism. Lydia Kukoff. Union of American Hebrew Congregations, 1981. (Reform perspective.)

Embracing Judaism. Simcha Kling. Rabbinical Assembly, 1987. (Conservative perspective.)

Others:

Great Ages and Ideas of the Jewish People. Leo W. Schwartz, ed. Random House, 1956.

Nine Questions People Ask About Judaism. Dennis Prager and Joseph Telushkin. Simon and Schuster, 1981.

The Jewish Book of Why, and *The Second Jewish Book of Why.* Alfred J. Kolatch. Jonathan David Publishers, 1981.

The Abandonment of the Jews: America and the Holocaust. David Wyman. Pantheon, 1984.

Toward Better Jewish-Christian Understanding

A Dictionary of the Jewish-Christian Dialogue. Leon Klenecki and Geoffrey Wigoder, eds. Paulist Press, 1984.

Christian Mission—Jewish Mission. Martin A. Cohen and Helga Croner, eds. Paulist Press, 1982.

More Stepping Stones to Jewish-Christian Relations: An Unabridged Collection of Christian Documents, 1975–1983. Helga Croner, comp. Paulist Press, 1985.

A Jewish Understanding of the New Testament. Samuel Sandmel. Ktav, 1974.

Faith and Fratricide: The Theological Roots of Anti-Semitism. Rosemary Radford Reuther. Winston Press, 1979.